# Contents

# 3

## Stakeholders and the
## Information Marketplace   56

### IN THEIR OWN WORDS

# 4

## Copyright in the Digital Age   96

### IN THEIR OWN WORDS

# 5

## Privacy and Intellectual Freedom in the Digital Age     148

### IN THEIR OWN WORDS

# 6

## Censors Take On the Net     190

### IN THEIR OWN WORDS

# 7

## Accessing the Digital Universe     226

### IN THEIR OWN WORDS

# Introduction

In 1994 I was teaching introductory Internet classes through a San Francisco group called Bay Area Internet Literacy. I found myself having to inform people who were eager to get connected to the Internet that all the programs they needed were available free—but the catch was that they had to be downloaded from the Internet. We'd all get a good chuckle out of this, and then I'd go about explaining to these enthusiastic beginners how they could break through this Catch-22 and get themselves online.

The situation is similar when it comes to finding information about the Information Highway. The discussions about where the Information Highway might be going all take place on the Internet and among people who are already well connected. Yet if this online technology is going to develop from its current role of serving an elite and educated public into a truly universal information system, a much larger part of our population is going to have to have a voice in determining its direction. But they can hardly participate in the debate if they can't get the information they need about what's going on.

The development of the new information technologies is happening so fast that even the most dedicated of information professionals is hard-pressed to keep up. This book is designed for librarians who are online, but with little time to explore the general areas of information policy, as well as for those who might not yet be connected to the Internet but need to understand its implications. In our key role as information providers we are well placed to influence the direction of the Information Highway, but only if we are able to understand the forces behind its development.

This book covers the main topic areas of the Information Highway debate that are particularly relevant to libraries and includes a short selection of documents in each topic area. In some cases these are the key Federal documents that have formed the core of the discussion; in other cases they illustrate the viewpoints of concerned groups. Wherever possible, relevant documents representing the library viewpoint have been included.

No book could begin to give a complete, much less an up-to-date, picture of these policy areas. This one should be seen as background reading, and perhaps even as history. Recent history, to be sure, but even two years is history in these fast-moving times. The Further Reading sections include some general World Wide Web sites where information on these same topics will be up to the minute. If I am successful in my goals, this book will be a launchpad for your further exploration of these areas, on the Internet and off.

We begin in Chapter 1 with a general introduction to the information society. The information society is not so much a change in technology as a change in attitude, what some social scientists would call a *paradigm shift*.

Chapter 2 gets us into the Information Highway with the *National Information Infrastructure: Agenda for Action*, the Clinton administration document that declared the goal of a new National Information Infrastructure. Then Chapter 3, "Stakeholders in the Information Marketplace," presents the economic view of the Information Highway from information pricing to the promise of a free market of information (and a number of challenges for libraries).

Chapter 4 covers an issue that is particularly important for libraries: copyright. In the world of digital information, copying becomes easier than ever before, to the point of threatening the revenue possibilities for the holders of intellectual property rights. The question here is whether we can maintain a workable balance between the information needs of the public and the needs of creators and publishers to earn from their work.

Privacy is of great concern to most of us as computers store more and more data about our lives, our buying habits, our incomes, even our medical records. For libraries the privacy issue centers around the relationship between privacy and intellectual freedom. This is covered in Chapter 5.

One of the hardest issues for libraries today is censorship, covered in Chapter 6. With a recent history of sensational media coverage that highlights the presence of sexual content on the Internet, free speech has been particularly under attack in the electronic information world.

From the first descriptions of the Information Highway, universal access has been declared as a goal. As often as not, public libraries are seen as the on-ramp the general public will use to gain this access. That there is not any single definition of universal access makes it very hard to respond to the expectation being fostered of libraries. Chapter 7 covers a number of different points of view, including voices from communities concerned that universal access may not include their members.

At the time of this writing, many important decisions are about to be made. Proposed changes to the copyright law are being discussed in Congress and on an international level. The Communications Decency Act has gone to the Supreme Court. By the time this book is printed, some of these questions will have been resolved and others will have surfaced. I have no predictions for the future of the Information Highway, just a steadfast belief that our future information services will be best served by the active presence of the library community.

[*Author's Note:* The opinions and interpretations expressed in this book, unless otherwise attributed, are my own.]

# 1

■ ■ ■

# The New Information
# Society

**W**e are living in the *information society*. This fact is touted in television news programs, popular magazines, and current trade paperbacks. We are so enamored of information that we even have the concept of "infotainment," which allows us to amuse ourselves and be informed at the same time. In fact, we seem to be caught in the grip of a new kind of mania, infomania. We hear about the Information Highway and the National Information Infrastructure almost constantly, as if information only recently became important to us.

Yet it's hard to separate human society from information. We build our cultures on a shared set of ideas about the world and about ourselves, and these ideas are based on information. These cultural ideas are the basis for our social structure, our religions, and our governments. We communicate these ideas with language—an evolutionary capability that sets our species apart from all others on the planet and that allows us great intellectual advancement ranging from science to philosophy. As we look at the big picture, it's hard to understand how information itself could be news.

From very early in the development of human society, we seem to have had an awareness of the value of what we know about ourselves. Earliest humans left their messages in carefully chosen caves where the information would be passed on to as yet unborn generations. (Little did they know that some of their drawings would survive thousands of years to be seen by people living in a world entirely different from theirs.) Even in those distant times, this self-knowledge was so precious that it was part of that culture's rituals—rituals that most likely had to do with birth, death, and the celebration of life. Many of the cave drawings are interpreted as representing important events in the history of the tribe, and thus serving one of human-kind's most common information functions, that of keeping track of the past.

Throughout our history, information of various kinds has been part of the power structure of tribes, states, and kingdoms. When what today we call science was still considered magic, information about chemistry was a well-guarded secret of a powerful group. Information on all topics was sequestered during the period we call the Dark Ages in a highly successful attempt to keep the common folk from hav-ing the means to question the medieval social structure. Even today, powerful segments of our population control the information that allows them to maintain their dominance in their particular areas of operation. From the early years of the modern medical profession, experts in the field have argued that laypersons should not have access to medical information since they would not know how to use this information wisely. Businesses sequester information that would be beneficial to their rivals. And today's CIA has such a store of documents classified top secret that the weeding and reclassifying of these documents after the end of the cold war is an impossibly large task.

The axiom "information is power" is only partly true, however. As Clifford Stoll, author of *Silicon Snakeoil*, remarked via E-mail to one librarian: "If information is power, how come librarians have zero power?" The answer is that the power lies in controlling and limiting access to the information; in giving it out to certain people at certain times in a chesslike rivalry for political or monetary ad-vantage. Libraries do the opposite of wielding power; libraries pro-mote democracy by spreading the power of information out to the general population. Freely disseminated, information loses its ability to concentrate power in the few. This was the original intention of the founders of the first democracy in the New World: to eliminate the concentration of power that the Old World royalty had enjoyed by making every citizen in the New World a full participant in civic decision making. In this worldview, equal access to information is an essential component of the democratic ideal. This ideal was visible in our country's early emphasis on education and literacy. The citizens of the New World colonies were avid readers of locally published newspapers and pamphlets, many of which were key to the formation of the ideas of the American Revolution.

So if all societies are, to some degree, information societies, what is the change that has come about? What is all of the current excitement about information?

## The Information Economy

A more accurate statement about our world than information society is that we have become an *information economy*. While information has always been an element of power, and has even been bought and sold, other products were key to the economic well-being of nations. We've relied on basic elements of production like steel, oil, and manufactured goods.

It has long been the case that the mere act of producing goods is not the key to economic achievement. It was in the last century that competition between manufacturers of similar products became the norm. Before that, there was no question of brand-names—people merely purchased the products available in their area. Improvements in manufacturing and transportation meant that companies were moving into each other's markets. To compete with each other it became necessary to build the idea of customer loyalty. Winning that battle for the market means knowing a great deal about consumers and about the competition. This is where marketing comes in.

The information resources of marketing became more sophisticated in the early part of the twentieth century as marketing became a "science." And in the latter half of this century, computers made it possible for us to gather and collate much larger amounts of information than ever before, increasing the complexity and sophistication of the game of competition. The success of a product today has as much to do with the image it projects and its presentation to consumers as it does to the substance of the product itself, and the elements of that success are made up of information about the market.

Information is also part of the machinery of our world. It drives our factories and our offices; it is the input and output of corporate decision making, and thus has great influence on our economy. We have become so dependent on information that our world could not survive today without it. Take away the information capability and factory owners no longer know how much to produce, shippers don't know where to send the goods, and retailers can't manage their inventory. So much depends on information management that we could not function today without it.

Today we have reached the point where information has taken on a value of its own as a commodity on the market. This stands in opposition to the earlier view of information as a public good and an essential element of democracy. If information is the product of the 90s, as it has been called, it implies that you will not be giving it away for free in an effort to equalize opportunity.

## The Information Highway

In 1985 few people outside the university and research community were aware of the existence of the Internet. The number of computers connected over the Internet was less than two thousand. These computers were of the less-than-friendly variety and it took some technical savvy to participate in the online community. Most Internet users were involved in research or higher education, and overwhelmingly in scientific and technical fields. The computers themselves were the size of large desks or good-sized armoires. Far from "personal" computers, they were each shared by as many as hundreds of different users.

By 1990 the number of computers directly connected to the Internet had grown to over three hundred thousand, and since then this number has doubled every twelve to eighteen months, until the figures for early 1997 will top sixteen million. Many factors contribute to this growth, not the least of which is the increase in the number of computers, especially personal computers on desktops and in homes.

The users of the Internet today are different from the original scientists who founded the network of networks, as the Internet is known. (The name *Internet* actually comes from an early description that referred to it as an "internetwork" of computers.) They would have to be—current estimates of the number of Internet users are in the area of ten to thirty million, and they can't possibly all be scientists and engineers. As more people have gotten onto the Internet, it has changed, and as it has changed more people have gotten onto it. The basic interface of the Internet until the early 1990s was really no interface at all—a blank screen where one had to type commands. Today's Internet presents itself with a graphical point-and-click interface familiar to Windows or Macintosh users. No longer do we have to know the underlying Internet protocols to make use of its resources.

Though Internet use is still the realm of the computer literate, today everyone knows that the Internet exists. It has been the topic of hundreds of news reports, and the presence of a URL (a uniform resource locator often starting with "http://") has become *de rigeur* for advertisers who wish to appear hip or modern. During the decade from 1985 to 1995, the Internet went from being primarily a tool for scientific and technical research to being part of the world of advertising. This is quite a transition, and it has happened with amazing speed. It was science fiction writer Bruce Sterling whom I heard say that Internet years are like dog years—there are at least seven of them for every calendar year.

Users of online systems, however, were estimated in 1996 to be only about 15 to 20 percent of the population of our country, and users of the Internet itself about 10 to 15 percent. Despite the fact that 40 percent of American households had some kind of personal computer, only 40 percent of those also had a modem. The fact is that most people in our society have never followed an Internet address to its place in cyberspace.

The term *Information Highway* was first used by Al Gore in 1989, but didn't come into common usage until 1993 when the Clinton administration announced its plans for a National Information Infrastructure (NII). Almost immediately, the NII was being referred to in the media by the catchier title of Information Highway (and later, Information Superhighway). The original Information Highway that Al Gore referred to was a Federal project called the National Research and Education Network (NREN). The NREN wasn't intended to bring networked computing to the general population; instead, it was a Federal bill designed to upgrade the telecommunications connections between major supercomputer centers in the United States. As originally proposed, it would benefit primarily the scientific research community. In only a few years this has become a promise to bring this new technology to all of the American people. Hardly anyone talks about the NREN program anymore, though it is still going forward. We have a new dream: the Information Highway.

A great deal of confusion surrounds the NII, the Information Highway, and the Internet. It isn't made any clearer by the fact that the Internet exists, and the other two are still just figments of a Federal agenda. People often start speaking about the Information Highway only to lapse into stories about the Internet, as if there were no difference between the two. And while the Internet is growing and changing at record speeds, very little visible progress has been made on the NII. It is natural for people to gravitate to what they can actually see today rather than to something that hasn't yet been clearly defined.

The commercial marketplace is also concentrating on the Internet. The development of the first easy-to-use graphical interface based on the World Wide Web (WWW) made it possible for advertisers to present their products in cyberspace. The WWW permits the on-screen presentation of both pictures and text and therefore maintains the logos and "look-and-feel" that is so important to advertising. The commercial world works on immediate results, and is not going to wait for a decade of development before taking advantage of a new technology that could mean increased sales or greater marketing advantage.

## The Future of the Information Highway

It is at this point that the term Information Highway no longer serves us well. What is actually being planned for the future is a general overhaul of our communications industry, including telephone, television, cable communications, and radio. This is prompted by the technological change of *digitization*. Where once voice was carried as analog signals over wires, and television was broadcast as waves through the air, both picture and sound can now be delivered through computer technology that digitizes the information for transmission. These digital signals can be sent over any number of transmission methods, both wired and wireless, and reinterpreted at the receiving end to produce sound or pictures. What this means for the communications industry is that telephone wires can carry more than voice (as they do today whenever anyone uses a modem to communicate with a computer); cable wires can carry voice or data as well as video; and we can receive almost any kind of communication from the wireless bandwidth in the atmosphere around us.

In the U.S. Department of Commerce document *The National Information Infrastructure: Agenda for Action,* which launched the NII, it was made clear by the Clinton administration that the role of the government is not to create the NII, but to facilitate its creation by commercial interests. The first step in this facilitation is the deregulation of the telecommunications industry to create a more competitive marketplace. The Telecommunications Act of 1996, signed into law in February of that year, opened a new era for the companies that have traditionally brought us telephone service, cable service, and our broadcast media. This complex law eliminates many of the restrictions that had been placed on these industries when they were given monopoly positions over sections of the market. Previously, the companies in these sectors were not allowed to compete in each other's areas—telephone companies couldn't own or operate cable services, nor provide content over the telephone system; and no parent company could own more than a small percentage of the media outlets (radio, television, and newspapers) in any given geographic area. It will now be possible for a company to provide a full range of services over any one or combination of communications technologies. The traditional separation between our communications media will soon melt away as the industry finds new alliances and shapes new markets.

Many public interest groups are concerned that the deregulated telecommunications companies will be more powerful than ever. Even before the passage of the law in the Federal legislature, companies had been preparing mergers that would most likely result in the formation of a small number of very large companies positioned to take part in the digital future. The 1996 law included only minimal requirements for public service on the part of those providing communications and media services. In general, requirements like universal service are considered to be anticompetitive in nature and therefore need to be eliminated or limited in scope.

## Information, Infotainment, and the Highway

Deregulation of the telecommunications industries not only allows cable companies, telephone companies, and broadcasters to compete in what were previously each other's separate jurisdictions, it allows all these companies to enter into the business of providing content. Under previous regulations that governed the telephone monopoly, telephone companies provided equipment and wiring but could neither regulate nor produce the messages carried across those wires. The idea was that for a company to own both the physical infrastructure and have control over the content would give that company the power to squelch any competition or dissenting voices. In essence, the television and radio industries do have this power—they alone decide the content of the messages carried across their signals. (Well, they and their advertisers.) Although this is supposedly offset by the requirement that stations carry public service information, we know that the overwhelming majority of the content of television is created by the media companies, not by citizen groups. Part of what limits widespread participation in broadcast media is the expense of program production. In addition, the scarcity of broadcast bandwidth determines the number of stations that are available. All of this makes it very difficult for anyone other than the primary media companies to produce and air programs.

There is a great deal of interest in making content available over the Information Highway, not only on the part of the telecommunications industry but also of those companies that already produce news, information, and entertainment. The Information Highway promises to create a market for services like video on demand, personalized news, and other value-added information products. It is widely assumed that the most lucrative business on the Information Highway will not be the wiring and transporting of digital products but the selling of programs and information services, regardless of how they are delivered to the home.

What exactly will these programs and services be? The NII plan requires the Federal government to disseminate its information electronically, and already many states and local governments are deciding to follow suit. There is also a specific interest in using electronic communications to further medical science and our health services. But other than these applications of government information and medicine, we have no idea what the content of the Information Highway will be.

## Designing the Information Highway

When beginning to create a new computer system, computer professionals will tell you that you must do what is called a *needs analysis* in which you attempt to understand what needs the system will fulfill and how it can do this best. Amazingly, no such analysis has been done for the Information Highway. This is strange in a consumer society where great study and testing are done on almost all products. We seem to have more information about the market possibilities of a new deodorant than we do for the entire Information Highway.

The fact is, we shouldn't really be concerning ourselves about hardware and delivery until we determine what it is that we will be delivering. The components of the system could change greatly, depending on what needs they are attempting to fulfill. Then we should build the system that best meets that goal.

Some tests of information delivery have been done, though most have been notable by their failure rather than by their success. Market studies of online shopping or banking through televideo technology have uniformly shown that people don't engage in enough of that kind of activity to pay for such a system. The shopping channel on cable television is successful, though when shoppers were interviewed they often stated that their favorite part of the service was that they got to call an 800 number and talk to people on the other end of the line. Had it been a totally automated mail order service, they would have been less interested.

Too often, expensive trial systems are built before their purpose seems to be thought through. The state of California decided that it wanted a kiosk system to deliver its information to the public. A test system was developed, at great expense, and about fifty kiosks were installed in such public locations as malls and supermarkets. The system's display was videolike, with full motion segments and audio instructions. But today's computer screens allow for only a small amount of information to be displayed at a time. So, for example, in the section of the program about the state tax system, there was room on the screen for only a half dozen typical tax questions, each of which, when touched, pulled up a single screen answer. In most cases, the "answer" was the address and phone number of the state franchise tax board.

The problem was that the kiosk was not a good way to deliver complex state information. It was necessary to stand when using it, so any text or multimedia presentation that lasted for more than a few minutes would soon tire the viewer's patience (and legs). The kiosks provided no privacy, so they couldn't be used to deliver information on any topics that users wouldn't want to access in public (for example, directing the user to local clinics that treat sexually transmitted diseases).

Even more disturbing, the state's measure of the kiosk program's success was to count the number of accesses with no follow-up on whether users had found what they were seeking. The day I stood in a grocery store watching people use the system, it was mainly being used by preteenaged children who were bored with the grocery store experience. It was a machine they could manipulate, and it didn't require quarters to keep it running.

The Federal government also proposed a kiosk plan to deliver its information. Initially, the kiosks were to be placed in post offices throughout the country. It took a group of librarians meeting with

Federal officials to convince them that many people accessing Federal information need expert help in finding appropriate resources. This expert help is not available in post offices—as a matter of fact, the original kiosk program did not include any help beyond what was present on the screen. The program was modified to include the placement of kiosks in libraries as well as other public places.

Rather than proposing information systems, we should be studying the information needs of our population, and how best to respond to them. These studies would need to reveal what information we use already and what information we might make use of if it were available to us. (It would be essential to include libraries in these studies, since we already have experience in delivering information to the general public.) From such studies we could then determine the proper way to deliver the information to the user. For some information, the best answer might be to use digital communications systems. For other information, other media, even print, may be more appropriate.

Computers are especially effective when the information is only useful when it is very up-to-date. An example of information that we need in its most up-to-date form is traffic reports. Today's radio stations that cater to the commuter crowd give traffic reports every ten minutes in metropolitan areas. Automobile commuters can listen to these reports while driving and can change their route according to the information they receive. This system currently works quite well. But in southern California, they are experimenting with a more sophisticated technology to deliver traffic information: sensors in the highways report traffic speeds to a central office where the information is made available via the World Wide Web (WWW) over the Internet. This would be a useful system except for one problem: its delivery mechanism. Motorists cannot search the WWW for this information while driving (and we hope that they do not try!) so they can't get updates on traffic conditions once they leave their homes or offices. Why gather this information if you can't deliver it to the users at the point that they need it?

The fact is that the traffic information might still best be delivered by the older technology of radio, just as it is today. An auditory rather than a visual display allows drivers to keep their eyes on the road, for the greater safety of all. In this example, focusing on the information need rather than on the technology will lead to better, more usable information systems.

Unfortunately, the Information Highway is not being designed from the point of view of information needs—it is being designed from the point of view of an economic need to expand the market for communications technologies. We have extensive systems of telephone lines, cable technology, and broadcast bandwidth (television and radio). The task that the current administration has taken on is to make these into the Information Highway. The task that we should be taking on is that of determining what the Information Highway should be and how it could best serve each community in this nation.

It is worth questioning whether our current approach will actually result in the creation of an information system, as opposed to a new form of entertainment. There is a large and powerful commercial contingent that clearly intends to make the Information Highway the next Hollywood. These people are not all wet. I was doing my usual Saturday afternoon at my neighborhood branch of the public library, showing people how to use the library's Internet access. I coaxed one young woman over to take a look and took her on a quick tour. After a minute she said to me: "Show me the really good stuff." I told her that she was looking at some of the best the Net had to offer, and asked her what she had expected. "But it's just a bunch of reading," she said. The great deal of hype about the wonders of the Internet had led her to expect something rivaling the latest Hollywood thriller. Not only is that more entertaining, but when you consider the level of functional illiteracy in our country—the number of people for whom text is a barrier—then you understand the push for multimedia or video on demand.

The question here of course is whether we will produce a televisionlike interface to market the Information Highway to nonreaders, or whether we will put our energy into increasing the literacy in our country so they can make use of quality information products. If we do not work on literacy, it is doubtful that the Information Highway will provide the same quality of content to nonreaders as well as readers.

We also have to wonder what information will be available over a purely commercially oriented system. As librarians, we know something that may not yet have entered into the consciousness of the upper echelons of the telecommunications industry: there is a lot of information that has very little, if any, commercial potential. Much of the information that we use every day is pretty mundane—weather and traffic reports, local bus schedules, community meetings, and so on. We don't pay for this information today, and we're unlikely to welcome the idea of paying for it in the future. Other information either has too small an audience (the schedule of a church's monthly events) or too poor a one (instructions on how to apply for welfare benefits) for it to even pay for itself in terms of gathering and delivery.

Remember that information is also an important component in any social service. For example, there is public health information that has to reach nearly everyone in our population—information on immunization programs for children, or information on safe sex. Getting these particular units of information out to the public cannot be left to chance. It also can't be left to the kind of self-selection that characterizes traditional commercial markets where ability to pay determines all. It isn't enough to reach members of the middle class about the main risk factors for HIV infection when those in our society who are most at risk are more likely to live in poverty. The commercial marketplace is unlikely to take on the task of providing this type of socially essential information.

The issue of universal access focuses on this problem of how the Information Highway will serve all members of our society. There is concern on the part of public interest groups that this new medium will be dominated, just as television and radio today are, by a few large media companies. This would essentially eliminate the promise that we have already seen in the community networking or Free-Net movement to create small-scale information systems that can nourish the particular needs of any size community within our borders.

There are numerous ideas on how to combine the commercial information function and the nonprofit and social services information functions in a single system. Some public interest groups have suggested that we have a public "lane" on the Information Highway. This designated portion of the Information Highway could be used by schools, government, libraries, and health services. Others want to retain a version of the nonprofit Internet separate from the Information Highway that will be developed by the commercial sector.

As of this writing, there is no plan for mediating the interests of for-profit and nonprofit information providers. It may be too early for such a plan since the nature of the future Information Highway is still in large part a mystery. The risk is that when we do finally understand the structure of modern communications technology, it could be too late to shoehorn in a place for the public sector.

# 2

## The Promise of the Information Highway

### A Librarian's History of the Internet

When I first encountered the Internet in the mid-1980s, I had no idea that it would or even could evolve into the rich information resource it is today. In those days, the content of the Internet was primarily programs, not documents. And to download a program you had to know its file name and the name of a computer on which it could be found. The first user-friendly retrieval tool released in 1990 was a program called Archie that allowed you to find the location of a file on the Internet, but you still had to know its file name or a good portion of its file name. Archie was the electronic equivalent of the hand-written title catalogs kept by twelfth-century monks, but the Internet users considered it the best thing since sliced bread.

In spite of its unfriendliness, some libraries had found ways to make good use of the Internet. The first of these were academic libraries whose parent institutions were universities with state-of-the-art network connections and expert technical staffs. The libraries made their online catalogs available to the public of Internet users through a simple remote logon interface. This allowed researchers and librarians at distant institutions to consult the catalogs of some of the foremost libraries in the world. In 1990 Peter Scott of the University of Saskatchewan released a program called Hytelnet that allowed the user to view a list of library catalogs available on the Internet and automatically made the remote logon connection to each. This meant that users who weren't familiar with Internet commands could easily "surf" from one library catalog to another. A new era had begun.

But the Internet still wasn't an information system, unless computer source code and online catalogs fulfilled all of your information needs. That was about to change. In 1991 researchers at the University of Minnesota computing center designed the Gopher protocol to help them deliver campus information through a single interface. Gopher allowed the development of menu-based hierarchies that pointed to resources on local computers or located anywhere on the Internet. Though originally intended as a campuswide information system, Gopher became a general organizing tool for the Internet. Libraries took to the creation of Gophers in a big way. After all, who knew better how to organize information into categories and subcategories? The library Gophers were the best and the most extensive and quickly gained the admiration of large numbers of Internet users.

Gopher had an unexpected but profound effect on the Internet. It encouraged people to make more information available, and it expanded Internet use beyond the computer elite who had dominated it in its early years. Encouraged by the ease of the use and the wide range of the audience, institutions, government agencies, and nonprofit organizations began placing their documents on the Internet for worldwide distribution. The Gopher software was improved over time and soon allowed users to download graphical files as well as text; full-color weather satellite images were posted hourly to the Internet, an enticing preview of a future of ubiquitous, real-time information services.

Gopher was the primary user interface to the Internet well into 1994. Its successor, the World Wide Web, was also developed in 1991 but didn't become known to most users until the software Mosaic was developed at the University of Illinois in 1993. Mosaic allowed users to view the World Wide Web through an easy-to-use graphical interface. And the Web offered a more sophisticated view of online documents, with the ability to create *hyperlinks* from one document to another and to incorporate pictures and even sound right into the online document itself. In 1993 use of the World Wide Web increased 341,634 percent, according to Hobbes' Internet Timeline.

As I write this in 1996, the Internet that I visit for news and information would have been totally unrecognizable to a user in 1985. Full-color images, often carrying commercial advertising messages, appear on nearly every screen that I encounter. Some of the images dance across the virtual page as tiny, "pixelated" cartoons. I have used the Internet to listen to conferences that I could not attend in person and have even watched a short video of myself answering a reporter's questions.

Somewhere along the way from the early 1980s, when the Internet began, to the present, a change took place that transformed a little-known scientific tool into a national program called the National Information Infrastructure (NII), also known as the Information Highway. To understand how this happened, we need to look at the official history, one that goes beyond libraries.

# The "Official" History of the Internet

A defense department project called Advanced Research Projects Agency Network (ARPANET) linked some military, research, and academic computer centers in the 1960s and 70s. University computers were connected to this network to the extent that they engaged in defense-related projects. By the late 1970s it was clear to the university community that it could make use of a computer network for a wide variety of research that wasn't necessarily defense-related. So in 1981 the university community formed its own internetwork of computer centers apart from ARPANET. This internetwork was soon dubbed the Internet.

The purpose of the Internet was to serve the needs of the high-tech research community. In a world of mainframe computers, users then were overwhelmingly scientists, engineers, and technicians, and computers themselves were relatively rare. The Internet began in 1981 with less than one hundred computers connected together.

The use of computers expanded greatly in the 1980s with mini- and micro-computers making these machines available to many more users. As computer use grew, so did the Internet. By the end of 1985, there were about two thousand computers connected to the interrelated networks that made up the Internet.

Recognizing the value of computer communications for the development of science, the National Science Foundation (NSF) created a program that funded high-speed data lines connecting the six NSF supercomputer centers in the United States. Called the NSFNET, this high-speed network also carried data traffic between the non-supercomputer Internet sites. Thus it became the backbone of the Internet, increasing the capacity of the system manyfold.

# HPCC, NREN, and the NII

By mid-1990 the number of computers on the Internet had grown to 300,000, and the network was feeling the pinch from this rapid growth in traffic. So in 1991 yet another piece of legislation was introduced in support of computer communications for the education and research community. Called the High-Performance Computing Act of 1991, it proposed the creation of a National Research and Education Network (NREN). This time, however, there was interest beyond that of a small community of scientists and engineers.

Computer use had moved beyond the original world of science and electrical engineering and was becoming common for basic office activities like creating documents, managing small business accounts, and database management. Internet use had also expanded beyond the strictly scientific community. For example, in 1991 there were already over two hundred libraries whose catalogs were available over the Internet. These were university libraries, and they were able to make use of the Internet through their parent institutions, where Internet access by now was common in all academic areas.

The more forward-thinking members of the library world realized that the future of libraries was in their use of computer networks. The American Library Association (ALA) had been closely following the discussions leading up to the NREN proposal, even providing statements to the legislature during its development phase. When NREN was announced in March 1991, ALA was ready and responded with its own set of requirements in a statement to the Subcommittee on Science, Technology and Space that positioned libraries undeniably in the "E" of NREN. Among other things, ALA asked for high-capacity network connections in all fifty states and direct connections for major national libraries and all state libraries. And it made the point that libraries—all libraries—should be part of the new digital communications infrastructure.

While specific amendments to the NREN bill that would fund connections to libraries and schools were not part of the final bill that passed, something important had happened during the discussions inside and outside of Congress: the idea had been planted, at least partly thanks to the ALA, that the time had come to extend computer networking beyond the academic and scientific environment to, as ALA termed it, "education in its broadest sense." This would include the nation's public libraries as the primary institutions of continuing education in our society.

When the Clinton administration released its plan for the National Information Infrastructure in 1993, it was clear that this role of libraries had been fully absorbed into the process:

> Most importantly, the NII requires building foundations for living in the Information Age and for making these technological advances useful to the public, business, libraries, and other non-governmental entities (NII: Agenda for Action).

# What It Is—and Isn't

It's common to see the terms National Information Infrastructure, the Information Highway, and the Internet used interchangeably. While they aren't the same thing, their meanings have become so intertwined that it isn't possible to create a complete separation between them.

## *The Internet*

The Internet is our largest existing network of computers. It is difficult to describe this network to anyone who has not used it because it has a very fluid structure. The type of governance that keeps the Internet running is best described as a *cooperative,* though it has also been called a *working anarchy.* There is no ruling body that plans Internet growth or that determines what content will be obtainable. Instead, expert Internet users form committees, known collectively as the Internet Engineering Task Force, as needed. These committees resolve technical problems and develop the standards that allow computers to exchange data or to participate in online offerings such as the World Wide Web.

User-driven, the Internet developed its capabilities in response to the needs of its community. The underlying structure of the Internet reflects the needs of the original academic and research community that first developed it. One of the needs that the Internet did not have at its inception was that of supporting commerce. During the early years of the Internet, it was actually a violation of the Appropriate Use Policy to use the Internet for advertising or promotion of commercial products. This was because the Internet received Federal funding and therefore couldn't be used for commercial gain. It wasn't until 1991 that the Commercial Internet eXchange (CIX) began carrying traffic, allowing companies to make use of the Internet for their business. The CIX user traffic was carried over commercially funded data lines, but CIX users could also intercommunicate on the Internet with other users like any other subnetwork of the Internet. Today there is very little separation between commercial and noncommercial traffic on the Internet.

The Internet has no sense of geography. The reason that users refer to the area covered by the Internet as *cyberspace* is because it has no relationship to real Earth space. On the Internet your only location is relative to the map of network connections, that is, your subnet and subsubnet in relation to the whole interconnection of computers. That map does not indicate in any way where you are located on Earth. For many people that is one of the marvels of Internet communications: you can be in the midst of a deeply interesting conversation before you discover that you are communicating with someone in another country. Geographical distances are irrelevant.

## The National Information Infrastructure

The first sentence of the *National Information Infrastructure: Agenda for Action* (see In Their Own Words at the end of this chapter) described the National Information Infrastructure as "a seamless web of communications networks, computers, databases, and consumer electronics that will put vast amounts of information at users' fingertips."

Development of a true NII is a big project and involves a number of different economic and social sectors. Telecommunications companies need to build the wired and wireless systems that will carry the information. The broadcast, publishing, and entertainment industries must begin creating the new content that will travel over those systems. The computer hardware and software makers need to create the consumer products that serve as the access points to the NII. Schools and libraries have to take on the educational roles that will prepare all users to make use of this new technology.

All of this requires thought and planning, and some of it requires government action. This latter is especially true of the telecommunications component of the NII. The telephone, cable, and broadcast industries in this country have all been traditionally regulated by the government. Regulation of telephone service dates from the Communications Act of 1934, which was based on the understanding that telephone service could not be provided in a nonmonopoly situation. This natural monopoly has been superseded by more modern technology, and the breakup of AT&T in 1984 into regional telephone systems was the first step in eliminating the barriers to competition in this area. Broadcast regulations are based on a finite bandwidth that limits the number of stations and channels that can exist. Again, modern networking technology virtually eliminates this barrier to open competition.

The telecommunications regulations were also based on a separation of functions in our communications technologies. The telephone carried voice, television had picture and sound, radio had broadcast sound only, and cable was a line-based delivery of broadcast signals. This neat division of telecommunications functions based on the underlying technology is no longer appropriate, however. When most communications are transmitted digitally, it really doesn't matter whether you use a telephone line, a cable, or radio waves. Once limited to sound transmissions, the telephone line today can just as easily carry data or video. The same cable that brings you television programming can, with the proper equipment at both ends, serve as a telephone line or an Internet connection.

By the end of the 1980s, many legislators were of the view that the kind of regulations put into place in 1934 and even 1984 to protect consumers were no longer necessary for that purpose. Instead, they were seen as hindering the development of new businesses and new technologies. It was the announcement of the NII program in 1993 that served to open up a wider dialogue among officials about the possible steps that could be taken toward deregulation.

So we can define the NII essentially as a government program to deregulate the telecommunications marketplace, to stimulate technical development, and to encourage the high-tech world to fully enter the telecommunications marketplace. The product of the NII is the "seamless web" lauded in the *Agenda for Action,* and that web will be created by a marketplace unhindered by regulation.

## The Information Highway

If nothing else, the choice of the phrase Information Highway to describe our future communications and information system has helped the vision of it to penetrate every level of our society. Though only about 15 percent of our population has any experience with modern computer networks, everyone can understand the highway metaphor.

The word *highway* brings up an image of speed for many people, and that is definitely one of the selling points of modern communications. Messages travel across computer networks at speeds that are measured in microseconds. Information arrives on our screens in fractions of seconds, whether it comes from around the globe or around the corner. In modern network terms Tokyo is no farther away from us than our nearest North American metropolitan center.

The highway metaphor also reminds us of commerce. Highways are used to move products from the place of manufacture to their market. The Information Highway is tomorrow's product delivery system. And highways are a part of our national defense system, harking back to the origins of the Internet as a Defense Department project. The defense component of that original network is no longer functioning as part of the Internet, but isolates itself in a secure network that is not accessible to others. Like our highway system, today we are aware mainly of its civil uses.

When we talk about the Information Highway, we aren't so much referring to a specific system or design or plan. We use Information Highway to talk about the big picture—the future of digital communications that began with the Internet and that will develop in as yet unknown directions.

# Goals

Though it may sometimes seem that the Information Highway is a haphazard development, it is being influenced by some clear goals. Different sectors of society have different plans for the Information Highway, of course, but some goals are surfacing that are shared by most.

## *Move Forward Economically*

The Information Highway has everything to do with economic growth, especially in the international market. In a speech before the National Net '92 Conference on March 25, 1992, Congressman Frederick C. Boucher (D-Va.) told the audience that Japan had committed to installing fiber optic cables to every home and business in that country by 2015. By his estimation the United States could accomplish the same thing by 2010. International competition in the high-tech end of business is key to our future economic strength. This economic goal is clearly foremost in the minds of those who guide our country in the legislature and of those whose business decisions have an impact on our national economy.

Today's industries are predominantly information-oriented, rather than reliant on manufacturing or heavy industry. In a global economy, success can be determined by having the right information at the right time. Even in the manufacturing sectors, delivery of a successful product to market is often as much dependent on information about the market as it is on the quality of the product itself. A well-functioning information infrastructure will make American business more competitive in future markets.

## Increase Scientific Activity

To perform scientific research today requires sophisticated computer systems. The Human Genome Project, which is mapping our genetic material, could not be done without supercomputers. Archaeology, ecology, materials science—all use computers in some part of their work. Computers on networks can be used to share databases or to expand the research community to include scientists not located in the same geographical area. For some projects multiple networked computers are needed to perform like a single computer, able to do tasks that no one computer can complete on its own.

Our future is driven by scientific achievement, and useful science can come from unexpected quarters. We are often reminded of the common household products that originated with the space program like Tang.

## Improve Delivery of Social Services

Like business, social services are information-intensive activities. It is important that services be delivered as efficiently as possible to those who need them, especially in these times of increasing need and decreasing resources. Information is key to that efficiency. Social services not only have to gather, organize, and analyze information about their target constituencies, they also have a need to reach out to people who might need their services. Reaching those in need of services is a difficult problem today. Our broadcast media, which are the main sources of information for most people, have only a few public service slots in their programming. Television and radio stations today cover huge metropolitan areas and can't possibly carry all of the messages for the many local communities in their area in the few time slots available.

A public service information network could target an unlimited number of communities, delivering information and information services. Community networks and Free-Nets are already experimenting with this kind of public service. Communication could be in the language of the recipient or geared to the person's age or educational level. To achieve this, however, we need a truly ubiquitous system—one that reaches into every home and is available even to the homeless and nomadic. It must be as common as television and accessible for the price of a phone call. That's a large order, but one some people are working toward.

## Boost High-Technology Industry

It is stating the obvious that the Information Highway will be a boon to the high-technology industries in this country and abroad. The high-technology sector is growing faster than our overall economy, which makes it vital to our country's economic strength.

What might be slightly less obvious is how the high-technology industry is intertwined with just about every other business in our world. A good example is the link today between high technology and Hollywood; our entertainment industry is highly dependent on the development of faster computers and more powerful graphical capabilities for its blockbuster movie hits. The selling of our entertainment products both here and abroad is due to our advanced special effects and computer-driven animation features, both of which are proving to be great audience pleasers.

High technology also reaches into the more traditional areas of our economy as well. Farmers rely on detailed information from orbiting satellites to make decisions affecting their crops. Banks, of course, do most of their business as digital information transmissions and will do so increasingly as physical cash is replaced by online transactions. Retailers stock their stores and take inventory over complex computer networks. The benefits of a strong high-technology industry are felt throughout our business community.

## Bring Government Closer to the People

The Internet is already being used to bring more government information to the public. Congressional bills are now made available online in their marked-up form, and a number of state legislatures are providing the same service for state bills. You can retrieve press releases, agency reports, and various documents that previously were not readily available outside the Washington Beltway. The Government Printing Office and the Depository Library Program are developing online services that could eventually make the entire published output of the Federal government instantly accessible by everyone in the United States.

## Who Will Build the NII?

The mere sound of the phrase National Information Infrastructure smacks of a big government project. It doesn't help that we often refer to the NII as the Information Highway, since the highway metaphor also can lead to the assumption that this digital highway will also be built with government monies. In addition, the Federal government involvement in the Internet through NSFNET and scientific research funding gave many people the impression that the NII would be just a continuation of that funding.

However, each of these assumptions is wrong. From the very first mention of the NII, the Federal government has made it clear that this future communications system will be built by the commercial sector. The *Agenda for Action* states: "By encouraging private sector investment in the NII's development, and through government programs to improve access to essential services, we will promote U.S. competitiveness, job creation and solutions to pressing social problems." The NII is first and foremost an economic agenda, evidenced by the fact that the planning process is taking place under the aegis of the Department of Commerce.

It's not a great leap to see the commercial sector as the builder of the NII. We already have a strong networking industry, employing technologies capable of creating the next generation of communication systems. That was not the case in 1985 when the National Science Foundation funded Internet networking as a scientific research project. Yet just two years later in 1987 when the NSF needed to expand the Internet backbone that it ran, it received bids from a number of telecommunications and computer companies. During those years computer networking had moved beyond the purely research sphere and into the commercial sector. When the proposals were made for the development of the NREN and then the NII, there were companies in the private sector that could provide network services for these projects, making it possible for the government to step out of its role as network provider.

Many users of the Internet who were online before the commercial sector entry into the network were unhappy to see the Internet go commercial. In fact, the whole nature of the network is changing. The

Internet was a small, elite system serving only our research and academic communities, and initially only the scientific branches of those institutions. Although Internet was ostensibly a "public" system (meaning paid for with public funds), the NII is intended to be "public" in the sense that it will serve every person in the country.

This makes the network more of a consumer product, and one that reaches out directly to the users. There will not be institutions intervening between the user and the network as there are when one uses the Internet from one's workplace or educational institution. To create a system that reaches such a large and varied user base, it is necessary to rely on organizations that have proven track records for such service. The telephone companies and cable companies are closer to that than the Federal government.

In terms of the building of the NII, the primary role of the Federal government is to clear the way for open competition among the many industries interested in participating in the NII through products and services. The first major step in this direction was the Telecommunications Act of 1996. First introduced in 1995 as the Telecommunications Competitiveness Act, this bill is a major reform of telecommunications law. It opened the door for competition among telephone, cable, and wireless communications companies and eliminated many of the regulatory constraints on the telecommunications industry that had been in place since the early part of this century.

That deregulation is not by any means absolute, and telecommunications companies are still obliged to provide equitable access to a basic set of products and services. In the latter half of 1996, the Federal Communications Commission held extensive hearings and discussion to define universal service in this new environment. Included in this universal service package were special discounts for schools and libraries to help them achieve the President's goal of full connection by the year 2000.

## The Public Interest

While major U.S. corporations were praising the Congress for introducing the telecommunications reform bill, public interest groups were expressing their concerns about the possible social impact of these changes. A coalition of nearly one hundred such groups formed the Telecommunications Policy Roundtable, which meets regularly in Washington, D.C., to discuss issues of interest. These groups plus other groups that formed directly out of the Internet community, such as the Voters Telecommunications Watch and the Center for Democracy and Technology, have been a major voice in defense of the public interest. But it's a small voice compared to that of the companies who stand to profit most from the deregulated marketplace.

At the core of the difference of opinion between the public interest advocates and the commercial sector is their view of information. In the commercial world, information has been called the product of the 90s, and the NII is the intended product delivery system. To many in the public sector, information is not just another product—it is an essential component of social services, government, and civic life. Libraries, of course, are the embodiment of the public view of information, and librarians and library groups are active in this debate, which sometimes becomes an open challenge from the commercial world. In the week that Windows 95 was released for sale, Microsoft ran a half hour "infomercial" that included a scene in which a student discovers that he no longer has to go to the library to do research for a school report. That infomercial also showed a classroom of children gathered around state-of-the-art equipment while the teacher explained that their school library no longer received funding, but that the children could now find whatever they needed on the Internet. These messages were mild compared to the Packard Bell commercial of late 1996 that showed downtrodden masses marching to a dreary library and kept at their desks by uniformed stormtroopers.

Public interest advocates often cite our mass media, such as television and commercial radio, as an example of how commercialized information fails to serve the full diversity of our nation. In addition, they are critical of the one-way information flow that mass media represent. The noncommercial Internet model gives each user the ability to provide information as well as receive it. For the first time in modern history, an individual can have a presence as influential as that of an institution or a company. Nonprofit organizations have taken to the Internet with their messages, partly because the cost of participation was low and the audience one could reach was very large. Many felt that the Internet promoted a newfound democracy.

The entry of the commercial world onto the Internet has already brought about great changes. The World Wide Web sites of companies are designed by professional artists and maintained by full-time staffs. These sites are more elaborate and generally more entertaining than those maintained by individuals or nonprofit groups. The cost of competing for the Internet audience is now much higher than it was just a few years ago when most information was presented in plain text. Even full participation as an information consumer means keeping up with the latest in hardware and software.

## Information Highway and Democracy

The experience of the Internet has encouraged many to see the Information Highway as a tool for political democracy, and many people are using the Internet to campaign for candidates and issues. In the future computer networks could allow representatives in Washington to discuss issues with constituents in their districts before they vote on key legislation. They could provide public interest groups with the same access to the legislative process as professional lobbyists. And they can help individuals form powerful grassroots movements that could have a real impact on our political life.

But there are also many barriers to democracy on the Information Highway. To begin with, less than 20 percent of our population was connected to online communications by mid-1996, and many of those were connected only through their work. This online population is not representative of our country as a whole, but has a higher than average income and level of educational achievement. For the Information Highway to be a democratic tool, we really need to have universal access to this form of communication, at least among those of voting age. Not surprisingly, most political campaigns where the users of the Internet have had an influence have been over issues primarily of interest to the high-tech community, such as encryption and digital telephony.

In addition, the members of our government must also be online. Only a small number of our members of Congress have publicized an E-mail account where they can be reached by their constituents. Among those who do have such accounts, most admit that they don't place the same value on the receipt of a piece of E-mail on a topic as they do on a telephone call, a fax, or a letter. In the words of some, E-mail is just "too easy." Public officials fear being inundated with more E-mail messages than their staffs can read and reply to. These attitudes are likely to change, though it may not happen as quickly as some people would like.

It's also important to realize that any technology that encourages communication can be used for any number of goals, some in direct conflict with others. A good example of this was in the battle over the Communications Decency Act (CDA). Both sides of the CDA debate used the Internet to present their point of view and encourage others to join them, and both sides were able to use the Internet itself as evidence of their point of view.

Many of these same predictions of a democratic upsurge were voiced in the early days of radio and television. As we can see from the current state of these media, technological possibility does not translate to certainty. Optimists like Nicholas Negroponte, author of *Being Digital,* are known to state quite confidently that this technology will indeed be the revolution we desire. Those more prone to pessimism fear increased centralization and a Big Brother-like control of our every electronic action. A more realistic view might be that we have to consciously build democracy into the NII as the system develops.

## Public Interest versus Economic Goals

Documents produced by the Clinton administration show a balance between public interest and economic goals. This balance may not be maintained, however, in the actual building of our information infrastructure. With the emphasis on the economic goals of the Information Highway, public-interest goals may be sacrificed for the good of the general economy. After all, public interest doesn't produce revenues, and, perhaps just as importantly, it doesn't pay for political campaigns or company mergers.

Both the Clinton administration and the corporate world have justified many of their goals relating to the NII with the argument that economic growth itself is in the public interest; it means more jobs, higher pay, and an overall better standard of living. Taking this even further, the Third Wave economic theory of Alvin Toffler describes an upcoming future in which technology gives us the ability to fulfill our own needs without reliance on large institutions. In this vision of the future, social services like schools, libraries, and health care are decentralized and individualized.

Whether or not the Third Wave is an accurate picture of our future, we don't see any lessening of the need for social institutions today. What we are seeing instead is that our current economy is leading to a growing gap between the rich and the poor. In terms of the Information Highway, many of the major players in the NII arena have made it quite clear that they expect Second Wave institutions like schools and public libraries to be the bridge between the information haves and the information have-nots.

The Telecommunications Bill of 1996 was over two hundred pages long at the time it passed. Of all of this text, only a few paragraphs spoke to the public interest. Instead, this will be taken up with some Federal and many state and local agencies that administer public services. At the time of this writing, the Federal Communications Commission (FCC) is still struggling with the task of defining universal service for the new, deregulated telecommunications industry. The FCC has to try to strike a very delicate balance between the need to subsidize the access to advanced telecommunications services and hindering the open, competitive market that will create those services. Public interest is often viewed as a hindrance by advocates of the commercial sector, and we rely on government agencies like the FCC to make sure that a reasonable balance is achieved.

## Information Highway and Libraries

The influence that the Information Highway will have on our libraries is enormous. It alters the information environment, changing the world in which libraries operate. The Information Highway will bring a wealth of resources to even the smallest libraries, allowing them to provide services that before were beyond their means. Though this means an added burden of training and continuing education for library administrations, most libraries feel that the increased service will be well worth the effort that they must expend.

There is a growing assumption that libraries will step in to fill the gap between the information haves and have-nots. Libraries have accepted this goal as part of their traditional role in making sure that information is available equitably in this country. What we don't know today is the extent of the need for publicly supported information access in the future. How many people will have personal access to the Information Highway from their homes? In mid-1996 about 30 percent of our households had a computer, and about 30 percent of those had a modem. Home computer purchases are at an all-time high. But is there a plateau to this increase? And how long will it take for the lower-income families, of whom only about 3 percent have a computer, to catch up with their wealthier neighbors? Note that 7 percent of today's households do not even have telephone service. Is there any hope of connecting these people to the Information Highway?

It isn't known if the library will be providing online access for 3 percent or 10 percent or 40 percent of the population. This makes it very hard to plan library services. We also don't know what the online systems of the future will look like. The NII program was announced over three years ago, as of this writing, yet we still don't have an information infrastructure. We don't even have a blueprint for an information infrastructure. Not having a plan means that the NII serves as a kind of telecommunications Rorschach test—everyone sees in it his or her vision for the future. The cable companies see the NII being served over cable, ending up at a televisionlike appliance in the home with a "set-top box" for controls. The phone companies talk about developing a telephone with a screen and keyboard for E-mail services. And librarians talk of the "library without walls," a world in which we would be awash in information access wherever we went. This suits the wireless communications companies who, if given enough bandwidth, are prepared to have us all connected through radio communications anywhere we go and all of the time. But which one of these visions should be we planning for?

In fact, the Information Highway is likely to be all these things, all at once, and through a variety of delivery mechanisms. There will be false starts and failures before the predominant companies arise, and there will be technologies that don't find a consumer base. It is important to keep in mind that we are just at the very beginning of the development of this new communications system. Not that there is an end—the Information Highway is not something that will ever be finished. Given the speed with which these new telecommunications technologies advance, we can expect that change will be the only constant in our communications future. If there is anyone capable of accurately predicting the direction of the Information Highway, she is keeping it to herself—and her stockbroker!

In its first two years, the National Telecommunications and Information Association (NTIA) gave out $60 million in grants to projects that had as their goal the extension of public access to online communications. Though this funding represented only a drop in the bucket in terms of the fiscal needs of those committed to providing access, in 1996 funding for this project was greatly cut after threats of eliminating the funds altogether. Most libraries that are providing Internet access are doing so "by the seat of their pants," gathering what funding they can from their already tight budgets and creating alliances with any and all community groups that can help them achieve their goals. Though this is an admirable effort on the part of libraries, it threatens to strain their already weakened budgets and to force them into more corners where they have to choose between one worthy service and another. Some patrons at the stunning and controversial new San Francisco Public Library voice their concern that the online connections and fancy workstations in their library will mean fewer books and shorter library hours. In spite of the library's desire to provide the very best service, lack of funding could make these fears come true.

But at this moment things are looking up. The new Library Services and Technology Act is providing grant monies to help libraries get connected to the world of digital information. Some libraries, like Seattle Public, are showing us how community and business alliances can place libraries once again at the center of civic life. The American Library Association is developing projects with major companies like Microsoft and MCI, as well as managing the Fund for America's Libraries, all of which benefit our nation's libraries. It's a new era with new economic models, but it looks as if libraries are catching on fast.

## IN THEIR OWN WORDS

**The National Information Infrastructure: Agenda for Action**
*(Executive Summary)*
U.S. Department of Commerce, 1993, 26 pp.
http://sunsite.unc.edu/nii/toc.html
http://www.cpsr.org/cpsr/nii/ntia_nii_agenda.txt

This is the document that started it all. *Agenda for Action* spells out the basic goals for the National Information Infrastructure. The document sets the scene for the deregulatory actions of 1995 and 1996 by stating clearly that the NII will be built by the commercial sector, not by the government. As you read the list of NII objectives, note the careful mixture of economic and social goals that are articulated there. Balancing these oftentimes conflicting goals will be the measure of the success of the NII.

**Principles for the Development of the National Information Infrastructure**
American Library Association, 1993
http://www.ala.org/oitp/principles.html

The underlying principles for the NII articulated in this document have indeed proven to be the main issues that have arisen for public interest advocates since 1993. ALA's first area of concern is intellectual freedom, foreshadowing the great battle over free speech on the Internet that was brought on by the Communications Decency Act. Intellectual property has also been the target of legislation. Nearly every point here has become a major battle ground, and many of those battles, like the goals in the *Agenda for Action,* are about the balance of economic and social goals.

**Connecting the Nation: Classrooms, Libraries and Health Care Organizations in the Information Age**
*(Executive Summary)*
U.S. Department of Commerce, June 1995
http://www.ntia.doc.gov/connect.html

This report is a first look at the state of network connectivity for the nation's schools, libraries, and health care organizations. The treatment of these three institutions as a single "problem" is in itself interesting, as is the implied exclusion of other organizations that provide vital social services.

### Serving the Community
*(Executive Summary & Principles)*
  Computer Professionals for Social Responsibility, 1993, 30 pp.
  http://www.cpsr.org/cpsr/nii_policy

> The *Agenda for Action* portrays a top-down view of the NII, which is natural given its Federal nature. Many public interest groups, however, see an opportunity for community-based, bottom-up information systems that could serve to revitalize our local services and government and to empower citizens in a decentralized network. CPSR has the advantage that its members understand many of the areas where technology will play a role in carving out new social institutions based on networked communications.

### Further Reading

Negroponte, Nicholas. *Being Digital.* New York: Vintage, 1995.

> Founder of the MIT Media Lab, Negroponte is one of the great enthusiasts of what he calls "the digital life." His vision of the Information Highway is one of economic security, social equality, and world harmony. I wonder, though, if he doesn't reveal too much of his personal stake in the technology in the book's opening words: "Being dyslexic, I don't like to read. As a child I read train timetables instead of the classics. . . ."

Stoll, Clifford. *Silicon Snake Oil: Second Thoughts on the Information Highway.* New York: Doubleday, 1995.

> Stoll, best-known for his computer-spy thriller *The Cuckoo's Egg,* takes a stand diametrically opposed to that of Negroponte; in this book Stoll can't say anything good about computers. While he may go overboard in his nay-saying, he expresses many common fears of a loss of quality in our schools, libraries, and our personal interactions as they become dominated by machines.

### Internet Resources

The Benton Foundation, Communications Policy Project
  http://www.benton.org/cpphome.html

> "The Benton Foundation's Communications Policy Project promotes public interest values and noncommercial services for the

National Information Infrastructure through research, policy analysis, print, video and online publishing, and outreach to nonprofits and foundations." A good source for basic policy documents, including many that speak directly about schools and libraries.

National Telecommunications and Information Association
http://www.ntia.doc.gov

This agency of the U.S. Department of Commerce is the planning arm for the NII. This site is the best general resource for documents on the planning process, and points to other sites across the Net that gather links to papers and discussions on a wide range of networking topics. This is also the site for the Telecommunications and Information Infrastructure Assistance Program grants for library and community connectivity projects.

# THE NATIONAL INFORMATION INFRASTRUCTURE: AGENDA FOR ACTION

## U.S. Department of Commerce

### *Executive Summary*

All Americans have a stake in the construction of an advanced National Information Infrastructure (NII), a seamless web of communications networks, computers, databases, and consumer electronics that will put vast amounts of information at users' fingertips. Development of the NII can help unleash an information revolution that will change forever the way people live, work, and interact with each other:

- People could live almost anywhere they wanted, without forgoing opportunities for useful and fulfilling employment, by "telecommuting" to their offices through an electronic highway;

- The best schools, teachers, and courses would be available to all students, without regard to geography, distance, resources, or disability;

- Services that improve America's health care system and respond to other important social needs could be available on-line, without waiting in line, when and where you needed them.

Private sector firms are already developing and deploying that infrastructure today. Nevertheless, there remain essential roles for government in this process. Carefully crafted government action will complement and enhance the efforts of the private sector and assure the growth of an information infrastructure available to all Americans at reasonable cost. In developing our policy initiatives in this area, the Administration will work in close partnership with business, labor, academia, the public, Congress, and state and local government. Our efforts will be guided by the following principles and objectives:

- Promote private sector investment, through appropriate tax and regulatory policies.

- Extend the "universal service" concept to ensure that information resources are available to all at affordable prices. Because information means empowerment—and employment—the government has a duty to ensure that all Americans have access to the resources and job creation potential of the Information Age.

- Act as a catalyst to promote technological innovation and new applications. Commit important government research programs and grants to help the private sector develop and demonstrate technologies needed for the NII, and develop the applications and services that will maximize its value to users.

- Promote seamless, interactive, user-driven operation of the NII. As the NII evolves into a "network of networks," government will ensure that users can transfer information across networks easily and efficiently. To increase the likelihood that the NII will be both interactive and, to a large extent, user-driven, government must reform regulations and policies that may inadvertently hamper the development of interactive applications.

- Ensure information security and network reliability. The NII must be trustworthy and secure, protecting the privacy of its users. Government action will also ensure that the overall system remains reliable, quickly repairable in the event of a failure and, perhaps most importantly, easy to use.

- Improve management of the radio frequency spectrum, an increasingly critical resource.

- Protect intellectual property rights. The Administration will investigate how to strengthen domestic copyright laws and international intellectual property treaties to prevent piracy and to protect the integrity of intellectual property.

- Coordinate with other levels of government and with other nations. Because information crosses state, regional, and national boundaries, coordination is critical to avoid needless obstacles and prevent unfair policies that handicap U.S. industry.

- Provide access to government information and improve government procurement. The Administration will seek to ensure that Federal agencies, in concert with state and local governments, use the NII to expand the information available to the public, ensuring that the immense reservoir of government information is available to the public easily and equitably. Additionally, Federal procurement policies for telecommunications and information services and equipment will be designed to promote important technical developments for the NII and to provide attractive incentives for the private sector to contribute to NII development.

The time for action is now. Every day brings news of change: new technologies, like hand-held computerized assistants; new ventures and mergers combining businesses that not long ago seemed discrete and insular; new legal decisions that challenge the separation of computer, cable, and telephone companies. These changes promise substantial benefits for the American people, but only if government understands fully their implications and begins working with the private sector and other interested parties to shape the evolution of the communications infrastructure.

The benefits of the NII for the nation are immense. An advanced information infrastructure will enable U.S. firms to compete and win in the global economy, generating good jobs for the American people and economic growth for the nation. As importantly, the NII can transform the lives of the American people—ameliorating the constraints of geography, disability, and economic status—giving all Americans a fair opportunity to go as far as their talents and ambitions will take them.

*    *    *

# PRINCIPLES FOR THE DEVELOPMENT OF THE NATIONAL INFORMATION INFRASTRUCTURE

## American Library Association

Representatives from 15 national library and information associations met September 8–10, 1993, in Washington, D.C., to discuss critical national policy issues dealing with the National Information Infrastructure (NII) sometimes called the Information Superhighway. The group reached a consensus on key principles and questions that must be used to guide the development of plans for the evolution of the NII in the areas of:

- First Amendment and Intellectual Freedom
- Privacy
- Intellectual Property
- Ubiquity
- Equitable Access
- Interoperability

There is strong agreement among the diverse group that libraries will play several key roles in the evolution of the national infrastructures,

- As both providers and consumers of information,
- As public access points to the information infrastructure,
- As responsible for protecting the public interest in access to information.

The Forum was supported through major funding from the American Library Association, the Council on Library Resources and the National Science Foundation as well as contributions from participating organizations. Each of the organizations participating will bring the principles to their governing bodies for review, development and potential formal endorsement.

The principles and questions will be useful tools in the shaping and testing of plans, legislation and approaches to the major issues involved with the ambitious national information infrastructure undertaking.

## PRINCIPLES FOR THE DEVELOPMENT OF THE NATIONAL INFORMATION INFRASTRUCTURE

### FIRST AMENDMENT AND INTELLECTUAL FREEDOM

1. Access to the NII should be available and affordable to all regardless of age, religion, disability, sexual orientation, social and political views, national origin, economic status, location, information, etc.
2. The NII service providers must guarantee the free flow of information protected by the First Amendment.
3. Individuals should have the right to choose what information to receive through the NII.

### PRIVACY

1. Privacy should be carefully protected and extended.
2. Comprehensive policies should be developed to ensure that the privacy of all people is protected.
3. Personal data collected to provide specific services should be limited to the minimum necessary.
4. Sharing data collected from individuals should only be permitted with their informed consent.
5. Individuals should have the right to inspect and correct data files about themselves.
6. Transaction data should remain confidential.

### INTELLECTUAL PROPERTY

1. Intellectual property rights and protections are independent of the form of publication or distribution.

2. The intellectual property system should ensure a fair and equitable balance between rights of creators and other copyright owners and the needs of users.

3. Fair use and other exceptions to owner's rights in the copyright law should continue in the electronic environment.

4. Compensation systems must provide a fair and reasonable return to copyright owners.

## UBIQUITY

1. Libraries should preserve and enhance their traditional roles in providing public access to information regardless of format.

2. Network access costs for libraries, educational organizations, government entities and nonprofit groups should be stable, predictable and location insensitive.

3. Resources must be allocated to provide basic public access in fostering the development of the information infrastructure.

## EQUITABLE ACCESS

1. The NII should support and encourage a diversity of information providers in order to guarantee an open, fair and competitive marketplace, with a full range of viewpoints.

2. Diversity of access should be protected through use of nonproprietary protocols.

3. Access to basic network services should be affordable and available to all.

4. Basic network access should be made available independent of geographic location.

5. The NII should ensure private, government and nonprofit participation in governance of the network.

6. Electronic information should be appropriately documented, organized and archived through the cooperative endeavors of information service providers and libraries.

## INTEROPERABILITY

1. The design of the NII should facilitate two-way audio, video and data communication from anyone to anyone easily and effectively.

2. Interoperability standards should be encouraged and tied to incentives for the use of those standards in awards for federal funding.

3. A transition phase should provide compatibility between leading-edge technology and trailing-edge technology to allow users reasonable protection from precipitate change.

4. The federal government should encourage interoperability standards and should tie incentives to the use of those standards.

5. Federal government information dissemination programs should adhere to interoperability standards.

6. Principles of interoperability should require directory and locator services, and nonproprietary search protocols, as well as a minimal set of data elements for the description of data bases.

## PARTICIPANTS

The organizations participating in the Telecommunications and Information Infrastructure Forum were:

American Association of Law Libraries (AALL)
American Association of School Librarians (AASL)
Association of College and Research Libraries (ACRL)
American Library Association (ALA)
American Library Association—Committee on Legislation (ALA)
American Library Association—Ad Hoc Subcommittee on
    Telecommunications (ALA)
American Library Association—Committee on Intellectual
    Freedom (ALA)
Association for Library Information Science Education (ALISE)
Association of Research Libraries (ARL)
Association of Specialized and Cooperative Library Agencies
    (ASCLA)
American Society for Information Science (ASIS)
Council on Library Resources (CLR)
Chief Officers of State Library Agencies (COSLA)
Coalition for Networked Information (CNI)
Library and Information Technology Association (LITA)
Medical Library Association (MLA)
Public Library Association (PLA)
Special Libraries Association (SLA)

\*   \*   \*

# CONNECTING THE NATION: CLASSROOMS, LIBRARIES, AND HEALTH CARE ORGANIZATIONS IN THE INFORMATION AGE

## U.S. Department of Commerce

*National Telecommunications and Information Administration, Office of Telecommunications and Information Applications*

## EXECUTIVE SUMMARY

Connecting every classroom, library, hospital, and clinic in the United States to the National Information Infrastructure (NII) is a priority for the Clinton Administration. It is critical for these public institutions to become and remain active participants in the NII, since they can use telecommunications and information technologies to benefit all Americans. To this end, the Clinton Administration is working actively with Congress, the States, local governments, private industry, public interest groups, and the public institutions themselves.

*Connecting the Nation* provides a status report on this critical national initiative by drawing from the most current data regarding Internet connectivity, a benchmark for NII access. This report concludes that there is much work to be done before the goal of connecting every classroom, library, and health care organization to the NII is accomplished. Nevertheless, this report highlights how Federal Government funding programs can serve as a catalyst in this effort, spurring public-private partnerships even in disadvantaged and remote areas of the country.

CLASSROOMS   As the transition to a knowledge-based economy accelerates, America's children must have access to communications

Ronald H. Brown, Secretary
Larry Irving, Assistant Secretary for Communications and Information
Author: Emilio Gonzalez
Project Coordinator: Michael K. Hamra
June 1995

and information technologies in the classroom. Without these tools, American children will lack the necessary computer skills to compete in the 21st Century. Deploying computers in classrooms and connecting them to the NII will enhance the learning process by providing students and teachers with access to information and teaching materials from around the world. In addition, as a result of the fiscal constraints and rising costs facing public schools, information technologies that offer new opportunities, efficiencies, and improvements in the education process are highly desirable.

LIBRARIES    Public libraries have traditionally served as a repository of information for citizens. In the Information Age, libraries will play an increasingly important role because a changing economy requires that workers continuously learn new skills. Connecting libraries to the NII is critical to ensuring that all Americans can obtain information and services and benefit from life-long learning opportunities, regardless of economic circumstances and geography. This report finds that individuals who are well trained in using information technology gain important economic benefits.

HEALTH CARE ORGANIZATIONS    In health care, information technology is also playing an increasingly important role in helping Americans access quality health care and in enabling health care providers to streamline their eligibility determination and billing procedures. A recent study has concluded that America's health care costs can be reduced by more than $36 billion each year by applying selected telecommunications applications nationwide. These cost reductions in the health care industry will flow to patients, employers, and government. Advances in data storage and communications technologies are also improving access to quality health care services through applications such as telemedicine.

CURRENT STATUS    A review of the status of Internet connectivity at public institutions reveals two important facts. First, these institutions are beginning to use information technology. A foothold has been made. Second, many still remain unconnected, especially those that serve Americans most at risk to become information "have nots."

Specifically, only three percent of K-12 classrooms are connected to the Internet. Recent surveys show that only 21 percent of public libraries are connected, and the vast majority of these connections are in urban areas. Although no data are available concerning the extent of Internet access in clinics, only 23 percent of the Nation's hospitals are connected. These deficiencies are relevant because economic competition in the 21st Century will demand that our public institutions are on the cutting edge in preparing society for the future.

Approximately one-fourth of American households have computers, but computer ownership is highly correlated to family income and education. Thus, public institutions will play a critical role in assuring public access to the economic and social benefits of the Information Age, especially for those who do not have computers at home. This report finds that low-income groups and rural areas tend to have less access to information technology at home and in public schools and libraries.

### Federal Government Role

The Federal Government has a critical role to play in ensuring that public institutions are connected to the NII. The Clinton Administration has created funding programs to assist in the connection of public institutions. Federal Government support and investment have led to an accelerated pace in connecting public institutions and have stimulated private-sector investment.

One example, which is creating many success stories, is the Telecommunications and Information Infrastructure Assistance Program (TIIAP), administered by the National Telecommunications and Information Administration. The TIIAP is exemplary of how the Federal Government plays a vital role in stimulating private investment and partnerships between public and private entities—two indispensable factors for ensuring that public institutions become and remain active participants in the NII. This program has enabled the Federal Government to leverage $24.4 million in Federal funding to provide a total of $64.4 million for cutting edge demonstration projects for non-profit institutions and state and local governments. Establishing demonstration projects also ensures that there are successful "models" that can be duplicated easily by other public institutions, serving as a catalyst for similar efforts.

The Federal Government is also instrumental in working with the private sector and public institutions to establish a strategic vision for NII development and deployment. A shared vision is important because economies of scale and scope can be captured by aggregating demand. Proactive Federal participation in NII activity also encourages equitable deployment of networks and new communications and information technologies, so that rural and economically distressed communities and low-income and disadvantaged individuals can gain access to the NII.

### Highlights

Chapter I of the report reviews the NII initiative and discusses the importance of being connected to the NII.

Chapter II provides an overview of the level of connectivity of U.S. public institutions to the NII.

Chapter III highlights how communities and government are successfully partnering with the private sector to promote the development of public "on-ramps" to the NII, with Federal Government funding serving as a catalyst.

Chapter IV describes NTIA programs and initiatives that are helping to accelerate the connection of public institutions to the NII.

\* \* \*

# SERVING THE COMMUNITY: A PUBLIC-INTEREST VISION OF THE NATIONAL INFORMATION INFRASTRUCTURE

## Computer Professionals for Social Responsibility

### PART 1

### *Summary of Principles, Concerns, and Recommendations*

One of the central goals of the Clinton administration has been to develop new policies that strengthen U.S. communications and information technology. The administration's vision of a new National Information Infrastructure was first presented in a February 1993 white paper entitled "Technology for America's Economic Growth: A New Direction to Build Economic Strength." That vision was later

Reprinted with the permission of Computer Professionals for Social Responsibility, PO Box 717, Palo Alto, CA 94302.

refined in a report entitled "The National Information Infrastructure: Agenda for Action" issued in September 1993 by the National Telecommunications and Information Administration (NTIA).

The Clinton administration believes that the National Information Infrastructure, or NII, offers enormous potential for the nation. The Executive Summary of the NTIA report concludes that:

> The benefits of the NII for the nation are immense. An advanced information infrastructure will enable U.S. firms to compete and win in the global economy, generating good jobs for the American people and economic growth for the nation. As importantly, the NII can transform the lives of the American people— ameliorating the constraints of geography, disability, and economic status—giving all Americans a fair opportunity to go as far as their talents and ambitions will take them.

CPSR also sees great promise in the NII. At the same time, we believe that its potential benefits are not solely economic. The NII must promote the public interest along with private interests. The success of the NII program will depend on the extent to which it empowers all citizens, protects individual rights, and strengthens the democratic institutions on which this country was founded.

## 1.1 FUNDAMENTAL PRINCIPLES

We believe that the design of the NII must be guided by a set of principles that reflect the importance of the public interest in communications and information technology. CPSR strongly endorses the following principles set forth by the Telecommunications Policy Roundtable in Washington, D.C., of which CPSR is a member:

1. Universal access. All people should have affordable access to the information infrastructure.
2. Freedom to communicate. The information infrastructure should enable all people to effectively exercise their fundamental right to communicate.
3. Vital civic sector. The information infrastructure must have a vital civic sector at its core.
4. Diverse and competitive marketplace. The information infrastructure should ensure competition among ideas and information providers.

5. Equitable workplace. New technologies should be used to enhance the quality of work and to promote equity in the workplace.

6. Privacy. Privacy should be carefully protected and extended.

7. Democratic policy-making. The public should be fully involved
   in policy-making for the information infrastructure.

Our experiences as both designers and users of networking systems lead us to formulate an additional principle:

8. Functional integrity. The functions provided by the NII must
   be powerful, versatile, well-documented, stable, reliable, and
   extensible.

## 1.2 AREAS OF CONCERN

The principles outlined in Section 1.1 are widely accepted. In public
discussions of the NII, most participants embrace a similar set of
goals. For example, much the same principles are expressed in the
"Agenda for Action" paper issued by the NTIA and in position papers
issued by the telecommunications industry. At the level of general
goals, there is broad consensus throughout the United States that the
NII cannot be limited to the commercial sphere but must also serve
the public interest.

As members of CPSR, we are encouraged by this consensus. We
also recognize that stating a goal and achieving it are profoundly
different things. Despite the general agreement regarding the public-
interest principles, it is not yet clear how much those principles will
influence the design of the NII. There are many other factors involved. When private interests conflict with the public interest, decisions must inevitably be made. In some cases, the decisions may
make it difficult to satisfy public-interest principles, no matter how
widely those principles are held.

After listening to much of the early debate concerning the NII, we
have identified the following areas of concern:

The NII may fail to provide universal access. The principle of
universal access is much easier to articulate than to achieve. If
network connections are not readily available, particularly in
rural or economically disadvantaged areas, the NII will fail to
serve those communities. If the pricing structure is not carefully
designed, individuals and public institutions lacking the necessary resources may be frozen out. Even if the network itself is

accessible at a reasonable price, the NII will remain outside the reach of most nontechnical users unless training programs and well-designed software tools are available. It is critical that the designers of the NII undertake the necessary measures to ensure full network access to people in all sectors of the United States.

A small number of companies may dominate the network and exert undue influence on its design and operation. The NII is an extremely large and ambitious program that will require substantial investment on the part of private companies who undertake the task of providing the physical infrastructure. Because of the enormous scale of the project, barriers to entry into the carrier market will be high, creating a situation in which it is difficult to rely on market forces to ensure effective competition. If a small number of companies end up dominating the market, it will be harder to guard against monopolistic tendencies in that market and to ensure that the public-interest goals are met.

There is a danger that carriers will control content on the NII. The enormous economic potential of the NII lies not in the network infrastructure itself but rather in the information and services that infrastructure carries. Even so, the carriers that own the network may seek to control the content that flows through it. Of serious concern, along with more traditional forms of censorship, is the danger that carriers may give preference to content that they control. The economic history of the United States provides convincing evidence that it is difficult to provide an equitable marketplace for content providers when single companies are allowed to control both carrier and content.

NII services may emphasize commerce at the expense of communication. Judging from the way information networks are used today, people value being on-line primarily because it gives them new ways to communicate with other people. Much of the recent discussion of the NII focuses instead on using the network to market information services. Failure to understand what people want from the NII may adversely affect the design. Over the past two decades, for example, many companies have conducted trials of videotext systems focused on shopping and information retrieval. All have been dismal failures. Now, as we stand poised to develop the NII, telephone, cable TV, computer, and broadcast companies are again focusing on providing systems to promote electronic consumerism. Why? Part of the explanation is that, just as engineers tend to emphasize the engineering aspects of what they design, business people tend to emphasize the business aspects. Most Americans are neither engineers nor business people. The NII must be designed to meet the needs of all.

Public access to government information may be restricted. In recent years, more and more public information has been turned over to private companies for distribution. In the absence of pricing regulations, much of this information has become unavailable except to the well-funded. If the trend toward privatization continues, the NII will be unable to satisfy its enormous potential as a source of public information.

The NII may fail to provide a vital public space. In recent years, public participation in the political process and civic life has eroded considerably. By providing a framework for communication and community-building, the NII has the potential to reverse this trend. To achieve that potential, individuals and groups that represent the public interest must be an integral part of the NII design process. Otherwise, the NII is unlikely to meet the needs of that constituency.

The NII may be used to justify the elimination of other essential public services. Although increased access to information can benefit and empower everyone in society, it is important to recognize that there are many other problems in society that the NII will not address. For example, making government documents available through the NII does not eliminate the need for reference librarians any more than providing on-line medical advice eliminates the need for local doctors.

The NII may fail to protect individual privacy. As the NII develops and the amount of data accessible through the network grows, concerns about individual privacy become more pressing. Using the NII, government agencies and private companies would have unprecedented opportunities to gather and disseminate information about individuals. If no protections are built into the infrastructure to guard against abuse, such data collection threatens to erode the rights of citizens. Similarly, if the network itself does not protect the privacy of its users, they will be unable to communicate freely.

Global communication using the NII may be restricted. Even more than the networks of today, the NII will be global in its scope.

Moreover, by providing a common medium for international exchange of information, the NII will open up unparalleled opportunities for economic, scientific, and cultural exchange. To take full advantage of those opportunities, however, the NII must support and encourage international participation. Unfortunately, there is some danger policymakers will use economic competitiveness or national security to justify restrictions on international traffic. While imposing such restrictions may benefit a particular industry or special interest, it also runs the serious risk of isolating the United States from the international electronic marketplace, cutting us off from the enormous benefits that come from greater cooperation in this area.

The hardware structure may be chosen without giving adequate consideration to the software implications. The NII requires considerable investment in physical connections, transmission lines, switching stations, and other forms of computing hardware. Even so, the most important challenges in the NII design lie elsewhere—in the software that makes it both powerful and easy to use. All too often, hardware considerations are allowed to dominate the initial design of such a project, to the point that the hardware choices end up placing severe constraints on what the software can achieve.

An imaginative view of the risks of an NII designed without sufficient attention to public-interest needs can be found in the modern genre of dystopian fiction known as "cyberpunk." Cyberpunk novelists depict a world in which a handful of multinational corporations have seized control, not only of the physical world, but of the virtual world of cyberspace. The middle-class in these stories is sedated by a constant stream of mass-market entertainment that distracts them from the drudgery and powerlessness of their lives. It doesn't take a novelist's imagination to recognize the rapid concentration of power and the potential danger in the merging of major corporations in the computer, cable, television, publishing, radio, consumer electronics, film, and other industries. We would be distressed to see an NII shaped solely by the commercial needs of the entertainment, finance, home shopping, and advertising industries.

CPSR believes that the principles outlined in Section 1.1 provide a standard by which to judge the success of the NII. If the design meets those principles, the NII will indeed serve the public interest, revitalizing our communities and the nation as a whole. On the other hand, if the potential dangers are ignored, the NII may fall short of its goals and thereby fail to bring the power of the information age into everyone's reach.

## 1.3 CPSR'S RECOMMENDATIONS

CPSR has developed a set of recommendations that we feel will help avoid many of the pitfalls outlined in the preceding section. Although there is some overlap, we have divided our recommendations into two groups. The first, directed primarily to the Information Infrastructure Task Force and other governmental agencies responsible for oversight and administration of the NII, consists of recommendations concerning policy. The second is directed toward designers and addresses more technical aspects of the NII.

### Policy Recommendations

CPSR agrees with the conclusion expressed in the NTIA document that "the government has an essential role to play" in the development of the NII. We believe that the NII cannot meet its public-policy objectives without some combination of government initiative and regulation. In particular, we recommend that the Administration seek to establish the following general policies.

P1. *Consider the social impact.*   Beginning with the initial design, the Administration must evaluate the impact of the NII on the society at large. It is essential to conduct periodic reviews as the NII is implemented and used to ensure that it continues to serve the public interest.

P2. *Guarantee equitable and universal access.*   To the extent that free-market principles cannot guarantee affordable access to a full range of NII services, the Administration must be publicly accountable for the achievement of this goal through some appropriate mix of legislation, regulation, taxation, and direct subsidies.

P3. *Promote widespread economic benefits.*   The Administration should evaluate the NII's economic success using measures that reflect its impact on the economy as a whole, not merely the profits of NII investors and service providers.

P4. *Promote diversity in content markets.* The Administration must recognize the distinction between the carrier of NII information services and the content that is carried over that infrastructure. In economic terms, the greatest potential of the NII lies in the marketplace it will create for content services, and the Administration must take whatever steps are necessary to ensure that the content market is both fair and open.

P5. *Provide access to government services and information over the NII.* The Clinton/Gore technology announcement of February 1993 explicitly recognizes that information technology can "dramatically improve the way the Federal Government serves the people," thereby making the government "more cost-effective, efficient, and 'user-friendly.'" The Administration must continue to make provision of government services a central aspect of the NII design.

P6. *Protect public spaces.* The Administration should promote the development of a vital civic sector by ensuring resources, training, and support for public spaces within the NII where citizens can pursue noncommercial activities.

P7. *Encourage democratic participation.* Government must prevent concentrations of economic power from controlling the design of the NII and the operational "rules of the game." Decisions that affect the public's use of the NII must be conducted openly and democratically. To this end, the Administration must ensure full public disclosure and actively promote democratic decision-making. In addition, the Administration should ensure that any committees, such as the soon-to-be-appointed Advisory Council on the National Information Infrastructure, include sufficient representation from the public-interest community to ensure effective participation and to reflect the diversity of that constituency.

P8. *Think globally.* The Administration should actively facilitate the seamless connection of America's NII with the information infrastructures of other nations by working to resolve such issues as security, censorship, tariffs, and privacy. Moreover, the NII should not be limited to the United States and the highly industrialized nations of Europe and the Pacific Rim. Because communication and information are vital resources for all nations, it is in the common interest to help the developing countries become part of the global information infrastructure.

P9. *Guarantee functional integrity.* To the extent that market forces alone cannot guarantee that the design recommendations discussed in the following section will be achieved, the Administration should take appropriate steps to ensure that the NII design satisfies these critical technical, functional, and safety requirements.

## Design Recommendations

Our breadth of experience with existing networks and communications technology lead us to make the following recommendations about the technical aspects of NII design:

D1. *Emphasize ease of use.* Existing computer networks have fallen short of serving the public interest because they are difficult for nonexperts to use. The most significant challenge facing NII designers is to reduce the barriers to entry into the information network that the NII provides, so that using the NII for simple inquiries becomes as easy as using the telephone.

D2. *Provide full service to homes, workplaces, and community centers.* From the beginning, NII designers must strive to provide a high level of service to users where they live and work—to private homes, libraries, community centers, and businesses. If the public at large is offered only restricted, second-class service, the NII will be unable to serve as a medium for individual and community empowerment.

D3. *Enable all users to act as both producers and consumers.* Perhaps the greatest strength of existing networks is the opportunity for all participants to act as both producers and consumers of new products and information. By making it easy for individuals and small groups to develop new on-line services, today's networks display a vitality and openness that is difficult to find in other media. Individual initiative and entrepreneurship must continue to be supported in the NII design.

D4. *Address privacy and security issues from the beginning.* As is the case with reliability, it is difficult to implement privacy and security as an afterthought. In order to provide sufficient safeguards, it is essential that privacy and security be considered throughout the NII design.

D5. *Develop open and interoperable standards.* The NII will never be a single, static entity. It will instead continue to grow, driven in part by the general progress of technology and the extension of service to developing networks throughout the world. The NII community must develop standards that facilitate the growth of the network and allow for the broadest possible participation in the process.

D6. *Encourage experimentation and evolution.* On the basis of our experience with existing networks, it is clear that the most significant source of new network services and capabilities will consist of contributions by the NII users themselves. Many of the facilities that are now considered part of the core of the network were once experimental projects. Someone using the network recognized a need, developed a new service in response to that need, and then made that service available to others. As the community of users expanded, the service was then refined and standardized to the point that it became a widely accepted tool. The NII must allow for and encourage the same sort of experimentation and evolutionary development.

D7. *Require high reliability.* As use of the network expands into more and more sectors of the economy, the need for high reliability and fault-tolerance will become increasingly important. To meet the requirements of its users, reliability must be a central theme of the design at every stage of the process.

\* \* \*

# 3

## Stakeholders and the Information Marketplace

For over a century U.S. libraries have quietly (perhaps too quietly) gone about the business of organizing and disseminating information. Some information resources, like journal indexes, were once only available to individuals in libraries. Encyclopedias were sold for home use in the latter half of this century, but still were heavily used by library patrons.

Information was something sought mainly by students and researchers, and these people had little choice but to use the library to fulfill their information needs. Today people in all walks of life, in all professions and occupations, are frequent, if not constant, users of information. And that information is available to them through a variety of online and off-line resources. No longer does the library have a monopoly over the traditional information sources like bibliographic indexes. Individuals can subscribe to online services that allow them to directly search a wide range of bibliographic databases as well as access business and scientific information. Homes with computers can add an encyclopedia to their personal information library for a fraction of the price of a multivolume hardcopy encyclopedia. The information market is undergoing a radical change.

# Information in the Economy

Information is key in today's market economy. You have to know what products to make, where to deliver them, when, and what price to charge. You have to know who your buyers are and what your competitors are doing. This economy is also global, which greatly increases the competition for markets. Whereas once many countries were able to compete in this global economy purely on the basis of their cheap labor force, now countries like Russia and Vietnam are trying to boost their economies with an increasing use of information.

All of this means that the information industries themselves are booming. All of us need computers, networks, and software, no matter what our underlying business. These are the tools of business today, like the machine tools of yesterday. The end-product of these tools is information, and information itself has been dubbed the *product of the 90s.*

# Major Players

The word *information* is used so frequently and so authoritatively that we may fail to recognize that it means many different things to different speakers. Theoretical discussions of the meaning of the word could lead us into great abstraction and wouldn't be very useful here. A look at some of the major players on the Information Highway shows us that information is easily defined by who you are.

## *Telecommunications Companies*

Transporting information is big business in our world, and the telephone and telegraph companies that deliver our information are powerful players in our economy. The telephone business has been a highly regulated monopoly since 1934, though recent changes, such as the breakup of AT&T into the Regional Bell Operating Companies (RBOCs) is the beginning of a process of deregulation that is furthered by the Telecommunications Act of 1996.

These companies have an advantage over other businesses that wish to participate in the Information Highway because they already have a large installed base of wiring and equipment linking virtually every household and business in this country. Because of the requirement of universal telephone service, part of the regulation of the telephone business mandates that these companies provide their service at equal and reasonable rates to all customers, regardless of their location. This means that there are telephone connections in every part of our nation, regardless how remote.

Telephone companies before the 1996 Telecommunications Act were prevented from providing any of the content that passed over their wires. Their system was only the transport medium for the content of others. In the telecommunications debate that has arisen around the Information Highway, telecommunications companies continue to emphasize the transport of bits, but the information content of the messages remains a kind of black box. They don't have an actual information component to their business—yet.

This might not be a great disadvantage. There is ample evidence that what many people want to do when they get online is to communicate with other people. E-mail is still one of the most popular functions of the Internet and of commercial online services. Still, many argue that it is no longer sufficient to be in the business of just transporting information, especially in a regulated marketplace. In his 1996 book *Being Digital* Nicholas Negroponte says: "If the management of a telecommunications company limits its long-term strategy to carrying bits, it will not be acting in its shareholders' best interest. Owning the bits or rights to the bits, or adding significant value to the bits, must be part of the equation" (p.78).

## Cable Companies

In terms of communications wiring to the home, the cable companies come in second to the telephone companies, covering about 60 percent of American households. The model for cable communication is very different from that for the telephone. The telephone is designed for many small instances of equal two-way communication. Cable is designed for a large amount of one-way communication, from the cable company to the home.

Unlike the telephone companies, cable companies manage content. Their service is not just to provide the wiring—what they sell to the consumer is programming. But because of the one-way nature of the current cable system design, the cable industry is not prepared to take on interactive services. Their view of information is that of our broadcast media: a few large companies sending out programs to a mass audience. Even when cable companies predict a future of five hundred or more channels, think of that in comparison to the number of books in a library—it's still a limited information universe.

Cable companies know that they will have to add two-way communication to their design in order to win some of the Information Highway market, and some companies are already experimenting with two-way models. Because their equipment is not designed for two-way communication, such a changeover is expected to be very expensive. Some of the industry's members feel that there will continue to be a role for broadcastlike media in the future that will require a large amount of bandwidth going to the home, and only a small channel "upward" to the cable provider for the selection of video-on-demand and other services. Cable companies are in a good position to provide this type of service.

**Information Services**

We already have commercial online services. Companies like West Publishing and Dialog Information Services have been providing information online for decades. Today these systems don't look terribly modern to us: they are text-only systems that require the users to learn commands and search techniques unique to each system. They tend to carry what you might call "meta-information": that is, not the end information itself, but references to it. Dialog's traditional strength is in abstracting and indexing databases, while West provides references to case law.

Commercial online systems like CompuServe and America Online (AOL) have traditionally sold their services for their information component, though AOL is best known for its active real-time "chat rooms," where subscribers spend countless hours having conversations with others from around the country. Unlike the Internet, these systems do not use open designs that allow them to interconnect with other online systems. Instead, each one uses its own unique software, and they accept accesses only from registered users who then pay by their time on and the number of retrievals.

At the time that CompuServe was launched, the Internet was not available outside the university and research arena. Today such online systems have a lot of competition from the Internet, but they continue on the strength of their information services that cannot be found among the free information offerings of the Internet. It's not clear how much longer there will be a market for this kind of online service. Already there are companies that can arrange for online billing over the Internet, which will then provide a mechanism for value-added services that were once unique to the proprietary online systems.

## Computer Industry

The computer industry has always been in the information business but, like the telephone company, computer firms saw themselves primarily in the role of providing tools. Even the most sophisticated of software programs merely enables the production of information, influencing the form and the process but not the content.

The computer industry has not, however, been a bystander at the communications revolution. New developments in hardware and software have fueled all major developments. Interestingly, many of the software developments have not come out of the commercial computer industry but have arisen in the nonprofit academic world. As we saw in Chapter 2, our first true networked information retrieval system was Gopher, developed at the University of Minnesota as a convenient way to link the numerous information resources on the University of Minnesota campus.

The World Wide Web was developed at CERN (European Laboratory for Particle Physics in Switzerland) by Tim Berniers-Lee to allow the high energy physics community to share information. Based on a hypertext model, it lets authors include links to other documents or networked information resources right in their writings. The Web is, in effect, the implementation of Vannevar Bush's "memex," outlined in the July 1945 issue of the *Atlantic Monthly*. In Bush's vision, the memex was a desk and the resulting knowledge base reflected the interests and views of an individual researcher. In today's networked world, the end result is a combined view of all of the participants, and sharing of interesting links is virtually instantaneous.

With the rapid growth of the Internet, it became apparent to the software industry that there was a market for programs that facilitate online communication. After the success of Mosaic, the first WWW browser, its original inventor Marc Andreessen founded the Netscape company to carry on the work he had begun as a student at the University of Illinois. With Microsoft's entry into the Internet market, software for the Information Highway is truly becoming a consumer product and comes bundled with the traditional office software for word processing and spreadsheets.

But even these companies realize that the real money is in content. You can sell a user only so many software packages and upgrades to those packages. Content, in the form of games, multimedia programs, reference works, and networked information has an almost infinite market. Microsoft has expanded into reference works, like Encarta, and has entered into the news business with MSNBC, a news program that is produced by a joint venture of Microsoft and the National Broadcasting Company and that uses broadcast, cable, and the Internet to reach its audience. Every day, by its nature, there is new content for a news program, so every day there is something to sell to the viewers. MSNBC follows the broadcast model, but adds in an interactive component where viewers can make comments or ask questions.

The hardware industry is also interested in having a piece of the Information Highway pie. With more and more households buying personal computers, it has gained quite a bit already from the market. There will be a limit to how many families can afford a home computer, even though prices today are much lower then they were just a few years ago. Scott McNealy, chief executive of Sun Microsystems, sees a market for an inexpensive "network computer" designed solely to be connected to a network. It would act like a "smart terminal," running programs that are stored centrally on a server. Though the goal is to develop a computer that would cost little more than a TV set or a VCR and would therefore be within the reach of lower-income households, by late 1996 the announced price for this machine was closer to $1,000.

### Media, Entertainment

When I first heard of the Information Highway I made the mistake of interpreting the word *information* too narrowly. I thought of encyclopedias, census data, biographies, and other factual forms of expression. I forgot about fiction, and I forgot about other forms of storytelling such as movies and television. And I didn't think of the visual arts, which I tend to put in a category of their own, much less music.

So I was a bit taken aback when companies like Disney and Viacom and Time-Warner began announcing their plans for the Information Highway. This is an example of when the Information Highway name doesn't really help us understand the role that this future system will play. The Information Highway has room within it for all forms of communication, from the sciences to the arts, from the global to the personal. As a matter of fact, the only products that the Information Highway won't work for are those than cannot be digitized: it's not going to do your dry cleaning or get your muffler fixed, though it can aid in the communication process for those activities.

At the hearings on copyright that were held in late 1994, many members of the entertainment industry spoke to the committee from the Department of Commerce. One of these speakers was Jack Valenti of the Motion Picture Association of America, who summed up a basic if oft-ignored truth about the Information Highway: ". . . people don't buy wires and digital and head ends and all of the technology in its arcane form. What they buy and subscribe to and want to have come into their home is programming that they want to see, when they want to see it."

Entertainment will not be a trivial function of the Information Highway. Our entertainment industries are financially strong, both in domestic sales and foreign earnings. It can probably be successfully argued that the entertainment aspects of the Information Highway will be the ones that motivate the majority of people to invest in the equipment and connection to get online.

# Other Players

A great deal of our information comes from nonprofit sources: government resources, public services, health agencies. Nonprofit doesn't mean that there is no element of economy to this information. The gains, rather than being monetary profits, are in greater efficiency, better service, and richer cooperative agreements with other agencies.

As we have seen over the last decade in response to government information, there is some tendency to consider this noncommercial information a threat to commercial interests. But the vast majority of nonprofit information would not make any money on an open market. In many cases the intended audience is not an "interesting" market—for example, one could not expect to sell information on how to apply for welfare or for minimum wage jobs.

## Government

The Federal government has often been cited as the largest producer of information in the world. I always wonder what the unit of measure is for that statement—the most titles, the most pages, the greatest tonnage? Whatever the measure, there's little question that huge numbers of documents as well as large amounts of raw data are made available by the Federal government, and most of it is in the public domain.

Much of the raw data that feeds into commercial information products as well as research and development is initially gathered and distributed by the Federal government. Without the public invest-ment in data like the census, there would be no other source of this information because of the prohibitive cost of gathering it.

At the same time, the Federal government does not have unlimited funding for the distribution of information. As has been chronicled in the ALA's publication "Less Access to Less Information by and about the U.S. Government," the amount of information being distributed has been greatly reduced over the last two decades, at least partially as a result of financial considerations.

One of the stated goals of the NII is to "provide access to govern-ment information." Through the Depository Library Program (DLP), libraries are the distributed public access points for all published Federal information. The Government Printing Office produced a study in June 1996 on transitioning the DLP to an electronic deposi-tory program. A program of electronic dissemination has the poten-tial to make Federal information available to all U.S. residents through computer networks, either in their own homes, if they have a personal connection, or through their local library. And all libraries, even the smallest ones, can deliver the information to their patrons immediately, without having to wait for an interlibrary loan request.

Local government information is often a source of income for the issuing agency. Unlike Federal information resources, state and local information is not necessarily in the public domain—that depends entirely on the local public records law. Local government is an excellent source of business information and many a city or county has supported some of its functions by selling property tax, zoning, and other business-related information. These agencies may find that the NII helps them expand the customer base for their information. It can also help citizens get more out of their local government—in the Los Angeles area a group of cities began putting their requests for bids for city contracts out on an electronic bulletin board. More contractors were able to apply for the jobs because more of them had access to the requests, and the cities saved money because they got a wider range of bids from which to choose.

## Academia

The world of higher education and university-related research pro-duces information as part of its basic mission. Oftentimes the re-search itself is sponsored by Federal grants and the results of the research must be made public. This is done through publication in professional journals or through presentation of the research results at a conference or meeting. The general view of the academic community is that the exchange of information is essential for continued research. Authors are usually not remunerated directly for their writing and most publications are nonprofit, some even supported at a loss by professional organizations.

It may seem unfair that the academic authors are not given royalties, but the fact is that their writings are unlikely to be profitable. The audience for their works is small and specialized. Instead, in this environment information is an exchange between scholars that is facilitated by publication. The authors themselves are rewarded with job security and increased prestige in their field.

In those instances where there isn't a great profit to be made in academic publishing, disciplines are beginning to publish their information exclusively in electronic journals and making these available for free over the Internet. Other disciplines have online sites where research results and papers are stored for unlimited downloading.

## *Nonprofit Organizations*

Nonprofit organizations often have an information component as part of providing their service. Some nonprofits, like the League of Women Voters, are first and foremost information distributors. Others, like Planned Parenthood, need to reach potential clients before they actually require the organization's services. Because of low levels of funding, these organizations have always been somewhat disadvantaged in terms of using standard media to reach out to their audiences; placing information in newspapers through advertising is very expensive, and there is a limited amount of public interest time available through broadcast media.

Many nonprofits do give their information away for free. The constituencies they wish to reach may not be able to purchase the information, regardless of its value. Or the information may be of the type that needs to reach everyone, whether people would be willing to purchase it or not, such as information on child immunization programs or the schedules for school enrollment.

The Information Highway mainly promises a better way for nonprofits to reach members and potential members, raise funds, and make the public aware of their activities. As with current media, the real question for nonprofits is whether they will be able to afford to participate in the Information Highway. The social costs of their lack of participation would be very hard to calculate, as would the value of the gains with their full participation, but it would be interesting to experience an election year in which the information from the League of Women Voters was as readily accessible as the campaign ads we now see.

## Putting a Price on Information

One of the issues coming up in the information economy is How do we put a price on information? Many people on the Internet assume that digital works should be very inexpensive because there is no cost to print the works. If you look at the costs involved with book production, the actual producing of the physical book is a very small part of the total cost, around 10 percent. The biggest cost is what is called *distribution*. Distribution isn't the same as shipping costs; it's the cost to get a work into the whole loop of wholesale and retail markets.

Digital information will have a different pattern of distribution. It already does. We have a fair amount of experience with the commercial distribution of digital information through systems like Dialog or CompuServe. These systems are generally considered to be expensive, which would seem to indicate that the price of information isn't directly related to the cost of duplicating or distributing it. Like most products, the first rule of thumb for determining the value of information is "whatever the market will bear." Already, business information is priced much higher than consumer information, partly because businesses are willing to pay more.

Another determinant is competition. Unlike products like toasters or automobiles, there often isn't an equivalent information product that can compete with one already on the market. More competition may arise in the future, but many of our current information resources have virtual monopolies on a type of information, such as the case of West Publishing's monopoly on case law or the lack of alternatives in most subject areas for abstracting and indexing services. Without competitors, information providers can charge just about any price they would like within the ability of their customers to pay.

Where there is competition for similar information resources, pricing can vary based on *added value*. As a matter of fact, added value is seen as the true product of the future in the information business. Adding ease-of-use factors, information alert services, and other features that save the time of the customer, information providers will in the end be selling a service rather than an information unit.

Some people who see the Information Highway as a "get rich quick" opportunity have been sorely disappointed when they have tried to start up information businesses. What many people don't realize—yet something that librarians are quite aware of—is how much work must go into a quality information product. While it's true that anyone can put information out on the Internet with little expense, the effort to gather and organize information is usually much greater than it seems to those outside the process. It is no wonder that we have very few competing abstracting and indexing services—those are very labor-intensive businesses with large payrolls. The dream that it can all be done with just a home office and a moderate-priced computer remains just that—a dream. For the foreseeable future, our main commercial information products will undoubtedly continue to be produced by reasonably large companies that have significant investments in their information product. And those costs will have a role in determining the prices we pay.

# Pricing Models

There is a lot of discussion of pricing models on the Internet though the primary pricing model of Internet use is still flat-rate pricing. This seems to be the model favored by users, probably because one can easily spend many hours at a time "surfing" the Net. Subscribers to time-based services, where each hour online is charged at a rate of a few dollars an hour, find that on the Internet time really flies. As they move from accessing the information resources of the commercial service to using that service as an entry point to the Internet, they are spending much more money on the Internet use. Most Internet-only service providers give users a flat rate, though sometimes with limited service.

Some observers of Internet economics now argue that flat-rate pricing is not going to be viable as the Internet grows beyond its current capacity. New services, like multimedia games, use far greater amounts of the basic Internet "stuff," known as bandwidth. You can send thousands of E-mail messages for the same amount of Internet stuff that a few seconds of video will require. Even the motionless graphics of the World Wide Web have greatly increased the number of bytes of data that travel through the wires of the Internet connections. Yet a person sending a single E-mail message a day and one downloading millions of bytes of graphics files are paying the same rate. As the Internet struggles with greater congestion, this pricing model cannot continue to work.

One proposed solution to this is usage-based pricing. Under this pricing mechanism, multimedia and other high-bandwidth applications would be charged at a rate in relation to their load on the system. Plain text and E-mail use would be inexpensive. In addition, use of the Internet could be discounted during nonpeak times.

Some people have lauded this plan as a victory for universal access—text-based services on the Internet would be so inexpensive they could easily be affordable for all. What these people seem to forget is that those same text-based services may not be the appropriate ones for our lower-income populations. With a high national rate of illiteracy and an ever-growing level of functional illiteracy, those same high-bandwidth multimedia functions may be the only ones that can make the Information Highway accessible to a large portion of our population. The usage-based pricing model could make these unreachable for those people who need it most.

It could also make the Information Highway unreachable for schools and libraries, at least unless these are given significant discounts. The problem that they face will be true for any organization or individual that depends on a fixed and limited income—with usage-based pricing, it is very hard to guarantee that you will stay within your budget. Think of what it would be like for libraries if they were charged each time a user checked out a book—the more successful the library is in serving the public, the quicker its budget would be exhausted. The library would have no control over its own expenses. Libraries had a taste of this when they budgeted portions of their book budget for online searching. Many of them used up their allocated online searching funding long before the fiscal year ended. After that they had to charge users for each online search.

Another model is *pay-per-view pricing,* though this is less favored by economists. As we know from the experience of attempts to introduce pay-per-view television, this is not a model that consumers take to in large numbers. In online searching users report that the pay-per-view model is a deterrent to the information discovery process, since it exacts a charge even on the function of browsing through documents that users reject as irrelevant. Pay-per-view is also quite complex in terms of the accounting required since it is assumed that at least part of the payment will be allocated to the owner of the intellectual property rights of the viewed item. Because some information is less expensive than other information (and some even in the public domain) the user faces a complex billing mechanism that makes it very difficult to make good consumer choices. Imagine if every time you accessed a document, you first had to go through a screen that told you how much you would be charged to view it, or print it, or download it, and then asked you if you wanted to continue. It would be maddening, and all but the most determined consumers would be discouraged from using the online system at all.

Some of the costs of using online systems may be defrayed by advertising revenues. Internet services like the popular search engines of Magellan and Excite are already advertising-based. There are companies that will give you a free E-mail account if you agree to receive advertisements. This is a model very familiar to us, since advertising subsidizes the entire cost for our commercial broadcasting channels. The sheer number of Internet information providers, however, makes this model less viable as a whole—advertisers will be willing to place their ads on a few very popular Internet sites, but are unlikely to be interested in the many thousands of medium- to low-use sites. The advertising model could lead to a televisionlike NII where only a few large information providers survive.

Pricing mechanisms are an important part of the user interaction with the Information Highway. Though it may sound like an esoteric struggle between brands of economics, it actually is one of the basic factors in making the Information Highway available to all users. The wrong pricing mechanism can lock out some users or simply discourage others. It will be important to find a way to price the Information Highway for universal access while still making it a strong and reliable market for the providers of information.

## The Information Infrastructure As Market

The main business taking place on the Internet today is the same as the business conducted in magazines or on television: marketing. Like other forms of communication, the Internet is an ideal medium for advertising. What Internet sites have to sell is exactly the same product as what television, radio, and magazines have to sell—people's attention. Add to this the fact that the average Internet user has an above-average income and is interested in high-tech "toys," and you understand why marketers are flocking to this medium.

Marketing online has some difficulties along with its advantages. Users have a lot of options, like turning off images, that allow them to ignore or skip advertising. And there are millions of Web sites that can draw people's attention, so how do you get them to come to yours? Some advertisers are experimenting with interactive sites where users play games and win prizes as a way of gathering an audience for their products. Others vie to appear on the most frequently accessed sites like Yahoo, the most popular entry index to the subject matter of the Internet. Keyword search engines now allow an advertiser to buy a word—that is, when a certain word is searched that advertiser's graphic will appear on the results page. This assures advertisers that they will be seen by users interested in their product.

Marketing on the Internet is such good business that there are Web sites that market to marketers. Surveys are done that help advertisers target their products. New theories of marketing are arising that are trying to show that the online environment will require a different set of marketing tools. Some argue that because the Internet is by its nature a two-way communication, consumers will have more input into the development of products. Companies can actually engage potential customers in discussions about their needs.

Marketing, however, can collide with user privacy. In the two-way communication of the Internet, communication depends on both the Web site's computer and the user's computer having each other's addresses. When you contact a Web page, it can only respond because it knows "who" you are. "Who" in this case means the exact address of the computer you are using to connect to the Internet. A Web site may not know who you are in real life (your name and phone number, for example), but it can know how often your computer accesses its site, what information is viewed, and how long each piece of information is viewed. This is a gold mine for marketers, but privacy advocates are horrified.

## Catching the Third Wave

> The First Wave of change—the agricultural revolution—
> The Second Wave—the rise of industrial civilization. . . .
> —Toffler, *The Third Wave*.

The Third Wave is a bit more difficult to define. Toffler describes a world very different from the one we live in today, but of which we can see some seeds of development. In the Third Wave world the media will be "de-massified"; instead of a few television channels beamed out identically to each home, it will be possible to create personalized information and entertainment for each consumer. And news will be tailored to an individual profile, creating what Nicholas Negroponte called the "Daily Me." A similar thing will happen with mass production as products can be almost infinitely customized, like the services today that will take your measurements and make a pair of jeans that fits just you. Companies will get smaller as more can be done with fewer workers, and more workers will be setting up offices in their homes rather than commuting to large corporate buildings. In essence, institutions as we know them today will cease to exist.

The future world will also be an "intelligent" world. Our social memory will be ubiquitous and available to all through high-tech communications systems and wide application of artificial intelligence.

## Libraries in the Information Economy

Where does this leave libraries? Toffler puts libraries solidly inside the Second Wave: "Second Wave civilization smashed the memory barrier. It spread mass literacy. It kept systematic business records. It built thousands of libraries and museums. It invented the file cabinet" (p. 176). (This is the only mention of libraries in Toffler's book, by the way.) In the Third Wave economy each individual will have his or her own private library not unlike Vannevar Bush's memex machine that allows each person to store all the information and reading that interests him or her and to organize it according to the individual's personal scheme. Information itself will be so individualized that it essentially becomes private property.

While we are far from this vision today, some of the players are already advocating the move to a personal information space. Ads for computer products like Microsoft's Encarta show school children who are saved from a trip to the library because they have a computer and a network connection at home. A 1996 Packard Bell computer ad goes further and presents the library and the city it exists in as dreary and overcontrolled, and urges users to "do it all from home." The multisyllabic term for this phenomenon is *disintermediation*. Third Wave economists like Don Tapscott, who spoke at the 1996 LITA/ LAMA conference, see the future as a general elimination of middle men. He gives the example of travel services, where more and more travelers are making their own reservations over online systems rather than using a travel agent. In this disintermediated world users are able to access information directly, bypassing libraries and bookstores altogether.

Some librarians concur with at least part of this vision. Francis Miksa of the UT Austin Graduate School of Library and Information Science sees the library being transformed beyond the institution it is today to a value-added service where trained professionals help others create their own personal information space. Discussion on library lists breaks down between those who see the library as a place for social activities (story hours, literacy classes, public meetings) and those who see the library's proper function as information delivery.

It isn't clear how or even whether businesses will be able to make money selling information directly to the public. Our past experience shows that there is a market for online information services, but at this time only a handful of them are able to survive, meaning that the demand is not great. But there is great hope that the Information Highway will be a kind of gold rush for America's businesses. In this atmosphere, the idea that libraries might undercut profits by providing the same information services for free is being received with great alarm in the business community. It is significant that more than one computer company has tried to position its products as alternatives to the inconvenient trip to the "old-fashioned" library. We might argue, as some have, that this proves that libraries themselves are significant players in the information game—otherwise there would be no reason to try to steal our customers. But putting libraries in direct competition with the producers of commercial information products is a true David and Goliath situation, perhaps without the happy ending. Libraries aren't able to respond "in kind" to national television commercials. As a matter of fact, libraries not only don't compete with commercial information services, they often provide them to their own users. Libraries themselves are customers.

In the traditional library of books and magazines, libraries freely lent materials of commercial origin. Though there has been some tension between publishers and libraries—particularly between publishers of expensive academic periodicals and university libraries—the current wave of hostilities is unprecedented. What's different today?

One major difference is that many companies that are leaping into the information business have little experience with this type of product. Even if they have experience in the hardcopy information world, the Information Highway is a whole new product. It isn't yet known what the marketplace will look like or how competitive it will be. If it is highly competitive, then libraries might present a danger to the commercial world.

It would be good to remind these businesses that libraries have existed alongside bookstores, video rental outlets, and online services for years and there is no evidence that library lending has had a negative impact on those other markets. At the same time, libraries are a solid market for some information products and publishers can count on the libraries as a customer base. Yet in absence of proof that libraries and the Information Highway can coexist, the fears of hopeful marketers seem to take over.

The next difference is in the growing commercialization of our information resources. Though book publishers have been for-profit enterprises for centuries, the publishing business has not been one of sudden, tremendous wealth. Publishers were generally satisfied with profit margins in single digits, whereas our newer content sources like television and film work on overall profits of 12 to 15 percent. These businesses are very aggressive at pursuing their markets and will not be tolerant of any loss of revenue that can be attributed to public access libraries.

As is the case today, it is probable that libraries in the future will be providing a service that is not the same as that of commercial information providers. Some publishers wishing to move onto the Information Highway have understood that their paying customers want not just the raw information that can be shipped over computer networks—they want an entire information service. Such a service saves the customer time and guarantees a high quality of retrievals. With such a service, members of our society who can afford to pay for the convenience of receiving their information at home or at work with little effort on their own part will become subscribers. Like the readers who happily patronize bookstores, these online consumers will be the bread and butter of the new information services.

Libraries will hopefully have access to the same basic information sources as the commercial providers and will offer their own value-added service to patrons. It will be less slick and probably less tailored than the commercial services, but no one will be denied access because of a lack of an ability to pay. Libraries will also carry a vast array of noncommercial information that the commercial providers may ignore because of its lack of a strong market. Local information relating to the town or neighborhood of the library will be a primary example of information that the larger commercial providers will not be interested in.

Libraries will not be able to, nor will they wish to, compete with the entertainment services that promise to be the real moneymakers on the Information Highway. Though libraries do support a number of leisure activities relating to information and cultural sources, they don't run full-screen movie theaters or television networks today, and they won't be offering the equivalent of those programs in the future. The entertainment offerings envisioned for the future will require advanced computer networking services that will only be within the capabilities of a few large media companies. Libraries will be no threat to these services.

I think the best thing that libraries can do at this time is to continue to serve their patrons, using all of the information resources at their disposal, both hardcopy and digital. As the commercial market begins to settle down and the various stakeholders have found their customers, the fears of libraries as competitors will fade. We have to weather this time of transition with unwavering determination, however, and a continued dedication to serving the public.

## IN THEIR OWN WORDS

**Cyberspace and the American Dream: A Magna Carta for the Knowledge Age** *(Excerpts)*
> Progress and Freedom Foundation, Release 1.2, August 22, 1994
> http://www.pff.org/pff/position.html

> The Progress and Freedom Foundation is a nonprofit organization whose stated mission is "[t]o restore, to renew, and to re-create America's sense of its future." Often called a "conservative think-tank" it represents the Third Wave thinking of Alvin and Heidi Toffler on the Internet and has been linked to Newt Gingrich. The Magna Carta presents a utopian view of cyberspace as a new frontier where we get to re-create the world based on dynamic competition. Authorship of the Magna Carta is attributed to Esther Dyson, George Gilder, Jay Keyworth, and Alvin Toffler in the document itself, but most likely it was written by PFF staff based on their thinking.

**Pricing Information Goods**
> Hal R. Varian, June 1995
> http://www.sims.berkeley.edu/pub/Papers/price-information-goods.pdf

> How do we put a price on information, especially now that it is no longer printed or bound or boxed? Professor Varian is an economist whose main interest is this very question. This article discusses some basic economic concepts, such as price discrimination and bundling, as they apply to information and information services.

**The Cultural Legacy of the "Modern Library" for the Future**
*(Excerpt: The Challenge of a New Environment)*
> Francis Miksa, in *Journal of Education for Library and Information Science,* v. 37, n. 2, Spring 1996, pp. 100–119.

> This article by Professor Francis Miksa of the University of Texas at Austin Graduate School of Library and Information Science puts a historical perspective on the role of the library in society. The selection excerpted here presents a vision of librar-

ies in a Third Wave-like future where traditional institutions are no longer the dominant force.

## Further Reading

MacKie-Mason, Jeffrey K., and Hal R. Varian. *Some FAQs about Usage-Based Pricing.* 1994.
http://www.sims.berkeley.edu/-hal/people/hal/papers.html

> One of the great controversies in terms of telecommunications services is whether they should be flat-rate or if charges should be usage-based. MacKie-Mason and Varian, both economists, argue that usage-based pricing will likely come to the Internet.

Harnad, Stevan. *The Postgutenberg Galaxy: How to Get There from Here.* May 12, 1995.
http://cogsci.ecs.soton.ac.uk:80/-harnad/THES/thes.html

> Harnad suggests that academic writing can evolve onto the digital platform with relative ease precisely because it is not commercial in nature. He offers a model for the future.

Hoffman, Donna L., and Thomas P. Novak. "A New Marketing Paradigm for Electronic Commerce," *The Information Society,* Special Issue on Electronic Commerce, v. 13 (n. 1), 1997.

> While some are struggling to make use of the Internet as a market, others are trying to discover what marketing means in a networked environment. Hoffman and Novak maintain that those doing business on the Internet are going to have to change their methods, making use of a more interactive style where the consumer is a larger part of the marketing activity.

Schiller, Herbert I. *Information Inequality: The Deepening Social Crisis in America.* New York: Routledge, 1996.

> Schiller is professor emeritus of communications at the University of California at San Diego, and a longtime observer of the communications industry. He sees an "information crisis" brought on by the privatization of our information resources and services. His view is essentially the exact opposite of that of the Progress and Freedom Foundation, which sees the new information technologies as universal and personally liberating.

Sterling, Bruce. "Free As Air, Free As Water, Free As Knowledge." Speech to the Library Information Technology Association, June

1992, San Francisco, Calif. gopher://gopher.well.sf.ca.us:70/00/
Publications/authors/Sterling/freeknow.up

> Bruce Sterling is considered one of today's most influential
> science fiction writers. Clearly one of his skills is an uncanny
> ability to see into the near future. His speeches are even more
> entertaining than his writings, in my opinion, and in this
> pointed but compelling talk he asks the all-important question:
> "Knowledge is power—but if so, why aren't knowledgeable
> people *in* power? And it's true there's a Library *of* Congress. But
> how many librarians are there *in* Congress?"

### Internet Resources

The Information Economy
  http://www.sims.berkeley.edu/resources/infoecon/

> Organized by Hal Varian, whose piece is included here, these
> pages cover "The Economics of the Internet, Information
> Goods, Intellectual Property and Related Issues." A good basic
> starting point for the topic in general.

CommerceNet
  http://www.commerce.net

> There are a number of technical and not-so-technical issues that
> need to be resolved before business can take place on the
> Internet. Standards are needed for virtual commerce in a num-
> ber of areas, and CommerceNet, whose members are busi-
> nesses, sees its role as "transforming the net into a global
> electronic marketplace." Though not by any means the only
> organization working in this area, CommerceNet's Web pages
> provide a good outline of the range of the issues that businesses
> are facing.

## CYBERSPACE AND THE AMERICAN DREAM: A MAGNA CARTA FOR THE KNOWLEDGE AGE

### Progress and Freedom Foundation

*Excerpts*

## PREAMBLE

The central event of the 20th century is the overthrow of matter. In technology, economics, and the politics of nations, wealth—in the form of physical resources—has been losing value and significance. The powers of mind are everywhere ascendant over the brute force of things.

In a First Wave economy, land and farm labor are the main "factors of production." In a Second Wave economy, the land remains valuable while the "labor" becomes massified around machines and larger industries. In a Third Wave economy, the central resource—a single word broadly encompassing data, information, images, symbols, culture, ideology, and values—is *actionable* knowledge.

The industrial age is not fully over. In fact, classic Second Wave sectors (oil, steel, auto-production) have learned how to benefit from

Release 1.2, August 22, 1994. Copyright © 1994 by Progress and Freedom Foundation.

This statement represents the cumulative wisdom and innovation of many dozens of people. It is based primarily on the thoughts of four "coauthors": Ms. Esther Dyson; Mr. George Gilder; Dr. George Keyworth; and Dr. Alvin Toffler. This release 1.2 has the final "imprimatur" of no one. In the spirit of the age: It is copyrighted solely for the purpose of preventing someone else from doing so. If you have it, you can use it any way you want. However, major passages are from works copyrighted individually by the authors, used here by permission; these will be duly acknowledged in release 2.0. It is a living document. Release 2.0 will be released in October 1994. We hope you'll use it is to tell us how to make it better. Do so by:

Sending E-Mail to MAIL@PFF.ORG
Faxing 202-484-9326 or calling 202-484-2312
Sending POM (plain old mail) to 1301 K Street Suite 650 West, Washington, DC 20005

(The Progress & Freedom Foundation is a not-for-profit research and educational organization dedicated to creating a positive vision of the future founded on the historic principles of the American idea.)

Third Wave technological breakthroughs—just as the First Wave's agricultural productivity benefited exponentially from the Second Wave's farm-mechanization.

But the Third Wave, and the *Knowledge Age* it has opened, will not deliver on its potential unless it adds social and political dominance to its accelerating technological and economic strength. This means repealing Second Wave laws and retiring Second Wave attitudes. It also gives to leaders of the advanced democracies a special responsibility—to facilitate, hasten, and explain the transition.

As humankind explores this new "electronic frontier" of knowledge, it must confront again the most profound questions of how to organize itself for the common good. The meaning of freedom, structures of self-government, definition of property, nature of competition, conditions for cooperation, sense of community and nature of progress will each be redefined for the Knowledge Age—just as they were redefined for a new age of industry some 250 years ago.

What our 20th-century countrymen came to think of as the "American dream," and what resonant thinkers referred to as "the promise of American life" or "the American Idea," emerged from the turmoil of 19th-century industrialization. Now it's our turn: The knowledge revolution, and the Third Wave of historical change it powers, summon us to renew the dream and enhance the promise.

## THE NATURE OF CYBERSPACE

The Internet—the huge (2.2 million computers), global (135 countries), rapidly growing (10–15% a month) network that has captured the American imagination—is only a tiny part of cyberspace. So just what is cyberspace?

More ecosystem than machine, cyberspace is a bioelectronic environment that is literally universal: It exists everywhere there are telephone wires, coaxial cables, fiber-optic lines or electromagnetic waves.

This environment is "inhabited" by knowledge, including incorrect ideas, existing in electronic form. It is connected to the physical environment by portals which allow people to see what's inside, to put knowledge in, to alter it, and to take knowledge out. Some of these portals are one-way (e.g. television receivers and television transmitters); others are two-way (e.g. telephones, computer modems).

Most of the knowledge in cyberspace lives the most temporary (or so we think) existence: Your voice, on a telephone wire or microwave, travels through space at the speed of light, reaches the ear of your listener, and is gone forever.

But people are increasingly building cyberspatial "warehouses" of data, knowledge, information and misinformation in digital form, the ones and zeros of binary computer code. The storehouses themselves display a physical form (discs, tapes, CD-ROMs)—but what they contain is accessible only to those with the right kind of portal and the right kind of key.

The key is software, a special form of electronic knowledge that allows people to navigate through the cyberspace environment and make its contents understandable to the human senses in the form of written language, pictures and sound.

People are adding to cyberspace—creating it, defining it, expanding it—at a rate that is already explosive and getting faster. Faster computers, cheaper means of electronic storage, improved software and more capable communications channels (satellites, fiber-optic lines)—each of these factors independently add to cyberspace. But the real explosion comes from the combination of all of them, working together in ways we still do not understand.

The bioelectronic *frontier* is an appropriate metaphor for what is happening in cyberspace, calling to mind as it does the spirit of invention and discovery that led ancient mariners to explore the world, generations of pioneers to tame the American continent and, more recently, to man's first exploration of outer space.

But the exploration of cyberspace brings both greater opportunity and in some ways more difficult challenges than any previous human adventure.

Cyberspace is the land of knowledge, and the exploration of that land can be a civilization's truest, highest calling. The opportunity is now before us to empower every person to pursue that calling in his or her own way.

The challenge is as daunting as the opportunity is great. The Third Wave has profound implications for the nature and meaning of property, of the marketplace, of community and of individual freedom. As it emerges, it shapes new codes of behavior that move each organism and institution—family, neighborhood, church group, company, government, nation—inexorably beyond standardization and centralization, as well as beyond the materialist's obsession with energy, money and control.

Turning the economics of mass-production inside out, new information technologies are driving the financial costs of diversity—both product and personal—down toward zero, "demassifying" our institutions and our culture. Accelerating demassification creates the potential for vastly increased human freedom.

It also spells the death of the central institutional paradigm of modern life, the bureaucratic organization. (Governments, including the American government, are the last great redoubt of bureaucratic power on the face of the planet, and for them the coming change will be profound and probably traumatic.)

In this context, the one metaphor that is perhaps least helpful in thinking about cyberspace is—unhappily—the one that has gained the most currency: The Information Superhighway. Can you imagine a phrase less descriptive of the nature of cyberspace, or more misleading in thinking about its implications? Consider the following set of polarities:

| *Information Superhighway* | / | *Cyberspace* |
|---|---|---|
| Limited Matter | / | Unlimited Knowledge |
| Centralized | / | Decentralized |
| Moving on a grid | / | Moving in space |
| Government ownership | / | A vast array of ownerships |
| Bureaucracy | / | Empowerment |
| Efficient but not hospitable | / | Hospitable if you customize it |
| Withstand the elements | / | Flow, float and fine-tune |
| Unions and contractors | / | Associations and volunteers |
| Liberation from First Wave | / | Liberation from Second Wave |
| Culmination of Second Wave | / | Riding the Third Wave |

"The highway analogy is all wrong," explained Peter Huber in *Forbes* this spring, "for reasons rooted in basic economics. Solid things obey immutable laws of conservation—what goes south on the highway must go back north, or you end up with a mountain of cars in Miami. By the same token, production and consumption must balance. The average Joe can consume only as much wheat as the average Jane can grow. Information is completely different. It can be replicated at almost no cost—so every individual can (in theory) consume society's entire output. Rich and poor alike, we all run information deficits. We all take in more than we put out."

## THE NATURE AND OWNERSHIP OF PROPERTY

Clear and enforceable property rights are essential for markets to work. Defining them is a central function of government. Most of us have "known" that for a long time. But to create the new cyberspace environment is to create *new* property—that is, new means of creating goods (including ideas) that serve people.

The property that makes up cyberspace comes in several forms: Wires, coaxial cable, computers and other "hardware"; the electromagnetic spectrum; and "intellectual property"—the knowledge that dwells in and defines cyberspace.

In each of these areas, two questions must be answered. First, what does "ownership" *mean?* What is the nature of the property itself, and what does it mean to own it? Second, once we understand what ownership means, *who* is the owner? At the level of first principles, should ownership be public (i.e. government) or private (i.e. individuals)?

The answers to these two questions will set the basic terms upon which America and the world will enter the Third Wave. For the most part, however, these questions are not yet even being asked. Instead, at least in America, governments are attempting to take Second Wave concepts of property and ownership and apply them to the Third Wave. Or they are ignoring the problem altogether.

For example, a great deal of attention has been focused recently on the nature of "intellectual property"—i.e. the fact that knowledge is what economists call a "public good," and thus requires special treatment in the form of copyright and patent protection.

Major changes in U.S. copyright and patent law during the past two decades have broadened these protections to incorporate "electronic property." In essence, these reforms have attempted to take a body of law that originated in the 15th century, with Gutenberg's invention of the printing press, and apply it to the electronically stored and transmitted knowledge of the Third Wave.

A more sophisticated approach starts with recognizing how the Third Wave has fundamentally altered the nature of knowledge as a "good," and that the operative effect is not technology per se (the shift from printed books to electronic storage and retrieval systems), but rather the shift from a mass-production, mass-media, mass-culture civilization to a demassified civilization.

The big change, in other words, is the demassification of actionable knowledge.

The dominant form of new knowledge in the Third Wave is perishable, transient, customized knowledge: The right information, combined with the right software and presentation, at precisely the right time. Unlike the mass knowledge of the Second Wave—"public good" knowledge that was useful to everyone because most people's information needs were standardized—Third Wave customized knowledge is by nature a private good.

If this analysis is correct, copyright and patent protection of knowledge (or at least many forms of it) may no longer be unnecessary. In fact, the marketplace may already be creating vehicles to compensate creators of customized knowledge outside the cumbersome copyright/patent process, as suggested last year by John Perry Barlow:

> One existing model for the future conveyance of intellectual property is real-time performance, a medium currently used only in theater, music, lectures, stand-up comedy and pedagogy. I believe the concept of performance will expand to include most of the information economy, from multicasted soap operas to stock analysis. In these instances, commercial exchange will be more like ticket sales to a continuous show than the purchase of discrete bundles of that which is being shown. The other model, of course, is service. The entire professional class— doctors, lawyers, consultants, architects, etc.—are already being paid directly for their intellectual property. Who needs copyright when you're on a retainer?

Copyright, patent and intellectual property represent only a few of the "rights" issues now at hand. Here are some of the others:

Ownership of the electromagnetic spectrum, traditionally considered to be "public property," is now being "auctioned" by the Federal Communications Commission to private companies. Or is it? Is the very limited "bundle of rights" sold in those auctions really property, or more in the nature of a use permit—the right to use a part of the spectrum for a limited time, for limited purposes? In either case, are the rights being auctioned defined in a way that makes technological sense?

Ownership over the infrastructure of wires, coaxial cable and fiber-optic lines that are such prominent features in the geography of cyberspace is today much less clear than might be imagined. Regulation, especially price regulation, of this property can be tantamount to confiscation, as America's cable operators recently learned when the Federal government imposed price limits on them and effectively confiscated [billions] of their net worth. (Whatever one's stance on the FCC's decision and the law behind it, there is no disagreeing with the proposition that one's ownership of a good is less meaningful when the government can step in, at will, and dramatically reduce its value.)

The nature of capital in the Third Wave—tangible capital as well as intangible—is to depreciate in real value much faster than industrial-age capital—driven, if nothing else, by Moore's Law, which states that the processing power of the microchip doubles at least every 18 *months*. Yet accounting and tax regulations still require property to be depreciated over periods as long as 30 years. The result is a heavy bias in favor of "heavy industry" and against nimble, fast-moving baby businesses.

Who will define the nature of cyberspace property rights, and how? How can we strike a balance between interoperable open systems and protection of property?

### The Nature of the Marketplace

Inexpensive knowledge destroys economies-of-scale. Customized knowledge permits "just in time" production for an ever rising number of goods. Technological progress creates new means of serving old markets, turning one-time monopolies into competitive battlegrounds.

These phenomena are altering the nature of the marketplace, not just for information technology but for all goods and materials, shipping and services. In cyberspace itself, market after market is being transformed by technological progress from a "natural monopoly" to one in which competition is the rule. Three recent examples:

The market for "mail" has been made competitive by the development of fax machines and overnight delivery—even though the "private express statutes" that technically grant the U.S. Postal Service a monopoly over mail delivery remain in place.

During the past 20 years, the market for television has been transformed from one in which there were at most a few broadcast TV stations to one in which consumers can choose among broadcast, cable and satellite services.

The market for local telephone services, until recently a monopoly based on twisted-pair copper cables, is rapidly being made competitive by the advent of wireless service and the entry of cable television into voice communication. In England, Mexico, New Zealand and a host of developing countries, government restrictions preventing such competition have already been removed and consumers actually have the freedom to choose.

The advent of new technology and new products creates the potential for *dynamic competition*—competition between and among technologies and industries, each seeking to find the best way of serving customers' needs. Dynamic competition is different from static competition, in which many providers compete to sell essentially similar products at the lowest price.

Static competition is good, because it forces costs and prices to the lowest levels possible for a given product. Dynamic competition is better, because it allows competing technologies and new products to challenge the old ones and, if they really are better, to replace them. Static competition might lead to faster and stronger horses. Dynamic competition gives us the automobile.

Such dynamic competition—the essence of what Austrian economist Joseph Schumpeter called "creative destruction"—creates winners and losers on a massive scale. New technologies can render instantly obsolete billions of dollars of embedded infrastructure, accumulated over decades. The transformation of the U.S. computer industry since 1980 is a case in point.

In 1980, everyone knew who led in computer technology. Apart from the minicomputer boom, mainframe computers were the market, and America's dominance was largely based upon the position of a dominant vendor—IBM, with over 50% world market-share.

Then the personal-computing industry exploded, leaving older-style big-business-focused computing with a stagnant piece of a burgeoning total market. As IBM lost market-share, many people became convinced that America had lost the ability to compete. By the mid-1980s, such alarmism had reached from Washington all the way into the heart of Silicon Valley.

But the real story was the renaissance of American business and technological leadership. In the transition from mainframes to PCs, a vast new market was created. This market was characterized by dynamic competition consisting of easy access and low barriers to entry. Start-ups by the dozens took on the larger established companies—and won.

After a decade of angst, the surprising outcome is that America is not only competitive internationally, but, by any measurable standard, America dominates the growth sectors in world economics— telecommunications, microelectronics, computer networking (or "connected computing") and software systems and applications.

The reason for America's victory in the computer wars of the 1980s is that dynamic competition was allowed to occur, in an area so breakneck and pell-mell that government would've had a hard time controlling it—even had it been paying attention. The challenge for policy in the 1990s is to permit, even encourage, dynamic competition in every aspect of the cyberspace marketplace.

\* \* \*

# PRICING INFORMATION GOODS

## Hal R. Varian

Digital materials typically have the property that it is very costly to produce the first copy and very cheap to produce subsequent copies. It is often said, for example, that the "first copy costs" are more than 70% of the cost of an academic journal. Cost structures of this form pose special problems for pricing.

The first problem is that it is very difficult to sustain a competitive market with this sort of cost structure. Economists define a purely competitive market to be one where there are "several" producers of an identical commodity. The market for wheat, corn, shares of IBM stock, etc. are all examples of purely competitive markets. The market for automobiles is not purely competitive since there are not multiple producers of identical products. Instead, there are several somewhat different products some of which are close substitutes. Economists call this a situation of monopolistic competition.

The market for academic journals (or other sorts of information goods) tends to be much more like the automobile market than the wheat market. The high-fixed-cost/low-incremental-cost structure forces this outcome. To see why, let us suppose that there are several producers of a "generic" database. By this I mean a standardized set of data that anyone can produce: CD ROMs containing telephone directory listings, for example. There may be very large costs to producing the first copy of such a database, but subsequent copies can be stamped out at less than $1 a piece. Suppose that several firms have produced such CDs. If the products have similar user interfaces

Reprinted with the permission of Hal R. Varian. June 1995, current version: June 15, 1995.

*Abstract:* I describe some of the issues involved in pricing information goods such as computer software, databases, electronic journals and so on. In particular I discuss the incentives to engage in differential pricing and examine some of the forms such differential pricing may take. This paper was presented at the Research Libraries Group Symposium on "Scholarship in the New Information Environment" held at Harvard Law School, May 2–3, 1995, and will be published in the conference proceedings.

*Keywords:* Pricing, price discrimination, information goods.

and similar data, consumers will buy only from the cheapest producer. But then the producers with no sales all have an incentive to undercut the competition, and there is no natural floor on prices except the $1 a copy reproduction costs. Since this price is likely inadequate to recover fixed costs, producers will be forced out of business until only a single seller remains. This single seller can now operate as a monopolist unconstrained by competition.

Since a purely competitive market is not viable, we turn our attention to a market where producers have some market power. That is, the product that they sell is different enough from products produced by other producers that their primary concern has to do with the customers' willingness to pay for the product rather than their competition's behavior.

## PRICE DISCRIMINATION

If all customers for the product place essentially the same value on the product, the profit-maximizing pricing decision is easy: just price the product at this common value and charge what the market will bear. The difficulty arises when consumers' willingnesses to pay are heterogeneous. In this case the producer's choice is not so obvious, since fewer consumers will buy at higher prices. Furthermore, if willingness-to-pay differs across customers, the producer would generally find it advantageous to charge different users different prices. As we will see below, this will be true even for a producer who is only interested in cost recovery. I will illustrate some of these phenomena via a series of examples that involve the demand for an electronic book. In each example the cost structure will be the same: $7 to produce the first copy of the book, and the second copy can be produced at zero incremental cost.

> **Example 1**   There are two consumers, *A* and *B*. *A* is willing to pay $5 for a book, *B* is willing to pay $3 for the book.

Note that the total benefits $8 = 5 + 3$ exceed total cost, 7, so it is socially desirable to produce the book. However, the producer cannot recover his costs at any uniform price: if he charges $5, only one consumer will buy the book, so his revenues will be $5. If he charges $3, both consumers will buy, but revenues will only be $6. If the producer can price discriminate—sell to different users at different prices—then it will be possible to cover the development costs of the book.

**Example 2**   *A* is willing to pay $8, *B* is willing to pay $3.

In this case, total benefits minus total costs would be maximized if both parties got copies of the book. But again this outcome cannot be supported at any uniform price: the highest price at which both parties would buy is $3, and this generates inadequate revenues to cover the cost. However, if the producer could charge different users different prices, he would find it profitable to sell books to both consumers.

> **Example 3**   *A* is willing to pay $20, *B* is willing to pay $8. In this case, a producer who is only interested in cost recovery could price the book at $3.50 and be assured of recovering his costs. But a profit-maximizing producer would pursue a very different strategy: it is in his interest to price the book at $20 and sell only to the high end of the market. Note that this is the case *even though consumer B is willing to pay the entire cost of production!*

## Price Discrimination in Practice

The above examples show that it will typically be desirable for a profit-maximizing producer to practice price discrimination and it will often be desirable to do this even for a non-profit who is only interested in cost recovery. There are two problems with implementing price discrimination in practice: determining the willingness to pay of different consumers, and preventing consumers with high willingness to pay from purchasing the product intended for the consumers with low willingness to pay.

Since consumers will not willingly reveal their true willingness to pay, pricing needs to be based on something that is correlated with willingness to pay. For example, it is often thought that business users have higher willingness to pay than educational users, so many software manufacturers offer educational discounts. Similarly prices often depend on whether you are a large user, an on-peak or off-peak user, domestic or foreign, member of a particular group, etc.

Another dimension on which producers can price discriminate is on characteristics of the product. It is often thought that users who want the product immediately are willing to pay more than those who are willing to wait. Note that this has nothing to do with the cost of providing immediate service: the producer may want to charge differentially for different degrees of timeliness regardless of the cost of providing such service. A nice example of this is stock market quotations: quotations that are 5 minutes old demand a premium price, while those that are 1/2 hour old sell for much less.

Yet another dimension is the quality of the good itself. In an electronic text, one could price discriminate on resolution (screen, 300 dpi, 600 dpi, etc.), whether the data is formatted or unformatted, structured, unstructured, etc.

We turn now to the second problem: how do we ensure that the consumers with higher willingness to pay actually pay the higher price? One answer is to degrade the quality of the product offered to the consumers with a low willingness-to-pay.

Consider, for example, the case of airline pricing. There are two broad classes of travellers: business travellers and tourists. The airlines price discriminate between the two by offering a degraded product: a much cheaper ticket with restrictions (Saturday night stayover, advanced purchase, no changes, etc.). The consumers with low-willingness to pay tolerate this degraded product while those with high willingness to pay do not.

This strategy is common in high technology. Deneckere and McAfee (1994) describe several examples:

- Student versions of mathematical software that disable calls to the math coprocessor in order to slow down calculations.
- The 486SX chip, which is simply a 486DX chip with the co-processor disabled.
- Federal Express offers both morning and afternoon delivery. It appears that FedEx does not deliver afternoon packages in the morning, even if they arrive in time for morning delivery. Instead they will make two trips to the same location.
- The IBM Laser Printer Series E was a low-cost alternative to the IBM Laser Printer. The series E printed at 5 pages per minute rather than the 10 pages per minute of its higher cost brother. Apparently, both printers used exactly the same print engine, the only difference being 5 chips that inserted wait states to slow down the series E printer.

In each of these cases, the producer finds it advantageous to differentiate the product in order to support differential prices. Indeed, several of the strategies described above fall into this category: it may be just as costly to deliver delayed information as immediate information, but it is preferable to delay the information in order to maintain the two-tiered price system. Similarly with resolution: it would probably be cheaper to offer an image in one resolution, but low and high resolution products make price discrimination viable.

The fact that producers will find it advantageous to degrade the product in order to differentiate prices has been recognized for centuries. Witness the observation of an 18th century economist:

> It is not because of the few thousand francs which would have to be spent to put a roof over the third-class carriages or to upholster the third-class seats that some company or other has open carriages with wooden benches. . . . What the company is trying to do is to prevent the passengers who can pay the second class fare from traveling third class; it hits the poor, not because it wants to hurt them, but to frighten the rich. . . . And it is again for the same reason that the companies, having proved almost cruel to the third-class passengers and mean to the second-class ones, become lavish in dealing with first-class passengers. Having refused the poor what is necessary, they give the rich what is superfluous. (Dupuit [1849], quoted in Ekelund [1970])

As this quote suggests, observers typically find this sort of quality degradation unattractive. However, it may well be a big win from the viewpoint of consumers since the low-quality market may not be served at all without the degradation. By differentiating the product the producer can segment the market and recover revenue from the low-demand sector without destroying the revenue from the high-demand component. Indeed, Deneckere and McAfee (1994) show that the use of product degradation can, under some circumstances, make all parties to the transaction strictly better off!

## BUNDLING

Another very attractive form of price discrimination is known as product bundling. This occurs when distinct products are sold together as a package. Again, this is a common practice for information goods. One of Microsoft's most successful products in recent years has been Microsoft Office, which is a bundle of different software products. Similarly, academic journals are a bundle of articles, and a subscription to a journal is a bundle of issues. More recently, producers have been offering bundles of subscriptions of related journals at special rates.

In order to understand the economics of bundling, let us again consider a simple example of two mathematics professors and two journals, the *Journal of Addition* and the *Journal of Subtraction*. Professor A, an expert in addition, is willing to pay $120 for the *Journal of Addition* but only $100 for the *Journal of Subtraction*. Professor B is an expert in subtraction, and has just the opposite willingness to pay: $120 for the *Journal of Subtraction* and $100 for the *Journal of Addition*.

If the producer sells both journals at the separate prices, his profit maximizing strategy is to set a price of $100 for each. Each mathematician will buy both journals, yielding a revenue of $400. But suppose that the producer offers a bundle of the two journals: if the willingness to pay for the bundle is just the sum of the willingness to pay for the components, each professor would then be willing to pay $220 for the bundle. This yields the producer a revenue of $440!

Bundling is profitable in this example because it reduces the heterogeneity of the consumers' willingness to pay: as I indicated initially if consumers have different willingnesses to pay, and the producer cannot price discriminate, all the consumers who buy the product buy at the price of the buyer with the lowest willingness to pay. By creating the bundle, the producer can sell at the average willingness to pay, and this will typically be more profitable.

Indeed, this is one of the rationales for having journals in the first place. A journal is simply a bundle of articles and it is likely the case that there is much more heterogeneity in valuations of individual articles than there is in bundles of articles. Hence bundling articles together will generate more revenues than selling each individual article at a flat price.

Of course this sort of revenue enhancement is not the only reason for bundling. Collecting articles on similar topics together helps to reduce consumer search costs, lowers production costs, etc. However, these cost and search based effects are less compelling in an electronic environment, whereas the revenue effect may still be quite strong. It seems likely that producers will want to continue to use the subscription model even if it isn't warranted solely on cost grounds.

## SUMMARY

Producers of information goods such as electronic journals will want to consider the possibility of differential pricing, letting prices vary both across consumers and across qualities of the good. Quality variation may take the form of offering a degraded quality in order to sell to the low end of the market while still maintaining revenue from the high end of the market. Such quality variation can generate additional revenue to cover costs as well as increasing access to the good making all parties to the transaction better off. Bundling articles, journals and services together may be attractive as additional means of raising revenue.

### References

Deneckere, R. J., and McAfee, R. P. (1994). "Damaged Goods," University of Texas at Austin.

Dupuit, E. (1962). "On Tolls and Transport Charges." In *International Economic Papers,* vol 11. Macmillan, London. Translated by Elizabeth Henderson from the *Annales des Ponts et Chausées.*

Ekelund, R. B. (1970). "Price Discrimination and Product Differentiation in Economic Theory: An Early Analysis," *Quarterly Journal of Economics, 84,* 268–78.

\*    \*    \*

# THE CULTURAL LEGACY OF THE "MODERN LIBRARY" FOR THE FUTURE

## Francis Miksa

### Excerpt: The Challenge of a New Environment

The modern library and LIS education, which is the child of the modern library, now face the challenge of a new environment, a new environment which is itself a product of new roots appearing—new information technologies, new information professions and services. To me the chief issue is not to devise strategies which the modern library and LIS education can use to preserve itself against such

An expanded form of an address to the annual meeting of the Association for Library and Information Science Education (ALISE) in San Antonio, Texas, 17 January 1996. Reprinted with the permission of the Association for Library & Information Science Education.

change, as if they were some sort of sacred cows which must continue in their original forms at all costs. Rather, it is to identify the significant aspects of the new environment which give the most promise for assisting in the creation of a new library era, for assisting in the transformation of the modern library into a new expression of the library in society.

The first significant aspect of the new environment that will assist in the transformation consists of new information technologies which are slowly creating electronic alternatives to printed information and in so doing are challenging one of the basic reasons why the modern library appeared—the impossibility that many individuals could acquire and store large numbers of printed information-bearing entities. Information in electronic form and accessible through networking raises the distinct possibility that enormous numbers of individuals will be able to have their own libraries. In this scenario, a library will likely consist of a personal computer with some electronic (and, for a long time, some paper) documents stored locally and hundreds, perhaps even thousands of others accessible through links on the net. Think of it—a library seemingly contained in a small box. Further, given this capability to collect and store electronic information, the focus of the collection will also change because it will be possible to shape such collections and their access mechanisms precisely for the needs of the individual or the cohesive group of individuals who require them.

Only a little reflection will show that this new kind of library is not only a denial of the modern library's public space and general target population orientation. It actually represents something of a return to the library era that preceded the modern library when a library generally represented the private space of an individual or of a small group. Frankly, this reversion makes eminent sense to me for, ultimately, is not an excellent library one which is as personal in its selections and access mechanisms as the personal nature of the information seeking that prompted it? In this respect, it seems appropriate to paraphrase S. R. Ranganathan's second and third laws of library science. Instead of, "Every reader his book," and "Every book its reader," new technology appears to be making possible, "Every reader his library," and "Every library his reader."

Now, I must hasten to add to this picture that the mere existence of electronic technology will not by itself accomplish the shift to private space libraries. If that were the only ingredient required, one could rightly object to this scenario by emphasizing that the cost of electronic information, at least at the present time, makes collecting it by individuals just as prohibitive as collecting print products ever was. I would agree with this observation, but would add that I suspect the present costs are due primarily to present patterns of dissemination being tied to a publishing structure inherited from print culture. In the latter, a relatively small number of publishers are gateways for disseminating information to millions of clients who desire it. What will also be necessary for the new situation will be a social dissemination structure that replaces the present publishing structure with one which recognizes the new situation for what it is—an enfranchisement for all persons who participate in the networked society to become publishers. This phenomenon appears to be what is happening as we see an exponential increase in computers which are not merely clients but also servers. Servers are, in effect, publishers because they make information available, and when they make it available over the net they do not essentially function differently than a publisher of paper information products. We may mourn the loss of the control inherent in print culture publishing, but I suspect we will be able to do little about it and may each have to make our separate peace with the nature of information in a society in which everyone with a computer will have the opportunity to create, to sell, to give away information. In that context, there will be ample opportunity to collect enormous, dynamic libraries of information by anyone who cares to do so and at a cost which is as reasonable as buying any other widely disseminated product.

A second significant way that new growing roots hold significant promise for an emerging library different from the modern library has to do with funding. The modern library has been funded by government primarily as a practical matter as an economy of scale. However, if the necessity to preserve the social organization called the modern library is removed because the emerging library is becoming once again the realm of private rather than public space, what then remains for the government to fund? Can government funding be justified for what can no longer be justified as a public good based on a doctrine of jointness of consumption?

There is more to the issue than this, of course. Most complaints that I have heard about the possible loss of the modern library as a public space revolve around two issues. First, it will make information access purely an expression of the commercial sector with information being no less commercial than any other product—with a corresponding loss of "free" access to information. Second, if information accessibility does become primarily a commercial sector activity, a class of information deprived or "have-nots" will arise.

To the first of these two complaints, I can only say that the idea that published information is not commercial is a very romantic notion that has little reality in fact. Nevertheless, people in the library field often become upset today when they see the extent to which the development of new information technologies is driven by a profit motive and, increasingly, as information policy is debated, the extent to which the development of such technologies has become a political matter.

But, what is so new about this? When printing began, it represented both an economic and political innovation, economic because a profit motive was basic to it, political because its viability as an economic reality depended on an interplay with those who made political decisions. And for all of the period since the invention of printing, the creation and delivery of information has always been a matter of economics and markets, and it has always been a political matter. The only thing different over time has been where the charging mechanism has been plugged in and where control mechanisms have been exercised.

Government funding of information creation and delivery has been a successful solution to a problem for the past 125 years. But one should not thereby conclude that it is the only method of distributing information equitably and conveniently in society. If information creation and delivery were cheap enough, and the controlling political mechanism worked out, there is no reason why government has to be the prime mediator of the process. This is especially the case in a society which is imbued with the very social institution that the modern library helped to establish—that information accessibility is a necessity and a right to the members of a society.

As to the complaint that this scenario appears to insure that some people will be forever among the information dispossessed, I would say that there is some merit here. However, one must be careful about what this actually means. Some people are information poor because they do not know how to be information rich. They are, as our own field would say, information illiterate and their information illiteracy is the case despite the presence of public space libraries and despite formal education they have had. The solution to their information poverty is not first of all simply or even to make large collections of information-bearing entities available. It is for them to learn the value of information in their lives. Only after that, if they remain destitute of any connection to information products in the coming age, would I foresee some agency for connecting them to the net. Even then, however, I do not see that this will necessarily require a full-blown social organization called the modern library.

One may reasonably conclude that these two aspects of the contemporary situation constitute something of the handwriting on the wall for the modern library as society's grand social mechanism for storing and delivering information to its citizens. This may not happen immediately, but in my view it has a high probability of happening. The model of the modern library of the past century and a quarter will not hold, in other words, because the technology, economics and politics of the matter will find a different route to the same end. And what appears to have caused the rise of new information service fields is just this change going on—the creation of new paths (which together might be conceived to be "the" new path) to achieving that extraordinary social institution that the modern library has been so instrumental in establishing in the first place, that if a society is to endure, its citizens must absolutely have access to enormous amounts of information of all kinds and for all uses.

\* \* \*

# 4

## Copyright in the Digital Age

As librarians, we are generally aware of our basic obligations under the copyright law, although this often translates to no more than placing the appropriate notices over our public photocopy machines. However, we rarely think about the role that copyright plays in promoting the exchange of information and ideas nor of the fine balance between the author's rights and the interests of the public. The copyright law is not simply economic protection for the creators of intellectual property, it is a way to encourage the flow of those ideas to the widest possible audience.

The advent of the digital age has prompted a movement to reform the copyright laws for the protection of intellectual property in this new medium. Information delivered over computer networks has very different characteristics from the analog media like books and sound recordings. Protection of works in this new medium brings into question our basic assumptions about browsing, lending, and delivering information to the public, and some of the solutions may pose a threat to the balance between copyright holders and readers.

## Copyright and Libraries

The basis for our copyright law was drafted by James Madison in 1787 and added to the Constitution signed in 1790. This clause gave

Congress the power to "promote the Progress of Science and useful Arts by securing for limited terms to Authors and Inventors the exclusive Right to their respective Writings and Discoveries." This simple statement has been interpreted by many to promote a balance between the interests of authors to earn a living from their work and the interests of the public to have access to ideas and information. Or, to put it in another way, the copyright law exists not solely to assure the economic gain for authors but to make sure that knowledge will circulate readily in our society.

The copyright law itself, Title 17 of the U.S. Code, is understandably quite complex. But there are two sections of this law of special importance to libraries: the *first sale doctrine* and *fair use*. Both of these are complex legal issues, but we need only to understand their role in enabling the work of libraries. These two key aspects of the copyright law are brought into question in the protection of digital works, so we will return to them later.

## First Sale Doctrine and Library Lending

Libraries make information available to the public by lending copies of works. At first glance, this might seem like a violation of the authors' rights, but the copyright law includes an important section referred to as the first sale doctrine. This states that the owner of a particular copy, such as a library that has purchased a book, can then dispose of that copy without any further obligation to the copyright owner. Essentially, authors receive payment for their work only on the first sale of each copy. Lending or resale of the book takes place without any legal obligation to the author.

There are good reasons to deny copyright holders control over the resale and subsequent use of their works. Imagine if you had to secure the author's permission to discard a book or to sell it to a used bookstore. Not only would this be inconvenient for users of works, it would allow authors to retain control over their works beyond the making of copies. Such control could hinder the free flow of information that the copyright law is designed to encourage because it would put all distribution of the works in the hands of the copyright holder. An unscrupulous publisher could keep copies out of the hands of critics or not allow copies to be viewed by some groups of people.

It would also prohibit library lending, because any transfer of the work from one person to another would be an exclusive right of the copyright holder. So, in the United States, it truly is the first sale doctrine that makes the lending library possible.

### *Fair Use*

Some amount of copying of copyrighted works is permissible under the fair use guidelines. That said, it is important to note that fair use is often hard to define. In general, copies of single articles or portions of books can be made for personal and educational use, and passages can be quoted by other authors who are commenting on the work. Fair use allows the limited copying essential to education and private study and therefore promotes wider access to protected works. Copying by libraries is specifically covered in Section 108 of the copyright law and allows the single copying of material by libraries and archives under defined circumstances.

While the law upholds certain in-library copying as legitimate, many publishers, especially journal publishers, feel that library copying has been quite detrimental to their business. It is in this area of the interpretation of fair use where much of the tension surfaces between copyright holders and libraries, and nowhere is this tension more visible than in the discussions about the protection of digital and online information resources.

## Copying in the Age of Computers

When the copyright law was first enacted, copying meant setting type and printing copies, so only those members of society with access to a printing press were potential copyright infringers. Copying by individuals wasn't much of an issue until the invention of the photocopy machine in the latter part of the twentieth century. Suddenly anyone could make copies quickly and easily. It soon became possible for every library to have a photocopy machine for its own and for patron use, and we librarians faced a new challenge in adhering to the copyright law. Whereas libraries had previously been limited to circulating their original copies of journals to patrons, they could now allow patrons to copy individual articles for personal use. Interlibrary loan departments could deliver photocopies of articles to requesting libraries rather than sending issues or bound copies of journals. The amount of in-library copying increased greatly.

Copying doesn't only happen to paper materials. The VCR can be used to copy programs broadcast over television and cable; audio tapes can be used to copy other audio tapes or CDs; and anything on a computer disk can be copied in just seconds to another disk, another computer, or to tape. Provisions have been added over time to the copyright law to cover these newer nonprint forms of expression because emerging technologies have also made the reproduction of these works simpler and more accurate.

With computers it is not only possible to make any number of copies at the touch of a button, each copy is a perfect reproduction of the original. In most other forms of copying like audio tape or photocopying, the copy is often of somewhat degraded quality compared to a commercially produced master. Not only are the copies perfect, computer networks allow an individual to transmit these copies to hundreds or thousands of people with a minimum of cost and effort.

Beyond this deliberate use of computers to make copies, there is the fact that many functions performed by computers, by the nature of that technology, result in copies being made. For example, every time you click on a link on the World Wide Web, a copy of the information that appears on your screen has been made by the remote computer and sent to your computer for viewing. You cannot "surf" the Internet without making copies. Even when you view a document that you have stored on your own computer's hard drive, a copy of the document is made in the computer's memory during the time that you are looking at it. When you close the viewing program, such as your word-processing software, that copy in memory is erased, and a new copy will be made when you view it again in the future.

Although the computer seems to be the ideal tool for copyright infringers, this ability of computers to make perfect copies can also be of an advantage to the publishing industry. The distribution of works in digital form and over computer networks means that publishers will no longer need to produce a limited number of physical copies for sale. Instead, each time a file is accessed, a copy of it can be created and transferred to the requesting computer, in essence publishing the document on demand. This is to the benefit of the publisher who can then avoid overproduction of any work. The cost of producing the individual electronic copies is very low, so low that even very short runs may be financially viable.

The computer is, however, viewed by intellectual property holders as a particular threat to their business because all computer users, not just publishers, are capable of making copies. And if computers alone are a threat to copyright holders, networks like the Internet with millions of computers are a disaster in the making. A file or resource can be recopied any number of times to other computers on the network with very little effort. How are copyright holders to make use of this new technology and still protect their investment in intellectual property?

This was the question asked by the Working Group on Intellectual Property Rights of the Information Infrastructure Task Force on Information Policy. Chaired by Assistant Secretary of Commerce Bruce A. Lehman, this group produced its draft report in July 1994. Commonly called the *Green Paper,* this report examined the intellectual property implications of the National Information Infrastructure. The final report, called the *White Paper,* was issued in September 1995 and made recommendations for changes to the copyright law. The first laws proposed after issue of the White Paper didn't get too far in the 104th Congress. However, the White Paper may influence other proposed laws. It remains the most comprehensive statement of the Department of Commerce's stance on copyright law.

# Changing U.S. Law

Members of the Working Group on copyright were of the opinion that a wholesale rewriting of the copyright law was not necessary to protect digital information resources. The White Paper on copyright proposes only some "minor" changes to the copyright law for the protection of networked digital works. These minor changes, however, can have far-reaching implications for the use of digital and networked information resources.

## Transmission

The Working Group proposed defining the transmission of a digital work, such as over the Internet, to be an exclusive right of the copyright holder.

> 17 U.S.C. 106(3) "(3) to distribute copies or phonorecords of the copyrighted work to the public by sale or other transfer of ownership property, or by rental, lease or lending, *or by transmission*" (Proposed change is in italics).

Transmission itself was defined as "to distribute [a work] by any device or process whereby a copy or phonorecord of the work is fixed beyond the place from which it was sent." This means that every act of viewing files over the Internet or any other online system falls under this definition of a transmission.

## Copy Protection

Another proposed amendment to the copyright law has to do with new penalties for circumvention of copy protection schemes or for the provision of false copyright information. After all, the law may be the law, but it doesn't actually prevent copying at a technical level. The authors of the White Paper realized that for every technology that can be used to lock copies against unauthorized use, other technologies may be devised that could unlock those same works. So the Working Group proposed adding a new chapter to the copyright law that would prohibit the manufacture or distribution of any device whose purpose is to circumvent a copy protection scheme or technology.

### Database Protection

Proposals specific to database protection were not part of the White Paper, but were developed afterward by the Department of Commerce. Databases, or compilations of facts, are not covered by copyright law. For a work to be copyrighted, it has to have certain qualities, one of which is originality. When one telephone company claimed that its white pages were protected under copyright, the court decided (in *Feist v. Rural Telephone Services*) that an alphabetical list of phone subscribers did not meet the standard of originality. Although facts themselves cannot be protected under copyright, compilations of facts that are selected or arranged in significant ways may be protected because of the value-added nature of the compilation.

It can take an enormous effort and a great investment to compile a large database. Database publishers fear that their investment is at risk if they make their databases available over computer networks. Currently there is no law that would prevent users from making use of facts that they find in databases, either for other works or even to create competing databases. Bills regarding the protection of databases were introduced in the U.S. Congress in 1996, and the World Intellectual Property Organization (WIPO) proposed an international treaty of the same nature. The protection sought is not copyright but a new form of protection defined specifically for databases. This protection would cover a wide range of materials since *database* is being broadly defined to include any organized compilation of information (which presumably would also include library catalogs and other bibliographic compilations).

# What Could These Changes Mean for Libraries?

It's not easy to balance the needs of creators and the needs of the public, and clearly the digital environment places additional strains on this relationship. The implications of these possible changes to our copyright law are many and complex. Let's look in particular at how these changes might affect libraries.

## Library Lending

As we saw above, library lending of hardcopy works depends on the first sale doctrine. This pertains to a particular copy, which is much more easily understood as a material object than anything in the digital world. Because online works are not distributed in physical form but are essentially recopied from computer to computer, there is no physical copy to which to apply this doctrine. As a matter of fact, the first draft of the Working Group's report stated clearly that the first sale doctrine should not apply to works distributed by transmission over networks (though this wording was not included in the final report).

Eliminating "first sale" for digitally transmitted works essentially means that there would be no legal basis for the library's lending any information stored on a computer. The copy that the library would make available to its patron would not be the library's physical copy, but a digital copy that the library had made by transmitting the document to the patron. And if transmission is one of the rights of the copyright holder, the library would have infringed on the holder's rights.

Representatives of publishers associations have made clear that they do not consider it acceptable for libraries to be distributing copies of digital works to their patrons since this directly competes with the publishers' own digital products. As the International Publishers Copyright Council put it, ". . . disseminating printed and electronic works to individual consumers for their 'personal' or 'private' use is precisely the business authors and publishers are about." It's also precisely what libraries are about. That libraries and publishers have existed side-by-side, both disseminating works to the public for well over a century, seems to indicate that the balance supported by the copyright law is working quite well.

Note that this balance works at least in part because libraries and publishers have very different goals. A good example of this is in library lending of videotapes. At one time library lending of videotapes was hotly contested by video rental outlets because they saw it as being in competition with their business. My local library lends videos and yet new rental stores have opened on just about every available corner. So why don't all of the people who patronize the video store go to the library instead? Because these two institutions provide very different services. The selling point of the video store is that it has many copies of the latest popular films, plus candies and microwave popcorn at the checkout counter. The library carries some popular films, but just as the library's book collection has emphasized breadth, it also carries classics and educational films. Some patrons may visit the library video collection instead of going to a video store, just as some will borrow a currently published book from the library rather than purchase it, but other patrons are at the library precisely because the video collection is different from the one at the video stores. It's quite likely that the digital collections that libraries emphasize in their information services will serve different needs from those of the publishers and their distributors. Just as in the case of videotape lending, the predictions of disaster may be greatly exaggerated.

The publishers protesting the dissemination of works through libraries seem to assume that every visit to a library is a loss of business for the publishing industry. I haven't seen figures that would estimate the impact of libraries on the publishing industry (which would of course have to include on the positive side the purchasing of books and other materials by libraries), but many visits to a library are for works and services that could not be found elsewhere. Library patrons make use of reference services they could not purchase at a book store and borrow out-of-print items. But that some portion, whatever it is, of library visits competes with commercial publishing is not an argument for the tightening of the copyright law. The essence of the balance that has been carefully cultivated for intellectual property is that the owner has limited rights so that the public is assured the widest access possible.

## Fair Use

Fair use guidelines for digital materials is a much discussed but still unresolved area. It is important for libraries because this aspect of the copyright law is what allows the public to make specific uses of copyrighted materials without the owner's permission. There are also particular exemptions for library copying in Section 108 of the copyright law. Copying under the fair use guidelines is often for educational purposes, so this exemption to the general prohibition on copying is especially important to our educational institutions. Fair use also allows some copying for personal use, which supports a societal goal of continuing education for the public with libraries as our main institution of continuing education for the adults in our population.

One of the outcomes of the draft report of the Working Group on Copyright was to initiate a Conference on Fair Use (CONFU) to discuss the development of fair use guidelines for digital materials. Members of the CONFU, representing publishers, educators, and librarians, began meeting in September 1994. The group initially identified five areas that needed to be discussed by smaller working groups: distance learning, multimedia, electronic reserves, interlibrary loan, and image collections. Two other discussion areas were added later: music and software.

Negotiations between publishers and library and education representatives ran into difficulties very early on. Publishers felt that the CONFU talks were premature, and that it would be best not to formulate guidelines at this time. Carol Risher, executive director of the Association of American Publishers (AAP), explained at the LITA/LAMA conference in October 1996 that the publishers simply cannot agree to allow libraries to disseminate electronic works because they fear that library use will compete with commercial products. The publishers are particularly concerned with the idea that libraries may provide remote access to information resources, such as allowing a member of the public to access library resources from the home. The publishers anticipate a situation where home users would have a choice between equal online services, one of which would be provided by the library for free. We seem to be back to the situation we were once in with the video stores, where one side is arguing that the dissemination of these materials by libraries will be highly detrimental to the commercial vendors of these products.

Perhaps it is better not to make decisions about fair use at this time so that we can have more experience with the delivery of digital resources. It is possibly too early in the development of this technology for us to understand what types of services we might be providing in the future. Today anyone can send a plain text file easily over the Internet, but I rather doubt that our future information services will be of this simplicity of design. Future commercial information systems will no doubt employ complex—and eye-catching—multimedia features that will most likely not be delivered as whole files sent directly to a user's hard drive. Instead, they might be multipart programs with only the currently active segment temporarily residing on the user's machine. Already some Internet functions like RealAudio store only small portions of a sound file on the receiving system at any given time, and work is under way to develop similar systems for video delivery.

Some of these future online offerings will be oriented to entertainment and infotainment, much as movies and television are today. Libraries have never attempted to compete with the business of delivering first-run movies or televisionlike programming to the public. Others will be information services of the type that libraries are interested in providing to their patrons, and media companies may find that they can develop a charging system for these services under which libraries will become good customers for these works, just as they are today for reference works and other published fare.

Proposals to develop copy protection for databases also could have an effect on fair use. Should database protection legislation pass, there will be some restrictions on the use of facts taken from compilations such as databases and reference works, yet because the database protection is not covered by the copyright law, fair use limitations on the database owner's rights will not apply. This doesn't mean that there will be no use allowed of factual information, but it does mean that the legal history built into fair use will not be pertinent to this type of information. When database protection legislation was first introduced in 1996 it drew sharp criticism from a wide range of interests, including many organizations representing scholars and scientists who feared that any restriction on the use of factual information would be a threat to research. Members of these communities explained that under the proposed law a single vendor could essentially own such basic tools as the periodic table of the elements. Clearly this would be a great hindrance to "Science and useful Arts."

## Copy Protection

Another issue that can affect libraries is that of copy protection schemes. Publishers in the past have developed a variety of copy protection schemes for their works, some more successful than others. Copy protection on videotape does not interfere with normal viewing but alters the quality of copies made on normal home video equipment. This is a relatively successful scheme, although some video buffs claim to get good quality copies simply by adjusting their recording equipment. Copy protection for computer software was not so successful because it interfered with the legitimate need to make at least one backup copy of a program in case the original should become damaged. Most software manufacturers have given up the

use of copy protection schemes because their honest, paying customers found them so frustrating. There is no copy protection on sound
recordings, but the music industry put forth a great deal of effort in
an attempt to prevent the sale of certain home sound equipment that
would produce high-quality copies from music CDs. Their reasoning
was that as long as the home user can only create poor quality copies
from CDs onto sound tape, consumers will continue to purchase the
commercial sound recordings.

Current ideas for protective schemes for digital works go beyond
the mere encoding of files with password protection or scrambling of
signals. Computer files become fully vulnerable to copying once the
original user has opened them up with a password or key. Protection
needs to somehow relock the file after each viewing, at a minimum.
Some researchers are working on ways that a file can notify its
copyright owner each time it is opened or transmitted. If each such
notification can be tied to the digital credit card of the purchaser, then
it wouldn't be in that person's interest to give away copies to friends
since payment for these copies, and copies of the copies, would come
out of the purchaser's virtual pocket. Other schemes would mark
each copy with a unique signature and would detect if two files
contain the same signature; this would indicate that an illegal copy
had been made.

There are many potential problems with these proposed copy
protection schemes, not the least of which is the issue of privacy. It
is possible today to purchase a book or magazine without leaving any
record that would link you to the title you have bought. This means
that you can read certain highly controversial items like a self-help
book for cancer patients or a gay newspaper without having to worry
that this information will reach your health insurance company or
your employer. Libraries guard their patron files from public release
for this same reason, knowing that users are not free to explore ideas
if they fear that their choice of reading materials will be held up
to scrutiny in the future. Some copy protection schemes would link
the identity of the user to the protected work through the payment
system, and therefore eliminate the privacy of the reader. Some
schemes even imply that the copyright holder can know what files
you have on your own computer, which most people would feel is a
terrible invasion of privacy.

Copy protection schemes have other hidden problems. One of
these relates to the issue of archiving materials. Traditionally, libraries
are the archives of our culture's intellectual output. They often store

materials that the publishers themselves have lost interest in and have not preserved. Archiving of copy-protected materials would also mean archiving the key that opens the document. That in itself may not present a problem. But if that key is designed to interact with an outside system, such as a list of valid users, before allowing the file to be opened for access, the library's archived copy may essentially be unlockable in the future should that outside system have ceased to exist.

If publishers do develop and adopt copyright protection technologies, the question of fair use may be moot because if a document is copy-protected it may not be possible for the public to exercise fair use. Some defenders of the public interest in copyright see this denial of fair use to be a violation of the intended balance of rights between the public and the copyright holder. In their statement on the "NII Copyright Protection Act of 1995" (H.R. 2441), representatives of the library community shared their concern about this possible consequence of copy protection, saying: "The browsing, non-commercial sharing, and limited reproduction of works for educational and scholarly purposes now protected by statute will be available only to those able to pay for access to information." Copy protection could essentially give the copyright holder not only a monopoly on the making of copies but also on all use of the work. The right to control use has not been included in copyright holders' rights in the past, and this attempt to extend those rights has gained the nickname "the copyright grab," leading to a feature article of that name by law professor Pamela Samuelson.

## Browsing

Browsing is not a legal term, and there is no provision for browsing in our copyright laws. As an accident of the technology of text on paper, we are able to pick up and look at a printed work without copying it. One usually browses a work as part of the selection process, either in a bookstore, at a newsstand, or in a library. Browsing is actually an important part of the information retrieval activity, as we use clues from the work (table of contents, introduction, index) to determine if it meets our needs.

In the networked environment, to browse a text you must display it on the screen, and moving a text to the screen requires that the document be transmitted. What happens when this transmittal of a text comes under copyright protection? In essence, you may have to make a payment to the copyright holder in order to browse the text to determine if it meets your needs. Surely this will be a hindrance to research. As we know, some online searches retrieve hundreds of articles that must be viewed by the researcher to make a selection. And those doing in-depth research do many searches of this type. Is it fair to charge people for the items they browse but do not select?

The problem of browsing in the digital age may not be as difficult as it appears. Already some online services resolve the problem of browsing by providing document surrogates that help the reader make a selection without viewing the entire text. A surrogate is anything that substitutes for the document itself, and a common example of a surrogate is a citation and abstract for a journal article. Some authors advertise their books on the Internet by placing a single chapter online for free viewing, thus using the chapter as a surrogate for the book. In this way, the chapter has the same function as the movie trailer—it generates interest in the larger product without giving away the whole thing. Quality surrogates can both substitute for browsing and be an efficient tool in finding relevant items in a large information universe. Surrogates for networked materials could be provided free of charge, or with such greatly reduced fees that users are no longer constrained in their browsing activity.

## Contracts and Licenses

Digital information is rarely sold; instead it is leased to the user. If you look carefully at the envelopes in which your software diskettes arrive, you can see the contract that governs the license between you and the software company. You may have purchased a package with diskettes and documentation, but you are only licensing a copy of the software—you do not own it. The use of these resources is governed by your contract with the vendor, not by copyright law.

The same is true of online digital resources used by libraries. You do not purchase a copy of the Dialog database or the electronic version of the *Encyclopaedia Britannica,* you sign a contract for specified use of the content of those databases. That contract can be, and often is, more limiting than copyright law would be. It can designate that the information can be used only by certain classes of users, or can limit use to off-peak hours or to certain library computers. Copyright law can only restrict the making of copies and has no authority over the viewing of materials.

This is a fundamental change in the relationship of the library to the information that it makes available to the public. Libraries have independent control over the hardcopy works they own. No one can set rules for how, when, or to whom the library can lend the work. With online services, the data remains under the control of the publisher. This also means, at least in theory, that the publisher can deny a particular set of users access to its product. This has even happened, in at least one instance that I know of: in 1995, the Lexis/Nexis service was withdrawn from a college library because of a sign placed on the terminal which the online company felt was critical of the service. (Access was resumed a few weeks later after negotiations between the library and the company.) This has obvious implications for intellectual freedom in the digital age. You can criticize a book you find on the library shelf, and it will still be there, but digital resources can be withdrawn.

The issue of intellectual property, whether we are talking about books or Web pages, always must be measured by its impact on the public's access to information, and this brings us back to the all-important issue of the balance between the copyright owner and the reader.

## Libraries and the Copyright Question

The proposals to update the U.S. copyright law for the digital age are being formulated under the auspices of the Department of Commerce. This may seem odd, since we do have a Copyright Office, which is a department of the Library of Congress, but it is highly indicative of the interests that are being served. Library organizations, however, have been active in responding to the copyright proposals from the very beginning. In 1993 a group of seven library organizations issued a response to the first draft of the Working Group, *Fair Use in the Electronic Age: Serving the Public Interest* (available on the ARL Web site listed in the World Wide Web Resources of this chapter).

In the struggle for balance between copyright owners (which are often corporations) and the public, the voices heard most are those of the copyright owners. Few members of the public understand the role that intellectual property plays in their interaction with information resources and the entertainment that they enjoy. To the extent that the public interest is represented in discussion of copyright policy, librarians play a key role as advocates for public access to information. Preserving this public access in the digital age will be absolutely vital to assuring that libraries can serve future information needs.

## IN THEIR OWN WORDS

**Intellectual Property and the National Information Infrastructure: The Report of the Working Group on Intellectual Property Rights** (Executive Summary)

U.S. Information Infrastructure Task Force. Working Group on Intellectual Property Rights, September 1995, 232 pp.
http://www.uspto.gov/web/offices/com/doc/ipnii/ (available in a number of formats)

Also known as the White Paper, this report proposes changes to the copyright law aimed at protecting intellectual property in digital and networked environments. The proposal comes from a Department of Commerce working group and is unabashedly an effort to make cyberspace safe for commercial intellectual property.

**Taking on the Green Paper for Copyright: The Concerned Parties**

Information Infrastructure Task Force. Working Group on Intellectual Property Rights.
http://www.iitf.nist.gov/documents/committees_old/infopol/ intlprop-wg/nii-914.hrg, nii-916.hrg, nii-922.hrg, nii-923.hrg

Four hearings were held to receive public comments on the Green Paper for Copyright. These selected quotes, and my interspersed commentary, give you a taste of the discussion that took place.

## Executive Summary of Statement of the Nation's Libraries on H.R. 2441
American Library Association et al., February 8, 1996
gopher://ala1.ala.org:70/00/alagophwashoff/executive.summary

When the House Judiciary Committee's Subcommittee on Courts and Intellectual Property held hearings on the bill that was introduced to implement the changes to copyright proposed by the IITF Working Group, the American Library Association was among those invited to submit written testimony. ALA's testimony was submitted jointly with the American Association of Law Libraries, Association of Research Libraries, Medical Library Association, and the Special Libraries Association. Their statement summarizes the key concerns of librarians about the proposed changes to the copyright law that were embodied in the IITF's White Paper.

## The National Writers Union Critiques Government White Paper on Intellectual Property & the National Information Infrastructure
National Writers Union, October 1995

The National Writers Union (UAW Local-1981) represents freelance writers. While concerned about the earning power of authors in the digital environment, NWU is very supportive of the rights of the public to access information. More than any other group, NWU is aware that authors are among our heaviest information consumers as well as being information producers, and that the open availability of information is necessary to the quality of future intellectual output.

### Further Reading

*Statement of the Association of American Publishers (AAP) on Document Delivery.* AAP, April 1994. http://www.publishers.org/copyright/statement.html

The AAP and the publishers it represents are very concerned that document delivery and scanning of documents by libraries will eliminate the market for published works. Their view is that the current level of interlibrary loan through document delivery goes beyond the CONTU fair use guidelines. Also see the statement on scanning of works at http://www.publishers .org/copyright/scanning.html. These two papers essentially summarize the area of tension between publishers and libraries.

Bruwelheide, Janis H. *The Copyright Primer for Librarians and Educators.* 2d ed. Chicago: American Library Association, 151 pp.

A basic text on copyright law addressing real life situations and decisions for librarians and educators.

Dyson, Esther. "Intellectual Value." *Wired,* 3.07, July 1995. http:// www.hotwired.com/wired/3.07/features/dyson.html

Seminal thinker on the digital world, Dyson proposes that content should be free; the real cash value is in products and services, not intellectual property. In the spirit of Third Wave proponents like Alvin Toffler and Nicholas Negroponte, Dyson's view moves far beyond the minor modifications to the copyright law that are proposed by the Department of Commerce and suggests an entirely new paradigm for the future.

Samuelson, Pamela. "The Copyright Grab." *Wired,* 4.01, January 1996. http://www.hotwired.com/wired/4.01/features/white.paper.html

Samuelson is an outspoken professor of law, now at the University of California's Boalt Law School, who believes that the proposed changes to the copyright law amount to a grab of power by copyright holders, leaving the public with less legal right to access information. This paper, published in the highly fashionable magazine of the digital age, helped galvanize opinion in the online community.

National Writers Union. *Authors in the New Information Age: A Working Paper on Electronic Publishing Issues.* Oakland, Calif.: NWU, 1995. http://www.igc.apc.org/nwu/docs/aniabeg.htm

Another excellent document by the NWU covering electronic publishing, consumer issues, and end-user issues. Includes a chapter on "Libraries and Authors" that emphasizes the role of libraries in support of authors and their work. An interesting contrast to the statements of the publishers' organizations.

## World Wide Web Resources

Association of Research Libraries (ARL). Copyright and Intellectual Property. http://arl.cni.org/info/frn/copy/copytoc.html

> A good basic site on copyright and libraries.

Digital Future Coalition. http://www.dfc.org/dfc

> The Digital Future Coalition formed in 1996 expressly to co-ordinate protest against changes to the copyright law for the digital environment. This group wants to be sure that public rights to read and use information as well as fair use rights are maintained in the online world.

Library of Congress. Copyright Office. gopher://marvel.loc.gov:70/11/copyright

> The Copyright Office seems almost an uninvolved observer in the current battle over copyright, but this site is still the official online source for current copyright information including how to apply for copyright for your works.

Copyright and Intellectual Property Resources. http://www.nlc-bnc.ca/ifla/ll/cpyright.htm

> This bibliography of online articles and resources is maintained by the International Federation of Library Associations at their World Wide Web site in Canada. It covers U.S. and Canadian copyright issues as well as information on other countries such as Japan and Australia.

# INTELLECTUAL PROPERTY AND THE NATIONAL INFORMATION INFRASTRUCTURE: THE REPORT OF THE WORKING GROUP ON INTELLECTUAL PROPERTY RIGHTS

## U.S. Department of Commerce

### *Executive Summary*

Secretary of Commerce Ronald H. Brown, Chairman of the White House Information Infrastructure Task Force (IITF), has released a report on Intellectual Property and the National Information Infrastructure. The Report, written by the IITF Working Group on Intellectual Property Rights chaired by Assistant Secretary of Commerce and Commissioner of Patents and Trademarks Bruce A. Lehman, explains how intellectual property law applies in Cyberspace and makes legislative recommendations to Congress to fine-tune the law for the digital age.

## BACKGROUND

The convergence of computer and communications technologies has made possible the development and rapid growth of the National Information Infrastructure (NII). The NII will generate both unprecedented challenges and important opportunities for the copyright marketplace, and has tremendous potential to improve and enhance our lives. The NII affords the promise of:

- a greater amount and variety of information and entertainment resources, delivered quickly and economically from and to virtually anywhere in the world in the blink of an eye;

- access to rich cultural resources around the world, transforming and expanding the scope and reach of the arts and humanities and broadening our cultural experiences through diversity of content;

- support for our education and library systems;

- enhanced competitiveness for U.S. business and the promotion of job creation, economic growth, and well-being for Americans;

- new job opportunities in the creation, processing, organizing, packaging and dissemination of information, education and entertainment products;
- technology, trade and business opportunities for new products and new markets for U.S. industries; and
- a wider variety and greater number of choices for consumers of books, movies, music, computer programs and other copyrighted works; increased competition and reduced prices.

The availability of these benefits is by no means assured, however. Creators, publishers and distributors of works will be wary of the electronic marketplace unless the law provides them the tools to protect their property against unauthorized use. Advances in digital technology and the rapid development of electronic networks and other communications technologies dramatically increase the ease and speed with which a work can be reproduced, the quality of the copies, the ability to manipulate or change the work, and the speed with which copies can be delivered to the public. The establishment of high speed, high-capacity information systems makes it possible for one individual, with a few key strokes, to deliver perfect copies of digitized works to scores of others—or to upload a copy to a bulletin board or other service where thousands can download it or print unlimited "hard" copies. Just one unauthorized uploading could have devastating effects on the market for the work.

Thus, the full potential of the NII will not be realized if the legal protections that extend to education, information and entertainment products and their use in the physical environment are not available when those works are disseminated via the NII. Creators and other owners of intellectual property rights will not be willing to put their investments and their property at risk unless appropriate systems are in place—both in the U.S. and internationally—to permit them to set and enforce the terms and conditions under which their works are made available in the NII environment. Likewise, the public will not use the services available on the NII and generate the market necessary for its success unless a wide variety of works are available under equitable and reasonable terms and conditions, and the integrity of those works is assured. All the computers, telephones, scanners, printers, switches, routers, wires, cables, networks and satellites in the world will not create a successful NII, if there is no content. What will drive the NII is the content moving through it.

Of course, the NII could continue to serve as a communications tool and resource for Government, public domain and other material for which copyright protection is either not granted or not sought, but that would deny the public the NII's and GII's full potential to inform, entertain, enrich and empower. Unless the framework for legitimate commerce is preserved and adequate protection for copyrighted works is ensured, the vast communications network will not reach its full potential as a truly global marketplace.

Copyright protection is not an obstacle in the way of the success of the NII; it is an essential component. Copyright motivates the creative activity of authors and thereby provides the public with the products of those creators. By granting authors exclusive rights, the public receives the benefit of literature and music and other creative works that might not otherwise be created or disseminated. Effective copyright protection promotes a new Cybermarketplace of ideas, expression and products.

## DEVELOPMENT OF THE REPORT

The Working Group on Intellectual Property Rights was established within the IITF to examine the intellectual property implications of the NII and make recommendations on any appropriate changes to U.S. intellectual property law and policy. The IITF was established by President Clinton to articulate and implement the Administration's vision for the NII and to develop comprehensive telecommunications and information policies and programs that will promote the development of the NII and best meet the country's needs.

The Report is based on the Working Group's Preliminary Draft (Green Paper), issued in July 1994, and on extensive public comment and testimony. In September 1994, the Working Group convened four days of hearings in three cities. In addition, more than 1,500 pages of written comments were filed, in paper form and through the Internet, by more than 150 individuals and organizations—representing more than 425,000 members of the public. The open process instituted by the Working Group resulted in a well-developed, voluminous record reflecting the views of a broad spectrum of interested parties, including various electronic industries, telecommunications and information service providers, the academic, research, library and legal communities, and individual creators, copyright owners and users, as well as the computer software, motion picture, music, broadcasting, publishing and other information and entertainment industries.

The Working Group examined the adequacy of the intellectual property laws to cope with the pace of technological change. It found that the patent, trademark and trade secret laws need no adaptation at this time. It also found that the Copyright Act is fundamentally adequate and effective. In a few areas, however, it has recommended limited amendments of the Copyright Act to take proper account of current technology. Technology has altered the copyright balance—in some instances, in favor of copyright owners and in others, in favor of users. The goal of the recommendations is to clarify existing law and adapt it where the balance has shifted.

## SUMMARY OF RECOMMENDATIONS

### Clarification of Existing Rights

The Report recommends that Section 106(3) of the Copyright Act be clarified to expressly recognize that copies or phonorecords of works can be distributed to the public by transmission, and that such transmissions fall within the exclusive distribution right of the copyright owner. The Report also recommends related amendments to the definitions of "transmit" and "publication," as well as distribution-related provisions regarding importation of copies or phonorecords.

### Application of Fair Use Privileges

The Working Group recommends that the library exemptions be amended to allow the preparation of three copies of works in digital format; to recognize that the use of a copyright notice on a published copy of a work is no longer mandatory; and to authorize the making of a limited number of digital copies by libraries and archives for purposes of preservation.

The Working Group recommends that the Copyright Act be amended to provide an exemption for non-profit organizations to reproduce and distribute to the visually impaired—at cost—Braille, large type, audio or other editions of previously published literary works, provided that the owner of the exclusive right to distribute the work in the United States has not entered the market for such editions during the first year following first publication.

### Technological Protection Systems and Information

The Working Group recommends that the Copyright Act be amended to include a new Chapter 12, which would prohibit the importation, manufacture or distribution of any device or product, or the provision of any service, the primary purpose or effect of which is to deactivate, without authority of the copyright owner or the law, any technological protections which prevent or inhibit the violation of exclusive rights under the copyright law.

The Working Group recommends that the Copyright Act be amended to prohibit the dissemination of copyright management information known to be false and the unauthorized removal or alteration of copyright management information. Copyright management information is defined as the name and other identifying information of the author of a work, the name and other identifying information of the copyright owner, terms and conditions for uses of the work, and such other information as the Register of Copyrights may prescribe by regulation.

### Support of Pending Legislation

The Report also generally supports legislation that would amend the copyright law and the criminal law (which sets out sanctions for criminal copyright violations) to make it a criminal offense to willfully infringe a copyright by reproducing or distributing copies with a retail value of $5,000 or more (S. 1122). By setting a monetary threshold and requiring willfulness, S. 1122 ensures that merely casual or careless conduct resulting in distribution of only a few copies will not be subject to criminal prosecution and that criminal charges will not be brought unless there is a significant level of harm to the copyright owner's rights.

The Working Group also supports a public performance right for sound recordings. Two bills now pending, S. 227 and H.R. 1506, would grant such a right, although more limited than the Report recommends.

## OTHER RECOMMENDATIONS AND FINDINGS

The Report also includes recommendations that the Patent and Trademark Office (PTO) obtain public input related to measures that can be adopted to ensure the authenticity of electronically disseminated publications, particularly with respect to verifying the contents and date of first public dissemination of the publication, and evaluating the substantive value of the information contained in the publication as to its role in patentability determinations; and that the

PTO explore the feasibility of establishing requirements or standards that would govern authentication of the date and contents of electronically disseminated information for purposes of establishing their use as prior art. In addition, it recommends that the PTO, in the context of World Intellectual Property Organization meetings on the trademark International Classification system, propose changes to ensure that the system accommodates the goods and services of modern information technology; and that the PTO regularly update its trademark Manual for the Identification of Goods and Services to reflect new goods and services used on or in connection with the NII and GII.

In addition, the Working Group supports further study in the following areas:

The Working Group encourages copyright owners to explore with libraries and schools special institutional licenses, and endorses increased funding for libraries and educational institutions to assist in their ability to purchase and license works in digital format.

The Working Group supports the efforts presently under way to revise Article 2 of the U.C.C. to encompass licensing of intellectual property. Where parties wish to contract electronically, they should be able to form a valid, enforceable contract on-line.

Recognizing the important role of encryption technology in fostering a secure and useful NII, the Working Group supports efforts to work with industry on key-escrow encryption technologies and other encryption products which could be exported without compromising U.S. intelligence gathering and law enforcement. Proliferation of such technology will enable U.S. industry to meet the needs of the international marketplace for these products and continue to lead the development of the GII.

The Working Group believes it is—at best—premature to reduce the liability of any type of service provider in the NII environment. Exempting or reducing the liability of service providers prematurely would choke development of marketplace tools that could be used to lessen their risk of liability and the risk to copyright owners, including insuring against harm caused by their customers, shifting responsibility through indemnification and warranty agreements, licensing, education, and the use of technological protections. At this time in the development and change in the players and roles, it is not feasible to identify a priori those circumstances or situations under which service providers should have reduced liability. However, it is reasonable to assume that such situations could and should be identified through discussion and negotiation among the service providers, the content owners and the Government. The Working Group strongly encourages such actions in the interest of providing certainty and clarity in this emerging area of commerce.

The Working Group continues its work with the Conference on Fair Use and the Copyright Awareness Campaign. The Conference on Fair Use brings together copyright owner and user interests to discuss fair use issues and, if possible, to develop guidelines for uses of copyrighted works by librarians and educators. Some 60 interest groups are participants in the Conference and have been meeting regularly since September 1994. The Copyright Awareness Campaign, co-sponsored with the Departments of Education and Commerce, coordinates educational efforts of approximately 40 individuals and organizations to increase public awareness of the importance of intellectual property in the information age.

A copy of the Report may be obtained by calling the PTO Office of Public Affairs at 703-305-8341 or by sending a written request to:

> "Intellectual Property and the NII"
> c/o Terri A. Southwick, Attorney-Advisor
> Office of Legislative and International Affairs
> U.S. Patent and Trademark Office, Box 4
> Washington, DC 20231

*   *   *

# TAKING ON THE GREEN PAPER ON COPYRIGHT: THE CONCERNED PARTIES

## Karen Coyle

The concerned parties in the copyright debate are the creators (authors, songwriters, photographers), the commercial copyright holders (publishing and media companies), and the public. As pointed out by Professor Jessica Litman, whose words you will read later in this chapter, it is only the latter that has no official representatives and, unlike the commercial copyright holders, no bevy of attorneys to speak on its behalf. In the case of the hearings on copyright that took place in 1994, librarians stepped forward to promote the interest of the public.

## HEARINGS ON THE GREEN PAPER ON COPYRIGHT

At hearings in 1994, members of the public were invited to respond to the Green Paper on Intellectual Property and the National Information Infrastructure before a panel of members of the Working Group on Intellectual Property Rights. The meetings were held in Chicago (September 14), Los Angeles (September 16), and Washington, D.C. (September 22–23). The words of these people tell us more about the real meaning of copyright than the law itself or even the papers of the committee.

Speakers at the hearings represented a range of interests. Many were lawyers for industries or organizations that produce commercial intellectual property. As a matter of fact, the list of presenters at the public hearings reads like a Who's Who of commercial intellectual property interests, including online services (CompuServe, AOL), database services (Dialog), mass media (Motion Picture Association of America, American Association of Advertising Agencies, FOX), music industry (MCA, ASCAP, A&M Records), newspaper publishers (Times-Mirror, Chicago Tribune), and other big names (West Publishing, Microsoft, IBM). The major online services of CompuServe and America Online spoke to the issue of carrier liability. A surprising number of musicians, composers and songwriters appeared on behalf of themselves and their fellow artists. At each hearing, one or more members of the library profession representing the American Library Association, the Association of Research Libraries, The American Association of Law Libraries, and others, made an eloquent plea for public access.

There were also groups that were most notable by their absence. Schools were not represented. No producers of fine arts gave testimony. And no one appeared as a member of the general public. It's not surprising that these segments of our society were not present. The hearings were announced in the Federal Register and information about them was available at the Internet site of the Information

Infrastructure Task Force. These are not sources that reach the general public, and it can be assumed that even if they did, not many people would understand the impact of the changes being discussed on their lives. So the hearings were naturally populated by those with a professional interest in the topic.

There are three main groups of interested parties: the artists and creators of intellectual property; the companies whose products are intellectual property; and the public. The latter is spoken for by members of the library profession, other non-profit service organizations, and the occasional advocate for public access.

The quotes below are from transcripts of the hearings, which were made available on the IITF gopher site. The wording may be less eloquent than written pieces would have been, but the message is no less clear. The people quoted here were responding to the first draft paper from the Working Group on Intellectual Property. Very little changed between the Green Paper (1994) and the final White Paper (1995), which then became the guide for legislation introduced into the 104th Congress.

## CONCERNS OF CREATORS

Creators of intellectual property are authors, artists, musicians, playwrights, directors, and others. Their interest in the copyright law is as varied as the ideas they produce and they media they use.

Creators earn a percentage off of the sale of works, or, in the case of performed works, off of the performance rights. This is actually a small portion of the cover price paid by the public. In book publishing about half of the revenue goes to distributors and retailers and the publisher and author each earn only about ten percent.

This doesn't mean that creators of works are unconcerned— especially since the new online technologies hold the promise that self-publishing may be a more viable option in the future. Without the costs of printing and distribution, more authors may be able to market their own works, thus reaping more of the economic benefits. But even in today's intellectual property environment, artists rely on the sales of their works for their share of the money pie.

### Authors

Scott Turow, speaking for the Author's Guild, recognizes both the value of the NII to writers and the potential dangers:

*Scott Turow/Author's Guild*

The NII has every potential of being of enormous benefit to writers and authors, especially those of our membership who write non-fiction . . . [and] are highly dependent on research, and the breadth of the NII offers an opportunity to our members to do research that's both more comprehensive and quicker. . . .

The photocopying machine, notwithstanding the fact that whole books are seldom copied, still I think represents a device that's often used to circumvent author's rights and we would hope to see the NII structured in a way that doesn't allow those kinds of wholesale incursions into the rights of authors. . . .

Any step that would cut into the earnings that are really minimal for many authors would obviously imperil the cultural diversity that the NII itself both champions and benefits from.

Given that the intellectual property market is dominated by large companies that control the sale of those works, some artists fear that the benefits from the new technology will not be passed on to the creators. There is unfortunately a fairly clear history of corporate takeover of the creators' rights, and most analyses of the copyright proposals in the Green and White papers that come from outside the intellectual property industry point to a possible greater concentration of corporate power resulting from the changes proposed. As one speaker said:

*Thomas White/consultant, artists' rights*

Every new opportunity created by technology underscores for creators, such as screen writers, actors, directors, musicians, singers, record producers, song writers, film score composers, lyricists, dancers, choreographers, photographers and others, the reality that they will have little or no control with respect to how their artistic works or the excerpts or elements thereof will be used or exploited. And that they will obtain little or no money from the sale of their works in those new markets.

The online technology adds new threats to copyright. The Green Paper was responding primarily to the threat perceived in the ability of computers to make perfect, inexpensive copies of works. Adding networking to this formula increases that threat many-fold.

Some artists see the online systems as a threat. The larger commercial online services, like CompuServe and America Online, are aware of copyright law and are on the lookout for anyone using their service for any illegal ends, including the violation of copyright. But they argue that they can no more guarantee that their system will not be used to violate copyright than a library could claim that their copy machine was never used to make copies that fall outside of fair use.

*William Daniels/journalist, entertainment industry*

I accept CompuServe's argument that it cannot act as a gate-keeper of its own system. And I believe that if CompuServe and systems like that aren't held to account for the content in some fashion that they are distributing for a profit, we risk creating essentially electronic, not really free ports, but more like no copyright zones.

## Performing Artists

Artists in the performing media earn their primary revenues from performance rights, not from sales. The artist earns royalties each time the work is performed in a public setting. For textual works, a digital transmittal would be like the sale of a book. The same digital transmittal of a sound recording could theoretically either be a sale or a performance. For musicians and songwriters, this is a difference that will determine if they can earn a living from their work:

*Pat Rogers/Executive Director of the Nashville*
*Songwriters Association*

. . . the average songwriter depends upon performance royalties to feed and clothe his or her family. . . .

Royalties for the right of reproduction . . . cannot substitute for performance royalties. Songwriters have come to depend upon the concept of continued payment for continued use.

*Julie Gold/Songwriter*

I depend entirely upon my songs for my income. The vast majority of that income comes from my performance royalties. In order to keep writing I rely upon the fact that I'll receive royalties on a consistent and regular basis every time my songs are performed anywhere in the world.

## Moral Rights

European copyright law has a concept called "moral rights." Moral rights, not recognized in this country, protect the integrity of the artistic product even when copyrights have been sold. For example, under moral rights it probably would not be possible for the current copyright owner to colorize a film originally shot in black and white. Many artists in the U.S. have wanted this country to adopt moral rights in its copyright code, and there is even some international pressure for the U.S. to come into the European fold on this issue. Because networked information is global in nature, legal differences such as these could affect artists whose work is transported abroad.

Add to this the fact that in the digital world modification of a work is much easier than it was in the past and you will understand why some artists expressed their concern that moral rights were not added in this revision of the copyright law.

> *Glenn Gumpel/Director's Guild of America*
>
> . . . we are greatly troubled by the tone and tentative conclusions of the report in regard to the issue of moral rights. In our view the draft report shows a disregard for artist's rights, while focusing entirely on ways to facilitate economic rights.

> *Janel Hurrell/Author's Licensing and Collecting Society*
>
> It is disappointing that more emphasis is not given to moral rights in the paper. In the digital environment, the right of integrity is under severe threat. It is not only a threat to the integrity of the creator of an artistic work, but equally to the integrity and authenticity of scientific writers.

## COMMERCIAL CONCERNS

It is clear from this testimony, and from some of the conclusions drawn by the authors of the White Paper, that the promise of the Information Highway is economic. The report's introduction states: "Creators and other owners of intellectual property rights will not be willing to put their interests at risk if appropriate systems—both in the U.S. and internationally—are not in place to permit them to set and enforce the terms and conditions under which their works are made available in the NII environment." Our commercial providers of intellectual property, like publishers and media companies, have so far embraced cyberspace with great caution precisely because there is no incentive for them to give away their products in an environment that doesn't support commercial ventures.

### The Intellectual Property Producers

By far the greatest number of speakers came from the commercial producers and sellers of intellectual property, such as the publishing companies and media companies that market the works we buy. Most creators sign over their rights to publishers and distributors who have the means to manufacture and market their works. As George Vradenburg of Fox, Inc. put it:

> . . . our laws encourage the private transferability of the rights of copyright. . . . The ability of individual rights holders, be they directors, writers, performers, musicians or literary authors, to convey by contract their economic and other rights to a single rights holder creates, I think, a system of tremendous value and flexibility. The value to the individual artist, who can sell all the fruits of his creative labors, or her creative labors, to others better able to exploit the values in his or her creation.

In general, the members of this group had a very positive reaction to the increased protection that these changes in the copyright law would provide to works transmitted online. They made a strong case for the economic benefits of the changes:

*George Vradenburg/Fox, Inc.*

. . . the United States copyright industries are one of the healthiest and fastest growing sectors of the American economy. In 1991 the core copyright industries accounted for over $20 billion in revenues, 3.6 percent of the gross domestic product. In recent years those industries have grown at close to three times the rate of the economy as a whole. Total copyright industry employment in 1991 stood at close to five percent of all U.S. employment. And those industries delivered $40 billion in foreign sales, a performance exceeded only by the aerospace and agricultural industries.

*Mary O'Hare/Executive Committee of the Intellectual Property Section of the State Bar of California*

. . . the work of the Working Group cannot be seen by others in government as a nuisance, a side issue, or an afterthought in the debate concerning the building of telecommunication systems and information infrastructures. If our government institutions still remember, and can resurrect that sign saying, it's the economy, it may be appropriate to put right under it one reading, and intellectual property is the key.

*Priscilla Walter/law firm of Gardner, Carton & Douglas, Chicago*

. . . I also very strongly agree with the report's statement that the potential of the NII will not be realized if the information and entertainment products protectable by intellectual property laws are not protected effectively when disseminated on the NII. . . . I can certainly assure you that my clients will not continue to invest the millions they are now investing in building networks and developing entertainment and information products to be disseminated over them if they believe that they will not be able to protect that distribution or earn a fair return on their investment.

## Content, Content, Content

Jack Valenti explained to the panel that what would really make or break the NII was not the hardware, but the content, and that the creation of content will require large investments that must be protected:

*Jack Valenti/Motion Picture Association of America*

. . . people don't buy wires and digital and head ends and all of the technology in its arcane form. What they buy and subscribe to and want to have come into their home is programming that they want to see, when they want to see it. Now there is no question that programming arises from creativity, and creativity's life is nourished by copyright. . . . And I think that it is a given that huge private investments are going to be required to give shape and form to this highway or this infrastructure. . . . But no one is going to invest any private money in something [if] they think they are not going to get some kind of a worthy return. And that means that copyrighted programs ought to be and must be protected in the fullest sense of the word, which this Green Paper underscores very staunchly, I must say.

## Information Wants to Be . . . What?!

Some of the speakers found themselves at odds with the Internet culture of free and open exchange. To be sure, the commercial world of information is very different from that of the university environment that originally built the Internet, and where the rallying cry is "information wants to be free."

*Robert Thompson/Professor of Ethics at the Owen Graduate School of Business, Vanderbilt University*

. . . the word information connotes a certain free as air, free as water connotation to the average person. In that regard I might humbly suggest that some consideration be given to reformulating this process and perhaps even calling the highway the intellectual property network, or IPNET. . . . The reason I say that is to educate the general public to the fact that what they will be accessing through this technology is in fact property, private property in some cases.

*James Schatz/West Publishing*

West commends the Working Group's timely recognition that a strong and continuing education program at every educational level is necessary to reverse the present and growing attitude of many citizens that works should be free for the taking in the electronic environment.

*Edward Massie/President and CEO of Commerce Clearing House*

We're concerned about the use of metaphors for the NII such as information highway, digital library or universal service, that imply that all of the information available might be free.

*Robert Simons/Dialog Information Services*

The bad news is, of course, being college students to a large extent, they believe that if it comes from cyberspace it therefore must be free and unencumbered. I myself am not that far out of college, a few decades, but I had very similar views when I was young as well, until I was married and had a family and a mortgage.

## *What about the "Free" Library?*

Some speakers see libraries as a threat to their copyrights:

*John F. Dill/Chairman and CEO and President of Mosby Year Book Incorporated*

The dissemination of knowledge is the essence of publishing. There is no other reason to publish or to make public an author's work than to accumulate and refine the world's knowledge base. No publisher wants to restrict that flow of information. We have a responsibility, however, to our authors to insure that the fruits of their labor are protected. . . .

Recent years, however, have seen an increasing number of document delivery devices improperly labeled inter-library loans. The unauthorized transmittal of copyright materials between libraries threatens the very foundation of journal publishing in particular. The NII will provide a convenient relatively inexpensive means for libraries to continue and even expand this practice. We believe that the final report must address this issue and provide appropriate protection for the publishing community and the authors it serves.

## The Government As Publisher

Others are concerned about competing with government publishing:

*Robert Simons/Dialog Information Services*

Under the guise of being enticed by the potential for revenues, we're quite concerned about the potential within the government to get into the retail information business, which we do not believe is a fundamental government role in this country.

## Online Services and Liability

The online services, such as America Online and CompuServe, are concerned about their potential liability for the infringing activities of their customers:

*Ellen Kirsh/America Online, Inc.*

The strict liability standard has been imposed on print publishers of copyrighted materials, whether or not the publisher intended to infringe or had knowledge of the infringement. However, print publishers have the opportunity to review what they publish in advance of publication. This is not the case for on-line service providers. Our medium is interactive and participatory in real time. We have no means of knowing what will be made available on our services until it is posted there. . . . We are simply not publishers. We are something new and different from anything that we have known before. . . .

The only way for an operator to minimize risk would be to eliminate all member contributions to its on-line service and to own all of its own content.

*Allan Arlow/Computer and Communications Industry Association*

. . . the authors [of the Green Paper] seemed to suggest that mere transportation of works across the NII should trigger either direct infringement liability or the requisite knowledge for contributory infringement liability. We are very concerned about the implications of such a position, if that is indeed the case, because some NII service providers may be mere passive conduits, simply acting as a pipeline through which works travel under the command of subscribers or users.

## Browsing

The ability of information seekers to browse was threatening to some:

*Edward Massie/President and CEO of Commerce Clearing House*

. . . we note the report applies the notion of fair use to electronic browsing rather more broadly than we would like.

*William Barlow/Times-Mirror Company*

But I think that we want to make clear though that when you have public access that does not mean free access. . . . And I think that one of the concerns we have is we have newspapers. And nobody prints out a newspaper, they don't reproduce it. If we send it over on-line and make it available, people are going to browse that issue. And I don't think that, given the nature of our products, magazines, newspapers, that browsing should be something that would be a fair use . . . we want to make it clear that fair use is an area where private usage does not equate to public use and public access.

## Will Licenses Replace Copyright?

There was some recognition among the attendees that copyright is only part of the story. A great deal of intellectual property use is governed by contracts and licenses rather than copyright.

*Priscilla Walter/law firm of Gardner, Carton & Douglas, Chicago*

Although copyright offers very significant protection for content providers, many of our clients rely very heavily on contract, certainly to establish the terms of their licenses. Contract rights are especially important for those of our clients whose products contain primarily facts or otherwise non-copyrightable materials. After the *Feist v. Rural Publications* case, such clients rely almost totally on contractual protection.

*Lorin Brennan/American Film Marketing Association*

. . . there are two general models of licensing, what we would call per user licensing and per use licensing. Per user is a hard copy business. You hand someone the software program or a record. You don't care how many times they play it or that they use it because you're looking at the user to license the works. The motion picture business is based on per use licensing. Every public performance has a different use. You go in to see a movie a second time you pay a second ticket.

## Copy Protection

Many speakers expressed strong support for the development of copy protection technologies:

*Priscilla Walter/law firm of Gardner, Carton & Douglas, Chicago*

The technical developments addressed by the report, including access control, digital signatures and copyright management systems, will all be important to make electronic contracts practical. The role of the federal government should, in my view, be to encourage and to create an environment for the development of such technologies.

Speakers not only applauded the committee's proposal to make defeating of such technologies subject to criminal penalties, some wished to see those penalties expanded:

*James Schatz/West Publishing*

West believes that the Working Group should carefully consider making such actions criminal infringement under Section 506(a) of the Copyright Act. . . .

*Charlotte Gibberman/Tribune Company*

We could like to see the prohibition of the importation of copyrighted works by electronic transmission without authorization and to insure that these laws are enforced effectively. . . . Our concern is the hacker, the weekend user that may not rise to the level of fraud but certainly interferes with our work, and we would like to also see some sort of law, some sort of remedy that we can use against those people.

### Fear and Loathing

Not everyone is at ease with the coming digital age. This speaker expressed his fears about the future of the intellectual property industry:

> *Edward Massie/President and CEO of Commerce Clearing House*
>
> First, we're concerned about the technical ease of fast, clandestine conversion of printed works to digital format without authorization of the copyright owner. Second, we view the electronic network environment as one that makes it easier than ever for information shoplifters to operate and more difficult than ever to identify who they are. Third, we believe [in an] information on demand world, but we see no means to electronically create binding contractual terms and conditions by which intellectual property rights are currently protected. Fourth, we are unsure how the NII will permit copyright information to travel with copyrighted data and how its legal underpinnings will deter tampering with such information.

Others have already embraced the online world, and are proud of their role in its development:

> *Robert Simons/Dialog Information Services*
>
> . . . we believe that we actually were helpful in blazing the trail and cutting down the trees over which the highway will be paved in the near future.

## CONCERN FOR PUBLIC ACCESS

Public access advocates feel the proposed changes to the copyright law threaten our information democracy. No one denies that the changes would provide greater protection for digital works than they now have under the law. Where access advocates and commercial marketers differ is in the former's belief that the public has a right to equal access to information, regardless of one's ability to pay.

> *Robert Oakley/American Association of Law Libraries*
>
> Libraries are essential to the American democratic society where education and learning are available to all, not just to an aristo-

cratic elite. This idea that anyone in America can get the information they need simply by going into a library is threatened by the kind of technological controls over information now being developed and discussed at length in the draft report. If implemented, these controls will potentially give copyright owners a complete monopoly, allowing them to dictate who will have access to information and on what terms. Gone will be any notion of fair use. Gone will be libraries serving the community. Gone will be a society without an information elite. In its place we will have a society where users who can afford to pay will pay by the screenful.

## The Public/Private Balance

Probably the most common theme of those who spoke for the public interest in copyright law was the need to preserve a balance between the rights of copyright owners and the right of the public to have access to information. For many, especially the representatives of the library profession, the proposed changes to the copyright law put that balance in jeopardy:

*John Berry/University Library, Univ. of Illinois at Chicago*

The real genius of the United States copyright law, we feel, is that it balances the intellectual property rights of authors, publishers and copyright owners with society's need for the free exchange of ideas. . . . The preservation and continuation of these balanced rights in an electronic environment are essential to the free flow of information and to the development of an information infrastructure that serves the public good and the public interest.

*Gloria Werner/Association of Research Libraries*

First of all, the need to retain a balance, and I want to underline the word balance, of interests between the rights of copyright owners and users. . . . We believe that the Working Group's interpretation of transmission, and the related recommendation, is troublesome. The recommendation that all transmissions fall within the exclusive distribution right of the copyright owner would greatly expand copyright owner rights as they now exist and would limit current and acceptable practices that we now experience throughout the libraries of the country.

*Jessica Litman/Professor of Law, Wayne State University*

Copyright rights are limited because the system is designed to benefit all of us in a variety of creativity enhancing ways. My basic objection to the draft report is that, as I read it, it does not seek to preserve that balance.

## First Sale Doctrine

One aspect of this loss of balance is in the assumption in the report that electronic transmission cannot support the first sale doctrine:

*Gary Shapiro/Electronics Industries Association*
*& Home Recording Rights Coalition*

Electronic purchasing and distribution of copyrighted materials may supplement or ultimately replace traditional sales channels such as record and video stores. The methods of delivering books or movies to the consumer should not determine whether they are covered by the first sale doctrine.

*Alfred Willis/Art Library Society of North America*

. . . we agree that the recommendations made in this report with respect to copyright of works distributed by transmission must be reconsidered because they are skewed in favor of copyright holders without simultaneously granting limitations to balance reliably the purely financial interests of those holders with the interest of the public at large. . . . Publishers should be able to make a reasonable return on the first sale of material published by transmission without depriving readers and many authors of the benefits deriving from subsequent distributions essentially from the first sale doctrine as it operated in the print environment.

## Do Users Have Rights?

Professor Jessica Litman interprets the copyright law as giving some specific rights to users as well as the rights clearly assigned to owners of copyrights:

*Jessica Litman/Professor of Law, Wayne State University*

. . . copyright law has never given copyright owners control over all of the uses of their works. Instead, the law has given copyright owners exclusive rights over uses that lend themselves to public commercial exploitation. . . . Today, they have the exclusive rights to reproduce, adapt, distribute, perform publicly, and display publicly. Rights over essentially consumptive uses, like the right to read or see or listen to or discuss or think about or lend or resell or display privately or perform privately are rights that have been reserved to the public.

## Fair Use

Among these rights generally afforded to users is that of "fair use." Many of the public advocates who appeared at the hearings were concerned that fair use would be restricted in the digital information world:

> *Gloria Werner/Association of Research Libraries*
>
> It is . . . critical that they [researchers, students, members of the public] have opportunities on-line equivalent to their current opportunities off-line, to browse through copyrighted works. It is equally critical that they have on-line opportunities equivalent to their other opportunities off-line, to exercise such fair use rights in making individual copies of quotations, brief extracts from copyrighted works, or journal articles for research or scholarship purposes.

> *Lucretia McClure/Medical Library Association*
>
> The copyright law allows fair use of the intellectual content of materials, and that must not change because the container is electronic rather than print. It is essential that researchers, students, health professionals, and the general public be able to use the on-line equivalent of their current opportunities to browse through copyrighted works and to exercise their fair use rights in making individual copies of quotations, brief extracts, or journal articles for fair use or scholarly purposes.

Educational institutions are probably more affected by any change in the interpretation of fair use than any other organization:

> *Sandra Walker/International Visual Resources Association*
>
> I think the Working Group has not fully considered the implication of networking as it relates to class use by non-profit educational institutions. . . . As an example of how materials might be used in a networked environment for distance learning, an art history professor physically located in a university

might wish to relate images of art works and related text to students physically located at other sites. Will this use of the information infrastructure be construed as fair use or copyright infringement?

## Licenses and Contracts

Use of digital information resources is often governed by licenses and contracts. These contracts can be more restrictive than copyright law and can therefore limit public access to works:

> *John Berry/University Library, Univ. of Illinois at Chicago*
>
> . . . licensing agreements should not be allowed to abrogate the fair use and library provisions authorized in the copyright statute.

> *Robert Oakley/American Association of Law Libraries*
>
> Licenses have come into increasing use for library acquisition of all types of electronic information. However, too often such licenses fail to take into account uses permitted under the Copyright Act. Licenses should not be used to contract around otherwise legitimate uses of proprietary material.

## Communities with Special Needs

In one of the successes of public advocacy, pleas like this one by John Kelly resulted in the insertion of special exceptions into the White Paper for the reproduction of materials for the visually handicapped:

> *John Kelly/Recording for the Blind*
>
> Clearly, we need an NII environment in which the manufacturers and owners of intellectual property are comfortable with the protection of their material. The greater the assurances of protection, the freer the flow of information and the greater the benefit of all end users. However, as systems are developed to protect the copyright holder's material, we cannot afford to add further layers of inaccessibility to people with print disabilities to that information.

## The Bottom Line

Professor Litman questions the basic premise that amendments to the copyright law are needed to increase the amount of digital information available to the public:

*Jessica Litman/Professor of Law, Wayne State University*

And to the extent that it [the Working Paper] does offer reasons for enhancing rights in the copyright bundle, it relies on arguments, again, that we have heard repeated today that stronger copyright protection is required in order to entice authors and copyright owners to make their work available over the NII. And I doubt that. The report's working model for the NII is the current Internet now. As members of the Working Group or the audience who have made use of their Internet access are no doubt aware, whatever deficiencies the Net suffers from, and there are many, there is surely no lack of content.

And she suggests that there is a need to have an advocate for the rights of the public equal to the advocacy that the commercial interests bring to bear in this arena:

*Jessica Litman/Professor of Law, Wayne State University*

Current stakeholders have very able lawyers. . . . What I think is needed now is for someone to act as the copyright lawyer for the public. To examine these proposals as one would if the public had retained one as its copyright lawyer and said: here is a proposal—is this in my interest? . . . I believe that the public's copyright lawyer would seek an amendment expressly privileging individuals using their computers for ordinary reading, viewing, or listening to authorized copies of copyright works.

\*　\*　\*

# EXECUTIVE SUMMARY OF THE STATEMENT OF THE NATION'S LIBRARIES ON H.R. 2441

## American Library Association

*"NII Copyright Protection Act of 1995": Subcommittee on Courts and Intellectual Property, U.S. House of Representatives, February 8, 1996*

Testimony concerning the "NII Copyright Protection Act" (H.R. 2441) has been jointly submitted by five of the nation's principal library organizations on behalf of our 80,000 collective members and the millions of Americans who use our collections and services. Libraries have taken the lead and worked hard to make the vision of a National Information Infrastructure a reality. Both the President and the Speaker have acknowledged on many occasions that libraries play, and must continue to play, a critical role in bringing the benefits of digital technology to every American.

If that result is to be achieved in the digital future, however, it is vitally important to maintain in the Copyright Act the carefully crafted balance between the rights of information owners and users that has served the nation so well in the paper-oriented past. Libraries categorically reject the argument that H.R. 2441 accomplishes no more than "fine tuning" of the Copyright Act. Rather, if enacted as introduced, H.R. 2441 will shift that historic balance to favor copyright owners' desires over the needs of consumers and users. Perhaps most significantly, "fair use" under Section 107 of the Copyright Act will become a hollow right to the detriment of American industry, consumers, scholars, students and other library users.

Libraries believe that at least 3 important proposals are missing from the pending legislation:

H.R. 2441 proposes to amend Section 106 of the Copyright Act to "clarify" that the rights granted to copyright owners apply to electronic transmissions. However, no parallel change in the explicit scope of "fair use" (described in Section 107) is suggested. Accordingly, in order to maintain the balance at the core of copyright law, Section 107 also should be amended to refer specifically to electronic transmissions.

Legal precedent is minimal and mixed as to whether providers of on-line information services (which include libraries and educational institutions) should be liable for the copyright infringements of their users and under what circumstances such providers must remove allegedly infringing material from their systems. Librarians feel strongly that the uncertainty present in this legal environment, coupled with the potential for substantial financial liability, will chill the development of on-line information systems at a time when their expansion must be actively fostered. Accordingly, librarians support modification of H.R. 2441 to make clear that only the party who knowingly placed infringing material on-line or knowingly retransmitted such material should be legally liable for those actions.

Our library associations also support the efforts of the Digital Future Coalition to craft an amendment to Section 109 of the Copyright Act to update the "First Sale Doctrine" (codified at Section 109 of the Act) for the digital environment. Such language, now being developed with DFC, should make clear that—just as is now the case with print materials—the permission of the copyright owner need not be obtained by the lawful purchaser of a copyrighted work before the purchaser transfers that work to another person without retaining a copy.

Libraries are also specially concerned with 3 current provisions of H.R. 2441:

Expansion of the "distribution right" codified in Section 106 of the Copyright Act to expressly include all "transmissions," coupled with vague and unbounded protection for copyright encryption systems in proposed new Section 1201 of the Act, will effectively eliminate important limitations on the rights of copyright owners that are now part of the statute. It is those Congressionally-approved limitations which make many educational and private recreational uses of copyrighted information (such as home video and audio recording) legally possible. Moreover, as now written, the proposed revisions to Section 106 of the Act threaten to inadvertently neutralize the educational activities currently authorized by Section 110 of the statute and often supported by libraries.

Protection of "copyright management" information and licensing systems with sweeping new civil and criminal penalties (again viewed in tandem with the over broad, device-based restrictions proposed in new Section 1201) threatens to replace society's currently balanced regime of shared information resources. In its stead, a new, commercially grounded philosophy will "trump" the Copyright Act and all information, no matter how small the unit, can and will be licensed or otherwise accessed only pursuant to contract. The browsing, non-commercial sharing, and limited reproduction of works for educational and scholarly purposes now protected by statute will be available only to those able to pay for access to information. Such a regime threatens to make America a nation of information haves and have-nots.

Proposed modification of the "library exemptions" of the Act (codified at Section 108) to facilitate library digital preservation efforts are well intentioned. They require technical corrections, however, to provide libraries with the maximum flexibility possible in preserving the nation's cultural heritage and making it available to students and scholars.

Librarians look forward to working actively with Congress to craft balanced and farsighted legislation updating the Copyright Act for this exciting digital age.

\*   \*   \*

# NATIONAL WRITERS UNION CRITIQUES GOVERNMENT WHITE PAPER ON INTELLECTUAL PROPERTY & THE NATIONAL INFORMATION INFRASTRUCTURE

## National Writers Union

*Note to Readers:* The Information Infrastructure Task Force was created by the executive branch of the U.S. government to recommend policy and legislation on the so-called Information Superhighway. The IITF set up a Working Group to make recommendations on copyright law and intellectual property. The "White Paper" is the report of this Working Group. The legislation recommended in the White Paper was sent to Congress on Thursday, September 28, 1995.

The National Writers Union welcomes the release of the report, "Intellectual Property and the National Information Infrastructure," prepared by the Working Group on Intellectual Property Rights of the Information Infrastructure Task Force. Action is needed by government to address copyright law, and violations of the principles underlying that law, in the electronic information era. The NWU's initial critique focuses on a few major concerns of those who create intellectual property.

The NWU agrees with many of the points and policies in the IITF Working Group's document, and we differ on others. However, we cannot examine the content of the report without noting first that the document fails to address at all some of the most important issues facing individual creative people whose work will be central to the application of new information technology. That is to say, our major criticism of the Working Group's report focuses on what the report does not say. We are struck by the remote character of the report in that it misses the daily realities of the individual writer, artist or other creator.

National Writers Union, Local 1981/UAW, AFL-CIO, National Office East, 873 Broadway, Suite 203, New York, NY 10003, email: nwu@netcom.com, tel: 212-254-0279

New Technologies Campaign, 337–17th St., Suite 101, Oakland, CA 94612, email: nwu@netcom.com, tel: 510-839-0110

The NWU approaches the report from two perspectives. First, as the largest union representing nearly 4,500 freelance writers in the U.S., we are concerned about the economic future of writers and other creators whose works will be transmitted on the NII. Second, the NWU's philosophy embodies deep concerns for society as a whole. Clearly, the NII has the potential to reshape our culture and nearly every aspect of our lives. For that reason, we must voice concerns that favor the rights of information users at the same time that we seek fair compensation for our work.

From the perspective of creators, we believe that the report merits mixed reviews. On the positive side, the report comes out strongly in favor of protecting the rights of "authors" on the NII and a companion Global Information Infrastructure (GII). We agree with the report that "copyright protection is not an obstacle in the way of the success of the NII; it is an essential component. Effective copyright protection is a fundamental way to promote the availability of works to the public."

We also agree, as the report states, that an "effective intellectual property regime must (1) ensure that users have access to the broadest feasible variety of works by (2) recognizing the legitimate rights and commercial expectations of persons and entities whose works are used in the NII environment." Indeed, this is simply a current application of the language of the U.S. Constitution itself, that Congress has the power to "promote the Progress of Science and useful Arts, by securing for limited Times to Authors and Inventors the exclusive Right to their respective Writings and Discoveries." An important objective of copyright is to enable those of us who engage in creative work to pay our bills while we add to public knowledge.

We note that while both the Constitution and the White Paper refer to "authors," the modern term requires careful scrutiny. There is an important distinction between the creator of a written work and its owner. Too often the term "author" is used to mean the owner, not the creator, of the work. As economic power in the various communications media becomes increasingly concentrated, creators are being victimized by economic and power imbalances; often creators are not protected by copyright law despite the elegant language of the U.S. Constitution.

Repeatedly, the report praises "authors" and their contributions to the lifeblood of our culture. Yet, the report contains not a word describing the massive consolidation underway in the telecommunications industries. Not once does it mention the decline in the standard of living of most writers, as well as of other creators—a decline due in large part to the stagnation, or outright decline, in pay; the theft of our work by large media corporations which commercially exploit our work and pocket the profit; and the seizure of an ever broader spectrum of rights by publishers who pay the same or less money than was paid out for print publication rights. Indeed, when it comes to the rights and needs of individual creators, the "balance" the Working Group aims to foster is simply invisible.

There is no mention of the developments similar to the following, which threaten to erode the protections of copyright for creators. All of these are related to the advent of the NII:

1. The attempt by *The New York Times* to force all contributors to sign "work-for-hire" agreements. Although we have seen "work-for-hire" agreements before, the unambiguous, non-negotiable demand on the part of *The Times* attempts to achieve a new low in the standards of conduct by a powerful media conglomerate toward individual creative people. Clearly, this is a move on its part to control all content absolutely, with no sharing of future profits with the original creator. In effect, *The Times* would rip away the right of creators to claim ownership to the product of our minds. Along with a diverse group of international creators' organizations, U.S. authors groups view this as a dangerous step certain to be adopted by other media companies if *The Times* succeeds in imposing this new policy.

2. The daily, unauthorized exploitation of writers' work on electronic databases and CD-ROMs by scores of magazine and newspaper publishers. The report fails to mention, even in passing, that there is a serious dispute over who controls and owns works currently circulating on even the most rudimentary version of the NII. In a landmark lawsuit filed by 11 members of the National Writers Union (*Tasini et al.* v. *The New York Times et al.*), writers allege that a systematic violation of the copyright law is being committed every day, not by individuals or libraries, but by some of the largest media companies in the world.

3. All creators have been presented with contracts demanding the rights to a work for all technologies, including those not even currently existing. In our view, this makes a mockery of the notion of fair commerce, particularly because virtually all media companies seeking these broad rights for technologies not yet existing cannot define the value of the right demanded.

If current laws are not amended to prevent these abuses or such practices are not halted by other means, the concept of "author" will have one meaning: an entity embodied in a media monopoly. And, in essence, the true meaning of the Constitutional protection of copyright to promote culture will have been obliterated. Based on its report, the Working Group appears to be either oblivious to or does not care about the survival of individual creators.

## THE PUBLIC INTEREST

Our second overall concern relates to the broad public interest. Here, again, we detect a disconnection from reality on the part of the Working Group. In its report, the Working Group supports "increased funding for libraries and educational institutions to assist their ability to purchase and license works in digital form." But the Working Group gives no thought to the source of such funding. The Working Group's report ignores the terrible reality of unreasonable cutbacks in library funding, on all governmental levels, and neither challenges governments to do more, nor suggests a commercial alternative whereby those businesses profiting the most from the NII are required to devote a small portion of their profits to assure universal access.

Moreover, the Working Group explicitly releases from any responsibility the very sources who should be assisting in the funding of libraries and educational institutions. As will be discussed below, in the context of fair use, the Working Group explicitly rules out calling upon those who profit from the NII to fund universal access. We strongly disagree. If the forecasts of the NII are correct, the new industries created in this technological revolution will reap hundreds of billions of dollars in profit. They should be asked to assume some burden to include all people in the NII.

FAIR USE   The Working Group sidesteps the question of fair use pending the outcome of the Conference on Fair Use. Writers, copyright owners, and the public need a clearer notion of fair use today and in the future. Certainly, some use of copyrighted material is fair and must be allowed without violation of law or the copyright owner's rights. However, a murky definition of fair use has a chilling effect on both free speech and commerce. This important issue should have been addressed by the Working Group.

The NWU supports the extension of Fair Use principles to the electronic realm. We will consult closely with our friends in the library and educational community on how to achieve this.

We would be remiss before leaving the topic of fair use, if we did not take the Working Group to task for an outrageous comment worked into the brief Fair Use section of the report. The report states, "Some participants have suggested that the United States is being divided into a nation of information 'haves' and 'have nots' and that this could be ameliorated by ensuring that the fair use defense is broadly generous in the NII context. The Working Group rejects the notion that copyright owners should be taxed—apart from all others—to facilitate the legitimate goal of 'universal access.'"

If this comment means to suggest that a liberal interpretation of the fair use principle constitutes a so-called "tax," and to suggest that the "haves" have no obligation to the "have nots," then the NWU must strongly differ. This would be a callous abdication of social responsibility on the part of the Working Group.

JOB CREATION   The Working Group continues to argue that the NII "can boost the ability of U.S. firms to compete and succeed in the global economy, thereby generating more jobs for Americans." However, global economic trends indicate that the technological revolution may, in fact, be eliminating jobs faster than they are created. While it is strictly true that new jobs may be created, the end result may be a net loss of jobs. Moreover, a recent article in *The New York Times* confirmed what many economists have been arguing for some time: high technology jobs, particularly the kinds involved in moving data, are highly mobile and are moving offshore. We urge the Working Group to take a more balanced and circumspect view of the economics of the NII as it relates to job generation.

PUBLIC EDUCATION ON COPYRIGHT   We strongly support a nationwide educational campaign on copyright, which takes into account region, age and other factors liable to influence the effectiveness of such a campaign. However, the report also should recommend a way of funding the copyright awareness program.

## STATUTORY ISSUES

TRANSMISSION   Turning to the specific legislative proposals of the Working Group's report, we support the addition of "transmission" to the Copyright Act's delineation of the copyright owner's distribution right and to the statutory definition of publication. Clearly, transmission rights are valuable rights belonging originally to creators of copyrighted materials and the Copyright Act should be amended to reflect this reality. As with other provisions of the Act, this change must be balanced with clear, effective fair use protections to safeguard public libraries and public access to information.

**CMI & CPS**     The report and attendant legislative recommendations devote considerable attention to the related issues of Copyright Management Information and Copyright Protection Systems. The proposed legislation in the report provides severe penalties for alteration of Copyright Management Information or circumvention of Copyright Protection Systems.

Copyright Management Information is an extension to electronic form of the copyright notice that copyright holders attach to works today in hardcopy. In the future, this may grow into a tool to be used to track, calculate and, in theory, remit to authors the amount due to them from transactions involving the sale or resale of their works. In whatever copyright regime evolves, it is important that any attempts to undermine the integrity of our Copyright Management Information be vigorously punished.

Copyright Protection Systems encompass all technologies for prevention of unauthorized access or duplication. The statutory protections afforded to Copyright Protection Systems derive from the White Paper's focus on "piracy" as the primary threat to the creation of a flourishing information environment. Piracy is a legitimate concern, and may be the most serious threat perceived by publishers and distributors, but it is not the threat that most concerns creators of intellectual property. From the point of view of creators, the real threat is the usurpation, exploitation, and hijacking of our work without compensation by increasingly large and powerful publishers and distributors.

## COMPOSITION OF THE NII TASK FORCE

To some extent, we believe the deficiencies of the report stem from the original composition of the NII Task Force. Unfortunately, the Administration has chosen to regard the NII as primarily an economic instrument, rather than as a public resource. As a result, the participants sitting on the advisory and decision-making bodies for the NII are overwhelmingly representatives of business and government bureaucrats. While we understand that the capital to construct the NII will come largely from corporate investment, substantial public monies, through direct government subsidy or regulatory oversight, will be expended on the NII. Moreover, the NII's impact transcends one sector's interests and, therefore, the public interest's voice—including that of individual creators—must be heard. It is not too late.

## CONCLUSION

In summary, there are areas, as we have stated, in which we concur with the Working Group. However, the report would have to do a much better job of reflecting the concerns and needs of individual writers, artists and other creative people before we could consider an endorsement. The report's omissions and deficiencies are too great. We will follow closely developments in Congress. Legislation and regulatory action on intellectual property and the National Information Infrastructure must do a more complete job than has been done by this report to include the concerns of the creators of intellectual property and of the general public.

\*    \*    \*

# 5

## Privacy and Intellectual Freedom in the Digital Age

In early 1996 I had the opportunity to meet with a member of the task force that developed the privacy principles document for the Department of Commerce. I was one of a small group of "privacy advocates" and the only librarian. When it was my turn to make my presentation, I explained the library community's concern about privacy and intellectual freedom, and cited the American Library Association policy that protects patron records.

The representative of the Department of Commerce looked at me with an expression of surprise and said, "You mean libraries don't sell their customer lists?" My reply, of course, was that not only do we not sell them, we protect them as far as we can within the letter of the law. My fellow advocates had also not heard this before, and were extremely impressed by the resolve of libraries against invasions of patron privacy. By the end of the meeting, many people were convinced that the ALA policy was an admirable model that others should be encouraged to follow.

Libraries first confronted the issue of patron records after the Internal Revenue Service asked to examine the patron records of several libraries in 1970. Almost thirty years of thinking about the significance of privacy for intellectual freedom has put us far ahead of other institutions in this area.

Although colleges and universities typically have policies regarding academic freedom, they are unfortunately lax in terms of applying this thinking to the online communications of their students and faculty. Public institutions that provide online access, such as Free-Nets or community projects, may not be aware of the privacy implications of their services.

The danger with online communication is that every activity of seeking information can be recorded. Marketers are interested in logging personal accesses to sites that will provide information for their commercial activities. It would also be possible for government agencies to trace every access to targeted sites, such as those supporting "white power" organizations, disseminating unpopular information like bomb recipes, or sites suspected of carrying illegal materials such as child pornography.

There are currently no laws or policies that would protect the privacy of information seekers on the Information Highway. The Department of Commerce report *Privacy and the NII: Safeguarding Telecommunications-Related Personal Information* proposes that the communications industry should develop its own standards for consumer privacy, thus obviating the need for government action in this area. But the report fails to address the fact that "consumer" transactions will leave their traces throughout the online network, not just at the site where their account resides.

Privacy comes up also when we discuss how users will pay for the information that they access. Some people theorize a micropayment system where each access to a particular unit of information (whether a report, a database record, or a Web page) will debit the viewer's "electronic cash" account by a small amount. But such debit transactions could link an individual's identity to that viewing, creating a record of everything the person has browsed or read electronically. Concern about such microtracking of our online activities has led to interesting research into the development of digital cash accounts that will preserve the privacy of the online consumer.

Libraries can protect their own files of patron records, but they cannot protect the privacy of their patrons as they access materials on Internet sites outside the library. Patrons accessing online materials through library accounts may have more privacy than those using personal accounts from their home or office, since they are not easily identifiable as individuals. However, as more sites require users to register before being allowed access, the potential for loss of privacy increases. Libraries must continue to be strong supporters of intellectual freedom in all media, and in the meanwhile have a particular obligation to inform their users of the reality of privacy in cyberspace.

# Privacy on the Internet

If computers have been such a boon to the information market, providing a way to connect actions in the world to potential customers, the Information Highway promises to be everything these marketers ever wanted in data-gathering tools. Yet most users of the Internet are unaware of the data that can be gathered about them while online.

## Surfing the Net

Each activity on the Internet requires two-way communication. As you "surf" the Internet, you are making a connection between your computer and another computer each time you access a link. To respond to you, the computer on the other end has to know your exact Internet address. The Internet address is a number that only your computer has, something like a telephone number on the telephone system.

Systems offering information on the Internet can, and often do, keep logs of accesses. These logs can store the Internet address of each computer that views a file, the date and time of that viewing, and how long the viewer stayed. So, in essence, everything you do on the Internet may leave a record of your activity.

If this sounds frightening, it should be. But maybe less so than it seems in some cases. Much depends on how you define "your computer" in the scenario above. If you access the Internet through a service provider like America Online or Netcom, the return address that the other computer sees does not identify you as an individual. Instead, the address is one that is assigned to you randomly at the time you log on and reassigned after you log off. The remote computer's log of activity will tell it how many accesses it has from these large systems, but not which subscriber made them.

Here's what a typical log of accesses at a Web site looks like:

backdraft-bbn.infoseek.com—[03/Nov/1996:15:55:45 -0800] "GET /~kec/
     reach.html HTTP/1.0" 200 1580

hd05-039.compuserve.com—[04/Nov/1996:20:11:26 -0800] "GET /~kec/
     ethics.html HTTP/1.0" 304 -

198.76.84.95—[04/Nov/1996:11:55:16 -0800] "GET /~kec/
index.html HTTP/1.0" 200 6838

v34-ppp-101.nett.is—[04/Nov/1996:00:50:19 -0800] "GET /~kec/
infopeop.htm HTTP/1.0" 200 34058

On the other hand, if you access the Internet from a computer on
your desk at work that has its own Internet address, logs reveal the
activity from that one desktop computer.

coyle.ucop.edu—[09/Nov/1996:07:48:35 -0800] "GET /~kec/
copyrigh.htm HTTP/1.0" 200 933

That's only one side of the story, however. Most online services and
office systems keep some record of what their own users do from the
time that they log on until they log off. These records may be only
temporary, with the intention that they would be scrutinized if an
unusual system problem appeared that needed detailed debugging.
Other than that limited type of internal use, commercial Internet
providers are forbidden by law from revealing this kind of transaction
information to anyone outside the company except under a court
order.

## Electronic Mail

Electronic mail has its own privacy problems. The Electronic Communications Privacy Act (1984) protects the privacy of mail as it
travels through networks on its way to its destination. Unfortunately,
E-mail is all too easily viewed by outsiders, regardless of the law. E-mail
travels across the networks of the Internet "in clear," to use a phrase
from the cryptography community. In clear means that it is not en-
coded or scrambled the way it would be if the message had been
encrypted; it is plain readable text. A program or a piece of equipment,
both called *sniffers* in Net jargon, can tap onto the network at any
number of points and simply copy messages as they pass through.
Finding a particular person's E-mail messages this way is a kind of
needle in a haystack, but clever technology does make it possible.

Once E-mail reaches its destination, it is stored as a file on the
computer the recipient uses for her E-mail. Once again, this file is in
clear. Although her account is protected by a password, this E-mail
file can be viewed by anyone who has certain account privileges on
that computer. In most computing environments in offices and institutions, the person who runs the central computer system, often
called the *system administrator,* is able to read any file on the system.

This is necessary because this person may be called upon to fix any kind of problem that arises on the computer.

Most privacy experts advise that you shouldn't put anything in E-mail that you would not send through the U.S. mail on a postcard. This isn't bad advice, yet in reality most E-mail goes through the Internet to its destination without being read by others. System administrators, by and large, are both honest and busy, and you should not expect them to spend their time reading the E-mail on their systems. Hackers use their skills to break into computer systems and take a look around, but attacks of this nature are relatively rare.

## Employee Use of the Network

The story changes when the computer you use belongs to your employer. The computer and the network connection in this case are a tool owned by the employer and are to be used as part of one's job. The employer owns the computer and the work you do on it. In court cases, employer snooping in E-mail and other computer communications has been upheld as legal, as has punishing employees for things they've said in supposedly private E-mail messages on their work accounts. In the corporate environment where companies run their own Internet sites, employers can now install software that logs all of the Web sites their employees visit for the purpose of revealing accesses to nonwork-related sites like *Playboy* or online games.

An electronic mail message is simply a file stored on the computer where you have your account. Between the time it arrives and the time you delete it from your personal mailbox, it may be included on regular system backups that are standard in any well-run computer center or service. These backups may be stored for a period of months or even perhaps years. Remember, it was E-mail backups that were used as proof against Oliver North in the Iran-Contra scandal— messages he had deleted years before that were found on backup tapes of the White House computer system.

It's important to have a clear understanding in your library about staff use of the library's computer accounts. Every staff member who uses E-mail or Internet access needs to know what use is permitted. Is it okay to send E-mail to a friend in another library branch arranging a lunch date? How about using the library E-mail account to keep in touch with one's daughter or son away at college? Can you subscribe to E-mail discussion lists on library topics? On nonlibrary topics (such as personal hobbies)? It's essential that both the employer and employee have a clear idea of where the line is drawn between acceptable and not acceptable use.

Many employers treat E-mail accounts much like the telephone: some personal use is permitted as long as it doesn't interfere with the employee's work or the use that others will make of the system. (Remember that some E-mail lists can send out hundreds of messages a day, flooding the E-mail system and taking up precious disk space.) But it's important to note that no employer can guarantee employee privacy, and this must be made clear to all users of the system. Under certain conditions, E-mail messages can be subject to disclosure for legal reasons, such as investigations of fraud or disputed personnel matters. Even in cases where the employer had told employees that their communications were private, courts have upheld punitive actions against employees based on the content of their E-mail messages. The bottom line is that you should always be aware that your E-mail messages are written documents that, like the notes you passed in class during your school days, might be read by others.

## Marketing on the Internet

The Internet is making use of an advertising-based model not unlike that of television or radio. What an Internet site has to offer an advertiser is the viewer's attention, and hopefully that attention will translate into the viewing of advertisements. Advertisements on the Web may actually be better marketing tools than those in the non-interactive media. Unlike a television or newspaper ad, the Web ad is actually a link to the advertiser's own Internet site where potential customers can access detailed information about the company and its products, and in some cases can even order the product online.

But as we saw above, the Internet identifies Web site visitors not as people but as computers. This isn't the right information from a marketer's point of view. What marketers would really like is to be able to identify the individuals behind each visit to their Web site or the sites on which they advertise. Added together with other information, such as the income, geographical location, and buying habits of that person, marketers are hoping to be able to tailor their contact with customers on a person-by-person basis.

This type of individualized marketing might also be preferred by consumers. Rather than receiving messages about products they already have or have little interest in, they will receive only relevant product information. This "micromarket" of one is seen as the future of a new economy that goes beyond the mass marketing of today and reaches out to individuals for a greater variety of products and services. But these individualized services have privacy implications because they depend on our letting companies gather information about who we are and what we buy so they can develop products aimed at each of us individually. The NTIA report *Privacy and the NII: Safeguarding Telecommunications-Related Personal Information* issued in 1995 says, "the free flow of information—even personal information—promotes a dynamic economic marketplace, which produces substantial benefits for individual consumers and society as a whole."

The fact is, however, that many consumers are reluctant to give their personal information to companies. For one thing, we don't necessarily have a shared definition of what is meant by personal. Some of us find giving a complete stranger our home address a bit too personal, while the majority of people would not like their medical information to be used outside their own doctor's office. Somewhere in between is a balance sought by marketers. Consumers today tend to be wary of opening their private lives to the private sector, so the NTIA report stresses the importance of education, "helping consumers to understand how their personal information can be used in beneficial ways, thereby increasing their willingness to use the NII."

Since use of the Internet often doesn't reveal who you are, much less other personal information about you, marketers on the Internet must get consumers to reveal that information to them. Some sites block access until you have filled in an online form with your name, address, phone number, and E-mail address. Others offer value-added services to subscribers who provide their names and addresses.

Internet users have been particularly reluctant to reveal information about themselves. One of the cultural aspects that has carried over from the earlier, noncommercial era of the Internet has been a strong sense of privacy and individual liberty. When *Wired* magazine started its online site Hot Wired, it required a free registration to access materials that asked for a name and address. A group of privacy advocates who call themselves the "cypherpunks" set up an account on Hot Wired for which the logon name was cypherpunk and the password was also cypherpunk. People who knew about this account could use it to log onto the Hot Wired site, thus avoiding giving any personal information about themselves in the process. Word of this account spread, especially when it became apparent that the Hot Wired site allowed multiple users to log on at the same time with the same account. At one point in the early months of the site, one administrator admitted that nearly half of their accesses were coming in on the cypherpunk account. The Net culture had found a way to defeat the marketing goals of this site, and without a doubt clever site administrators have learned from the Hot Wired experience. Some sites now ask for an E-mail address and don't issue an account until they successfully send mail to that address.

Library patrons, although they are using a shared Internet account when they access the World Wide Web from a public access station in the library, can register as subscribers on Web sites. It is important that the library alert patrons to the privacy implications of their use of the Internet so they can make an informed decision when asked to give personal information at a Web site.

## Privacy and Child Safety

Some time in the future, 1995 will be referred to as the "year of the online child molester scare." During that year there were a number of horror stories of young children being approached inappropriately by adults in online conferences and chat rooms. We know that news stories of this type do seem to run in waves, and probably for some reason. In this case, 1995 was probably the year when youngsters first became a visible presence online. Many children were playing on their parents' AOL accounts or exploring online communications for the first time from school.

These children may have had more time to spend online than their parents, and definitely had more time for the social aspects of online communication that takes place as real time chat, where users type short questions and responses to each other either in a public "room" or bulletin board, or privately between two people. The child safety issue came up when it was discovered that adults were spending time in chat areas advertised for children and teens, and that some of these adults had less than admirable intentions.

These unfortunate experiences were a good lesson for all of us. It's easy to be lulled into a feeling of comfort and safety when communicating with people online. When you are sitting in your own home, there is no visible threat like the dark corners of the real world. All of the streetwise clues that we've learned or that we've taught our children are inapplicable in the online world. This doesn't mean that networked communications are more dangerous than our city streets. There is danger to your privacy online, but the physical dangers of our streets are absent.

Alert members of the online community realized that we needed to teach our children online smarts equivalent to the rules we give them for their off-line life. One of these people was Larry Magid, who authored the pamphlet called "Child Safety on the Information Highway." This simple set of rules addressed to parents gives them the advice they need to prepare their children for this new means of communication.

Libraries should be aware that many of their users, young and old, will be inexperienced on the "streets" of the digital age. And many parents have been frightened by the stories of child pornographers roaming the Internet looking for victims. No one should go online for the first time without being given some safety guidelines for online interaction—simple, commonsense rules like "Don't give your name and address to anyone you don't know." New users need to learn that they are in control of their online interaction and can act to protect their own privacy.

The parents of young Net-surfers must also be prepared to advise their children on how to handle difficult situations that might arise. Children need to be told that they can log out of any conversation that makes them feel uncomfortable, and adults must be present to provide advice for new and potentially frightening situations. Providing this education through handouts and training is one of the most valuable services that libraries today can give their online users. The library may be a child's first point of contact with the online world, and that means that libraries have an opportunity to educate a new generation of "netwise" cyber-citizens.

# Technologies of Privacy

While computers may be one of the main causes of our current lack of privacy, they can also be the cure, and one of the main cures in this area is that of encryption.

## Encryption

We've all played with a magic decoder ring in our youth, or in our later lives have enjoyed the cipher games in the local newspaper.

These simple versions of encryption substitute one letter for another and are much too easy to solve to be of use for protecting the privacy of a message.

Today's encryption technology is highly advanced and could not have become so without the great computational powers of computers. As a matter of fact, the advancement of computer technology is now such that everyone with a desktop computer can use modern techniques to encode messages that are virtually unbreakable. These new products of the science of cryptography go far beyond anything that could have been imagined only decades ago. But if secure encryption is possible on every computer, why aren't we using it today to protect the privacy of our online messages?

The answer to that question lies in issues of national security. Encryption technologies have been extremely important in wartime (and in times of uneasy peace) because of the need to transmit messages that must not be read by the enemy. Many histories of the Second World War tell exciting tales of breakthroughs in cryptography that allowed us to decipher enemy messages and take decisive action. Because of this role of encryption in defense actions, encryption is considered an armament—not unlike a missile or a tank. The U.S. Department of State maintains controls over the production, export, and sales of arms, including the new secure methods of encryption. While these encryption technologies can be used domestically, they cannot be exported for sale or use.

In a global economy such as ours, it is virtually impossible to ensure that a product will not cross the U.S. border, especially when that product can be transmitted electronically. This has essentially prevented U.S. software manufacturers from including secure encryption in their products even though their customers would very much like to have it.

Other barriers to the development of secure encryption products for the general consumer come from the law enforcement community. Members of this community fear that widespread encryption would eliminate their ability to discover and monitor criminal communications. Not only would E-mail messages with key evidence be unreadable, encryption could be used to hide some forms of crime like money laundering and industrial espionage.

Privacy advocates argue that honest citizens must not be asked to give up their right to privacy so that the few criminals among us can be apprehended. As some would say, should we all be required to send our mail on postcards so that no one can hide a crime inside an envelope? The requirement of law enforcement that we all send our messages in clear strikes some as being a bit too like the world of Orwell's *1984* where all communications between citizens were monitored by the government.

## Key Escrow

An encrypted message is readable only to the person or persons who have the *key*—essentially a secret password that can reverse the scrambled message and return it back to its original state of legibility. One compromise solution between having all messages be readable as they travel through networks and having all messages be so locked up that they can't be viewed by legitimate law enforcement, is the use of *key escrow*. Under a key escrow scheme, each user who sends encrypted messages leaves a copy of her key with a trusted escrow agent. This agent will not reveal the key to anyone except law enforcement or government officials with a proper court order.

This seems to be a neat solution to a difficult problem—citizens get their privacy, and law enforcement officials can conduct investigations as needed, going through the court system as they do for wiretaps. Unfortunately, there are some catches.

The first catch is that it's hard to agree on who should be the trusted agent. The problem is not so much that there isn't any agency honest enough to perform the duties, but that so far no agency has proven itself to have sufficient security. At the time that one key escrow proposal was being discussed by the Clinton administration, the CIA was undergoing an embarrassing scandal due to an agent who had sold secrets to the Soviet Union for over a decade for the rather paltry sum of $1.5 million. If the CIA can't keep its own information secret, who could be trusted to be the escrow agent for the keys to the privacy of everyone in the United States? In a world of multibillionaires, it seems as if someone will inevitably be able to buy her way into our escrow agent's confidences.

The next catch is that our need to encrypt doesn't end at our country's borders. Many online transactions are multinational, and it's unlikely that the residents of any foreign country are going to want to have their keys held by an agency representing the U.S. government. Since sender and receiver must share information, they also must share their keys. Perhaps the future will bring about international agreements that would make the key escrow scheme viable in a global economy.

## *Pretty Good Privacy*

Pretty Good Privacy, known universally as PGP, is a computer program written by Phil Zimmermann that will encrypt messages securely. This program is distributed for free over the Internet, though with some controls to avoid violating the laws against export of the product.

PGP is very well known to Internet users and is often cited as a solution to privacy problems. Used properly it will indeed keep others from being able to read your messages. Unfortunately, it has not yet been incorporated into the programs that we use every day and is therefore still difficult for all but the most skilled or determined of computer users. Hopefully this will change over the next few years as more products include PGP's encryption capabilities.

PGP is significant, however, because it has served to change the direction of the encryption debate. It is well-known that the PGP program can be found on computers outside the United States. Since this is the case, why are we still focused on controlling the export of encryption? As many Internet users like to say, "The cat is out of the bag." And although agencies like the FBI contend that without strong controls on encryption they will be unable to fight crimes like terrorism, child pornography, and illegal drugs, the existence of PGP abroad and in the United States does not seem to have caused any increase in crime in our country.

# The Future of Privacy

The erosion of our privacy takes place quietly, and many of us are unaware of how far it has already gone. In September 1996, the Lexis/Nexis information company announced a new Internet service called P-TRAK. It described P-TRAK as being like an electronic "white pages" that would display the name of an individual, a current address and up to two previous addresses, and the telephone number. It also included some women's maiden names and some individual's birth dates. What the company failed to mention in its online description of the service was that when it was first released it also displayed the Social Security number of the individual, and still allowed searches to be done by SSN.

When Internet users heard of the P-TRAK service they were shocked by the loss of privacy that it implied. E-mail messages raced around the Internet warning readers of this assault on privacy and conveying the instructions on how to have one's information removed from the database. What these Internet users didn't know was that this very same information was available from a number of different sources and had been for a long time. The reaction to the P-TRAK database, like a similar reaction in 1990 to a proposed CD-ROM white pages product from the Lotus Corporation, shows that people do value their privacy, but they are generally unaware of how much information about them is publicly available. When that existence of the information is brought to the attention of the public, the reaction is quite strong.

To avoid further erosions of our privacy, we will have to be very diligent. Getting privacy issues out in the public eye is the best way to assure that we won't lose what privacy we have today. Libraries can further this goal first by letting their patrons know how strongly the library values their privacy. Perhaps the library model of patron privacy really could become the standard for the future.

## IN THEIR OWN WORDS

**Privacy and the NII: Safeguarding Telecommunications-Related Personal Information** (Introduction)
U.S. Department of Commerce, October 1995
http://www.ntia.doc.gov/ntiahome/policy/privwhitepaper.html
NTIA order number: pb96–109–087

In this report the Department of Commerce looks at the relationship between the consumer and the online service provider. Like others who feel that direct marketing has benefits for consumers, the DOC concludes that consumers and information services can reach an agreement as to the type and amount of personal data that will be gathered and used. Not gathering the data at all is not one of the options proposed. (Note that the original report is highly footnoted. I have removed those for the sake of readability, but you can find them in the version of the report on the NTIA Web page.)

**Why We Made PGPfone, and Why You Need It** (Excerpt)
Philip R. Zimmermann. Pretty Good Privacy Phone. Owner's Manual. Version 1.0 beta 7–8 July 1996

Phil Zimmermann and PGP, a free encryption program, are famous in the Internet culture. Phil released his program in 1994 and started a revolution against the Federal regulations that limit the use of encryption. This excerpt from the user's manual for the latest PGP product explains in clear language Phil's philosophy about privacy and why we all need it.

**Privacy in Cyberspace: Rules of the Road for the Information Superhighway** (Fact Sheet Number 18)
Privacy Rights Clearinghouse. USD Center for Public Interest Law. 1996
http://pwa.acusd.edu:80/-prc/fs/fs18-cyb.html

From the PRC Web site: "The Privacy Rights Clearinghouse (PRC) is a non-profit consumer education and research program administered by the University of San Diego's Center for Public Interest Law. The PRC offers consumers a unique opportunity to learn how to protect their personal privacy. Its publications provide in-depth information on a variety of informational privacy issues, as well as practical tips on safeguarding personal privacy." This fact sheet is a comprehensive yet concise statement on online privacy. PRC fact sheets are available in both English and Spanish and in hardcopy as well as online.

### Further Reading

American Library Association. *Policy on Confidentiality of Library Records.* 1986. http://www.ala.org/ICONN/ICONN-website/policy.html

American Library Association. *Policy concerning Confidentiality of Personally Identifiable Information about Library Users.* 1991. http://www.ala.org/ICONN/ICONN-website/confidentiality.html

These two ALA policies reflect the concern with the protection of patron privacy as part of the defense of intellectual freedom. Few other public institutions take such a strong stand to assure the privacy of their users.

Banisar, David. *Big Brother Goes High Tech.* Covert Action Quarterly, n. 56, Spring 1996. pp. 6–10. http://www.worldmedia.com/caq/articles/brother.html

Just in case you think we have nothing to fear but fear itself, Banisar, one of the founders of the Electronic Privacy Information Center, tells how government surveillance is going high tech. Scary!

Center for Media Education. *Web of Deception: Threats to Children from Online Marketing.* 1996. http://www.cme.org/cme/cmwdecov.html

CME is concerned about Web sites that are targeted at children and that use the Web to solicit personal information about the children. Kids especially enjoy the interactive nature of online communication, so sites often employ chat sessions to keep their interest. CME is concerned that the public nature of this interaction may be dangerous to our younger Net surfers, especially those unable to resist the manipulative power of these commercial Web sites.

Computer Professionals for Social Responsibility. *Clipper Chip Archive.* http://www.cpsr.org/dox/program/clipper/clipper.html

CPSR was instrumental in the battle against the Clipper Chip, a government designed encryption chip that contained a special "back door"—that is, a means by which law enforcement could decrypt messages. A large part of the Internet community felt that privacy that could be overridden by the government was really not privacy at all. The government continues to provide Clipperlike proposals which the Internet user community is dubbing "Clipper II," "Clipper 3.2.1," etc.

Magid, Larry J. *Child Safety on the Information Highway.* Arlington, Va., National Center for Missing and Exploited Children, 1994. http://www.missingkids.org/information_superhighway.html

This document, also available in pamphlet form from NCMEC, is a guide to parents on reducing the risks to their children as they go online. It gives six simple rules for personal online safety that are as relevant to adults as they are to children.

### Internet Resources

Electronic Privacy Information Center. http://www.epic.org

This is the most comprehensive site for privacy matters, and includes a large section on issues dealing with privacy and children online. Their Privacy Resources pages is an excellent list of other privacy sites on the Internet.

# PRIVACY AND THE NII: SAFEGUARDING TELECOMMUNICATIONS-RELATED PERSONAL INFORMATION

## U.S. Department of Commerce

## EXECUTIVE SUMMARY

As the National Information Infrastructure (NII) is built, more and more individuals will use it for a wide range of transactions. In the course of using the NII, individuals will create information trails that could provide others, in the absence of safeguards, with the personal details of their lives.

In this White Paper, the National Telecommunications and Information Administration (NTIA) hopes to contribute to the broader privacy debate by addressing the privacy issues related to a specific sector—the telecommunications sector. Specifically, this paper focuses on the privacy concerns associated with an individual's subscription to or use of a telecommunications or information service. The overall purpose of the paper is to provide an analysis of the state of privacy in the United States as it relates to existing and future communications services and to recommend a framework for safeguarding telecommunications-related personal information (TRPI).

The analysis provided herein reveals that there is a lack of uniformity among existing privacy laws and regulations for telephony and video services. In fact, similar services are governed differently depending on how they are delivered. And, other communications services like those available over the Internet are almost entirely unprotected. Furthermore, NTIA believes that it will become increasingly difficult to apply existing privacy laws and regulations to communications service providers as services and sectors converge, and as new technologies evolve.

To rectify limitations in existing telecommunications privacy law and to provide consumers with a uniform privacy standard for TRPI,

Ronald H. Brown, Secretary
David J. Barram, Deputy Secretary
Larry Irving, Assistant Secretary and Administrator, National Telecommunications and Information Administration, Washington, D.C.
October 1995

NTIA proposes a framework that draws upon the Information Infrastructure Task Force's NII Principles for Providing and Using Personal Information. This framework has two fundamental elements—provider notice and customer consent.

Under this proposed framework, telecommunications and information service providers would notify individuals about their information practices, abide by those practices, and keep customers informed of subsequent changes to such practices. Service providers would be free to use information collected for stated purposes once they obtain consent from the relevant customer. Affirmative consent would be required with respect to sensitive personal information. Tacit customer consent would be sufficient to authorize the firm to use all other information.

NTIA believes that establishing minimum privacy protections across the communications industry would ensure that consumers are provided with a reasonable level of privacy protection. Uniformly applied, a common "base" standard could also prevent some industries from gaining an unfair competitive advantage.

## PRIVACY AND THE NII

> The real danger is the gradual erosion of individual liberties through the automation, integration, and inter-connection of many small, separate record-keeping systems, each of which alone may seem innocuous, even benevolent, and wholly justifiable.
>
> —U.S. Privacy Protection Study Commission

> The numbers dialed from a private telephone—although certainly more prosaic than the conversation itself—are not without content. Most private telephone subscribers may have their own numbers listed in a publicly-distributed directory, but I doubt there are any who would be happy to have broadcast to the world a list of the local or long distance numbers they have called. This is not because such a list might in some sense be incriminating, but because it easily could reveal the identities of the persons and the places called, and thus reveal the most intimate details of a person's life.
>
> —Supreme Court Justice Potter Stewart, *Smith v. Maryland*

## I. INTRODUCTION

An advanced national information infrastructure (NII) promises enormous economic, social, and cultural benefits to its users and to the nation—enhanced educational and employment opportunities for all Americans, greater citizen participation, and improved delivery of government services. The NII can produce these benefits because it will facilitate and expand the flow of information from people to people and from place to place. However, many people may be reluctant to use the NII if they are afraid that the personal information transmitted over it can be used in ways that are unexpected or inappropriate. Thus, if government and the private sector want to encourage the vigorous consumer activity needed to unlock the full potential of the information infrastructure, they must acknowledge and safeguard the legitimate privacy interests of NII users.

## A. The Nature of Privacy

More than sixty years ago, Supreme Court Justice Louis Brandeis characterized the right to privacy—the right to be let alone [as] the most comprehensive of rights, and the right most valued by civilized men. A 1993 public opinion survey by Louis Harris & Associates found that 83% of Americans are concerned about threats to personal privacy. This reflects a five point increase over responses to the identical question posed a year earlier, and a 49 point increase from a similar poll conducted in 1970. In addition, a survey of members of the U.S. Chamber of Commerce revealed a staggering 59.2% . . . stat[ing] that they view the emerging issue of privacy in telecommunications as very important; 34.8% felt it was moderately important. Furthermore, the Privacy Rights Clearinghouse (PRC) reports that consumers are "frustrated by a lack of control they have over the use of their personal information"; and "suffer" from a lack of understanding about how information about them is collected, used, and distributed and from a "misunderstanding" of existing privacy protection laws and regulations.

Privacy means different things depending on the context. Among the many notions of privacy, growth of the NII primarily raises concerns about information privacy. That term refers to an individual's claim to control the terms under which personal information—information that can be linked to an individual or distinct group of individuals (e.g., a household)—is acquired, disclosed, and used.

Information privacy promotes two principal interests. It recognizes that control over personal information is important because mere awareness by others of certain types of information is potentially harmful. For example, an individual may want to keep certain types of health data confidential from the general public because its disclosure could cause the person embarrassment. Information privacy also recognizes that personal information can be used improperly, unfairly, or for purposes other than those intended by an individual. For example, an individual may refuse to disclose his or her social security number or mother's maiden name, not because disclosure in itself would be harmful but because that information could be used to gain telephone access to banking records.

Concerns about safeguarding privacy will likely grow as the NII becomes a pervasive, functioning reality. As the NII is built, more and more individuals will use it to execute an ever-expanding range of transactions involving, for example, business, entertainment, banking, education, recreation, and even health care. These transactions—by their very execution on the NII—create electronic records, which are easily stored and processed.

Further, because the costs associated with storing, processing, and distributing personal records are continuously decreasing, accumulating personal information from disparate sources will become a cost-effective enterprise for information users with interests ranging from law enforcement to direct marketing. For example, in one case, journalists spent an average of $112 and 75 minutes on-line to find financial, legal, marital, and residential histories of various luminaries, such as movie producer George Lucas and White House Chief of Staff Leon Panetta. Finally, entirely new modes of communication and transactions may be created that are not contemplated by current privacy regulations and policies, which are typically tied to today's or even yesterday's technologies. For instance, interactive, switched, broadband communications networks, which will enable individuals to educate and entertain themselves, to shop, to receive health care, to bank, and to participate in government over a single network, could pose new privacy concerns. In the absence of subscriber privacy provisions appropriate to such networks and technologies, it will be possible for others to track and store information about the daily activities of one's life.

## B. NTIA's Inquiry

These developments presage an information environment in which more personal information will flow more quickly, more widely, more invisibly, and more cheaply with fewer legal and social constraints. To understand better the privacy issues implicated by that environment, the National Telecommunications and Information Administration

(NTIA) released a Notice of Inquiry on private sector use of tele-communications-related personal information. We received 46 formal comments from industry, the press, academics, privacy advocates, and individuals. These comments, supplemented by consultations with stakeholders in the privacy debate, feedback from experts, and independent research, form the basis of this report. NTIA hopes that this White Paper will serve as a catalyst, inspiring industry and consumer advocates to work together to instill the consumer confidence essential for the viability of the NII.

## C. Scope of the White Paper

As the President's adviser on telecommunications and information policy, NTIA in this paper will focus on private sector collection, use, and dissemination of telecommunications-related personal information (TRPI)—personal information that is created in the course of an individual's subscription to a telecommunications or information service or as a result of his or her use of that service. To illustrate the concept of TRPI, consider an electronic mail service that allows individuals to log on to the service via modem and send e-mail messages through the Internet. To subscribe to this service, the provider will typically collect some basic information about the customer, such as name, home address, home telephone number, work telephone number, type of e-mail service requested, and credit card (or other payment) information. Once the e-mail service has been installed, additional data will be generated each time the customer sends an e-mail message. That includes all the personal information created in the course of routing a message from the individual to the addressee (e.g., header information on an e-mail message), as well as certain accounting information, which, depending on how the service charges its customers, could include the date, time, subject line of message, and its length. All of this subscription and usage data constitutes TRPI.

Although most consumers are probably aware that telecommunications and information service providers collect a wide range of subscription data, they may be less aware of providers' accumulation of other TRPI and the uses to which that data can be put. Many consumers may have the same level of awareness as the woman who told a caller trying to sell long distance service that she did not make many out-of-town calls:

"I'm surprised to hear you say that," she recalls him saying. "I see from your phone records that you frequently call Newark, Delaware, and Stamford, Conn." . . . "I was shocked, scared, and paranoid," she recalls. "If people are able to find out who I call, what else could they find out about me?"

The risks for consumers will likely increase in the future as several related factors induce providers of telecommunications and information services to become more sophisticated and aggressive in their use of TRPI. First, the continuing growth of competition in those markets will increase the number of firms competing for consumer attention. In that environment, companies like the enterprising long distance service provider in the foregoing anecdote will find TRPI a powerful resource for identifying potential customers and tailoring the companies' marketing strategies to maximize customer response.

Second, as established service providers diversify into other lines of business, their existing reservoir of TRPI will help them sell those new services more effectively and at less cost. Thus, when MCI and Rupert Murdoch's News Corp. announced a joint venture to market on-line information services, MCI executives said that they would use TRPI in their "Friends and Family" database to offer these services to some of MCI's current long distance customers.

Third, as competition continues to squeeze profit margins, more and more telecommunications and information service providers may come to view the sale of TRPI as an additional, low-cost revenue stream. However, it is not clear to what extent consumers will accept such practices. For example, although companies have long made a practice of extracting information from local phone books and selling it to marketers, when telephone companies have announced their intent to sell customer listings, they have been met with opposition. In 1990, New York Telephone informed its customers through billing statements about its plans to sell customer listings, and 800,000 customers asked to have their names removed from the lists. Bell Atlantic experienced a similar reaction when it announced plans to sell its "white pages" directory lists in July 1995. Furthermore, in response to the public comments the Federal Communications Commission (FCC) received to its Notice of Proposed Rulemaking on Caller ID, it passed rules prohibiting the sale or reuse of automatic number identification (ANI)-derived information without first notifying the originating telephone subscriber, and obtaining his or her affirmative consent for such reuse or sale. ANI, a subset of TRPI, is a signaling protocol used by carriers to automatically identify a calling party's billing telephone number. Some states have adopted similar rules restricting the use of ANI.

## D. Recommended Approach

The coming years thus promise increasing tension between the desire of telecommunications and information service providers to expand the use of TRPI to market new services, many of which will doubtless benefit consumers, and consumers' desire to control the dissemination of potentially sensitive personal information. The relevant questions for policy makers are: what level of privacy protection adequately balances the legitimate interest of individuals and service providers; whether existing laws and regulations provide the desired level of protection; and, if not, what changes should be made.

The United States currently has no omnibus privacy law that covers the private sector's acquisition, disclosure, and use of TRPI. Instead, American privacy law comprises a welter of Federal and state statutes and regulations that regulate the collection and dissemination of different types of personal information in different ways, depending on how it is acquired, by whom, and how it will be used. Although these laws provide some level of privacy protection, they are not comprehensive in the sense that they do not apply uniformly to all service providers.

As discussed more fully below, this is particularly true with respect to the principal regulations governing the acquisition and use of TRPI by certain providers of telecommunications and information services—the FCC's rules pertaining to telephone companies' use of customer proprietary network information (CPNI) and the provisions of the 1984 Cable Act regulating the disclosure of personally identifiable subscriber information by cable television operators. Because those requirements were imposed on a limited group of service providers, they afford consumers little, if any, protection against inappropriate use of TRPI by other types of service providers. As importantly, the limited applicability of those regulations virtually guarantees that different firms will have differing privacy obligations even when they offer similar services, creating a situation that could be potentially disadvantageous to one competitor or group of competitors.

To rectify these limitations in existing telecommunications privacy law and to provide consumers with a uniform privacy standard, NTIA has applied the Information Infrastructure Task Force's (IITF) NII Principles for Providing and Using Personal Information to the telecommunications sector in order to offer a framework for the acquisition and use of TRPI by telecommunications and information service providers. We hope that this recommendation will contribute to the broader debate regarding privacy concerns and the NII, assist the Administration's IITF, its Advisory Council, the FCC, Congress, state and local governments, and private sector policy makers as they grapple with this important issue. NTIA also hopes that this application of the IITF's Principles will encourage other sectoral analyses.

As stated above, NTIA's proposed framework draws upon the IITF's Principles and has two fundamental elements—provider notice and customer consent. Under NTIA's proposed framework, each provider of telecommunications and information services would inform its customers about what TRPI it intends to collect and how that data will be used. A service provider would be free to use the information collected for the stated purposes once it has obtained consent from the relevant customer. Affirmative consent would be required with respect to sensitive personal information. Tacit customer consent would be sufficient to authorize the use of all other information.

This approach, if embraced by industry, would allow service providers and their customers to establish the specific level of privacy protection offered in a marketplace transaction, free from excessive government regulation, so long as the minimum requirements of notice and consent are satisfied. The uniformity contemplated by this approach means its adoption would not create competitive imbalances among rival firms, but would preserve their ability to compete on privacy as vigorously as they compete on price, service, and quality. Further, because NTIA's recommended framework gives companies considerable flexibility in giving notice and securing consent, implementation of that approach should not be overly burdensome. On the other hand, this approach would reassure consumers that their reasonable privacy expectations will be respected when they use the NII. Uniformity across the communications sector should encourage more consumer use of the NII which, in turn, would create and expand market opportunities for information and to service providers of all types. For these reasons, NTIA believes that it is in the private sector's interest to adopt the privacy framework outlined in this paper, without waiting for formal government action.

\*    \*    \*

# WHY WE MADE PGPfone, AND WHY YOU NEED IT

## Philip R. Zimmermann

It's personal. It's private. And it's no one's business but yours. You may be planning a political campaign, discussing your taxes, or having an illicit affair. Or you may be doing something that you feel shouldn't be illegal, but is. Whatever it is, you don't want your telephone calls to be intercepted or overheard by anyone else. There's nothing wrong with asserting your privacy. Privacy is as apple-pie as the Constitution.

The right to privacy is spread implicitly throughout the Bill of Rights. But when the US Constitution was framed, the Founding Fathers saw no need to explicitly spell out the right to a private conversation. That would have been silly. Two hundred years ago, all conversations were private. If someone else was within earshot, you could just go out behind the barn and have your conversation there. No one could listen in without your knowledge. The right to a private conversation was a natural right, not just in a philosophical sense, but in a law-of-physics sense, given the technology of the time.

But with the coming of the information age, starting with the invention of the telephone, all that has changed. Now most of our conversations are conducted electronically. This allows our most intimate conversations, both business and personal, to be exposed without our knowledge. Cellular phone calls may be monitored by anyone with a radio. Electronic mail can be routinely scanned for interesting keywords, on a large scale. This driftnet fishing approach has been readily applicable to email for a long time, but in recent years advances in voice recognition technology have begun to bring similar capabilities to filtering phone calls. Now the government can scan large numbers of phone calls for particular words, or for particular individual's voices. I'm not saying the government actually does this to domestic phone calls today on a large scale as a matter of policy, but they have acquired the technology nonetheless.

In 1991, Senate Bill 266 included a non-binding resolution, which if it had become real law, would have forced manufacturers of secure communications equipment to insert special "trap doors" in their products, so that the government could read anyone's encrypted messages. Before that measure was defeated, I wrote and released Pretty Good Privacy, my email encryption software that uses public-key encryption algorithms. I did it because I wanted cryptography to be made available to the American public before it became illegal to use it. I gave it away for free so that it would achieve wide dispersal, to inoculate the body politic.

The 1994 Digital Telephony bill mandated that phone companies install remote wiretapping ports into their central office digital switches, creating a new technology infrastructure for "point-and-click" wiretapping, so that federal agents no longer have to go out and attach alligator clips to phone lines. Now they'll be able to sit in their headquarters in Washington and listen in to your phone calls. Of course, the law still requires a court order for a wiretap. But while technology infrastructures tend to persist for generations, laws and policies can change overnight. Once a communications infrastructure optimized for surveillance becomes entrenched, a shift in political conditions may lead to abuse of this new-found power. Political conditions may shift with the election of a new government, or perhaps more abruptly from the bombing of a Federal building.

A year after the 1994 Digital Telephony bill passed, the FBI disclosed plans to require the phone companies to build into their infrastructure the capacity to simultaneously wiretap 1 percent of all phone calls in all major US cities. This would represent more than a thousandfold increase over previous levels in the number of phones that could be wiretapped. In previous years, there were only about 1000 court-ordered wiretaps in the US per year, at the federal, state, and local levels combined. It's hard to see how the government could even employ enough judges to sign enough wiretap orders to wiretap 1 percent of all our phone calls, much less hire enough federal agents to sit and listen to all that traffic in real time. The only plausible way of processing that amount of traffic is a massive Orwellian application of automated voice recognition technology to sift through it all, searching for interesting keywords or searching for a particular speaker's voice. If the government doesn't find the target in the first 1 percent sample, the wiretaps can be shifted over to a different 1 percent until the target is found, or until everyone's phone line has been checked for subversive traffic. The FBI says they need this capacity to plan for the future. This plan sparked such outrage that it was defeated in Congress, at least this time around, in 1995. But the mere fact that the FBI even asked for these broad powers is revealing of their agenda. And the defeat of this plan isn't so reassuring when you consider that the 1994 Digital Telephony bill was also defeated the first time it was introduced, in 1993.

Advances in technology will not permit the maintenance of the status quo, as far as privacy is concerned. The status quo is unstable. If we do nothing, new technologies will give the government new automatic surveillance capabilities that Stalin could never have dreamed of. The only way to hold the line on privacy in the information age is strong cryptography. Cryptography strong enough to keep out major governments.

You don't have to distrust the government to want to use cryptography. Your business can be wiretapped by business rivals, organized crime, or foreign governments. The French government, for example, is notorious for using its signals intelligence apparatus against US companies to help French corporations get a competitive edge. Ironically, US government restrictions on cryptography have weakened US corporate defenses against foreign intelligence and organized crime.

The government knows what a pivotal role cryptography is destined to play in the power relationship with its people. In April 1993, the Clinton administration unveiled a bold new encryption policy initiative, which was under development at NSA since the start of the Bush administration. The centerpiece of this initiative is a government-built encryption device, called the "Clipper" chip, containing a new classified NSA encryption algorithm. The government has been trying to encourage private industry to design it into all their secure communication products, like secure phones, secure FAX, etc. AT&T has put Clipper into their secure voice products. The catch: At the time of manufacture, each Clipper chip will be loaded with its own unique key, and the government gets to keep a copy, placed in escrow. Not to worry, though—the government promises that they will use these keys to read your traffic only "when duly authorized by law." Of course, to make Clipper completely effective, the next logical step would be to outlaw other forms of cryptography.

The government initially claimed that using Clipper would be voluntary, that no one would be forced to use it instead of other types of cryptography. But the public reaction against the Clipper chip has been strong, stronger than the government anticipated. The computer industry has monolithically proclaimed its opposition to using Clipper. FBI director Louis Freeh responded to a question in a press conference in 1994 by saying that if Clipper failed to gain public support, and FBI wiretaps were shut out by non-government-controlled cryptography, his office would have no choice but to seek legislative relief.

The Electronic Privacy Information Center (EPIC) obtained some revealing documents under the Freedom of Information Act. In a "briefing document" titled "Encryption: The Threat, Applications and Potential Solutions," and sent to the National Security Council in February 1993, the FBI, NSA and DOJ concluded that:

> Technical solutions, such as they are, will only work if they are incorporated into all encryption products. To ensure that this occurs, legislation mandating the use of Government-approved encryption products or adherence to Government encryption criteria is required.

In the aftermath of the Oklahoma City tragedy, Mr. Freeh testified before the Senate Judiciary Committee that public availability of strong cryptography must be curtailed by the government (although no one had suggested that cryptography was used by the bombers). A few months later, Senator Grassley introduced legislation that would outlaw placing cryptographic software on any computer network that might be accessible by a foreigner—in other words, any computer network. The only exception would be if the software were designed to escrow its keys with the government. At the time of this writing, the fate of Grassley's bill is still pending.

The government has a track record that does not inspire confidence that they will never abuse our civil liberties. The FBI's COINTELPRO program targeted groups that opposed government policies. They spied on the anti-war movement and the civil rights movement. They wiretapped Martin Luther King's phone. Nixon had his enemies list. And then there was the Watergate mess. The War on Drugs has given America the . . . largest per-capita incarceration rate in the world, a distinction formerly held by South Africa, before we surpassed them during the eighties even when apartheid was in full swing. Recently, we've seen the images and sounds of the Rodney King beatings, Detective Mark Fuhrman's tapes boasting of police abuses, and the disturbing events of the Ruby Ridge case. And now Congress seems intent on passing laws curtailing our civil liberties on the Internet. At no time in the past century has public distrust of the government been so broadly distributed across the political spectrum, as it is today.

If we want to resist this unsettling trend in the government to outlaw cryptography, one measure we can apply is to use cryptography as much as we can now while it is still legal. When use of strong cryptography becomes popular, it's harder for the government to criminalize it. Thus, using PGP and PGPfone is good for preserving democracy.

If privacy is outlawed, only outlaws will have privacy. Intelligence agencies have access to good cryptographic technology. So do the big arms and drug traffickers. So do defense contractors and some other corporate giants. But ordinary people and grassroots political organizations mostly have not had access to affordable "military grade" public-key cryptographic technology for telephone conversations. Until now.

PGPfone, like the original PGP, empowers people to take their privacy into their own hands. It seems that it is now once again time for direct action, before it becomes illegal to spread this technology. So here is PGPfone.

*Excerpted from:*

> Phil's Pretty Good Software Presents . . .
> PGPfone Pretty Good Privacy Phone
> Owner's Manual Version 1.0 beta 7–8 July 1996
> Philip R. Zimmermann (pages 7–10)

*   *   *

# PRIVACY IN CYBERSPACE: RULES OF THE ROAD FOR THE INFORMATION SUPERHIGHWAY

## Privacy Rights Clearinghouse

If you have access to a computer and a modem, then you are licensed to drive on the information superhighway. And you are one of a growing number of online participants. According to one study, over one-third of the nation's households now have a personal computer. Another study found that at least 24 million people in the U.S. and Canada have used the Internet.

The information superhighway can bring many benefits to our daily lives. Unfortunately, it may create many new threats to our personal privacy as well. Unless you know the privacy "rules of the road," your online activity may lead to significant privacy problems.

If you are new to online communications, turn directly to page 7 of this fact sheet for a list of online privacy terms. Otherwise, read on.

## WHAT ARE "ONLINE COMMUNICATIONS"?

"Online communications" are communications over telephone or cable networks using computers. Examples of online communications include connecting to the Internet through an Internet Service Provider (ISP), connecting to a commercial online service such as

Fact Sheet Number 18: Privacy in Cyberspace
Privacy Rights Clearinghouse, 5384 Linda Vista Rd. Suite 306, San Diego, CA 92110
Voice: (619) 298-3396, Fax: (619) 298-5681
E-mail: prc@privacyrights.org, Web: www.privacyrights.org

The PRC is a project of the Utility Consumers' Action Network. This publication was developed under the auspices of the University of San Diego.

America Online, CompuServe, or Prodigy, or dialing into a computer bulletin board service (BBS). Increasingly, the differences between ISPs, the commercial services, and BBSs are blurring. The larger commercial services and many BBSs now provide Internet access.

The Internet raises some unique privacy concerns. Information sent over this vast network may pass through dozens of different computer systems on the way to its destination. Each of these systems may be managed by a different system operator ("sysop"), and each system may be capable of capturing and storing online communications. Furthermore, the online activities of Internet users can potentially be monitored, both by their own service provider and by the sysops of any sites on the Internet which they visit.

ISPs, commercial services, and BBSs are managed by sysops who may have different attitudes toward online privacy. Additionally, there are a tremendous variety of activities provided by all types of online services, each of which may raise specific privacy concerns.

## WHAT LEVEL OF PRIVACY CAN I EXPECT IN MY ONLINE ACTIVITY?

Often the level of privacy you can expect from an online activity will be clear from the nature of that activity. Sometimes, however, an activity that appears to be private may not be. *There are virtually no online activities or services that guarantee an absolute right of privacy.*

### Public Activities

Many online activities are open to public inspection. Engaging in these types of activities does not normally create an expectation of privacy. In fact, according to federal law, it is not illegal for anyone to view or disclose an electronic communication if the communication is "readily accessible" to the public (Electronic Communications Privacy Act, 18 U.S.C. § 2511(2)(g)(I)).

For example, a message you post to a public newsgroup or forum is available for anyone to view, copy, and store. In addition, your name, electronic mail (e-mail) address, and information about your service provider are usually available for inspection as part of the message itself. Most public postings made on the Internet are archived in searchable databases. . . . Thus, on the Internet, your public messages can be accessed by anyone at anytime—even years after the message was originally written.

Other public activities may allow your message to be sent to multiple recipients. Online newsletters, for example, are usually sent to a mailing list of subscribers. If you wish to privately reply to a message posted in an online newsletter, be sure you address it specifically to that person's address, not to the newsletter address. Otherwise, you might find that your message has been sent to everyone on the newsletter mailing list.

You should not expect that your service account information will be kept private. Most services provide online "member directories" which publicly list all subscribers to the service. Some of these directories may list additional personal information. Even individuals with direct Internet accounts may be identified with commands such as "finger," which let anyone with Internet access find out who else is online. Most service providers will allow users to have their information removed from these directories upon request. Be aware that some service providers may sell their membership lists to direct marketers.

### "Semi-Private" Activities

Often the presence of security or access safeguards on certain forums or services can lead users to believe that communications made within these services are private. For example, some bulletin board services maintain forums that are restricted to users who have a password. While communications made in these forums may initially be read only by the members with access, there is nothing preventing those members from recording the communications and later transmitting them elsewhere.

One example of this kind of activity is the real-time "chat" conference, in which participants type live messages directly to the computer screens of other participants. Often these activities are described as private by the service provider. However, chatline users may capture, store, and transmit these communications to others outside the chat service. Additionally, these activities are subject to the same monitoring exceptions which apply to "private" e-mail (see next section).

### "Private" Services

Virtually all online services offer some sort of "private" activity which allows subscribers to send personal e-mail messages to others. The federal Electronic Communications Privacy Act (ECPA) makes it unlawful for anyone to read or disclose the contents of an electronic communication (18 U.S.C. § 2511). This law applies to e-mail messages. However, there are three important exceptions to the ECPA.

- The online service may view private e-mail if it suspects the sender is attempting to damage the system or harm another user. However, random monitoring of e-mail is prohibited.

- The service may legally view and disclose private e-mail if *either* the sender or the recipient of the message consents to the inspection or disclosure. Many commercial services require a consent agreement from new members when signing up for the service.

- If the e-mail system is owned by an employer, the employer may inspect the contents of employee e-mail on the system. Therefore, any e-mail sent from a business location is probably not private. Several court cases are pending which could affect whether or not work-related e-mail messages can be considered private. . . .

Once a sysop has intercepted e-mail for any of these lawful reasons, the sysop generally may not disclose the contents to anyone other than the addressee. Certain exceptions to this disclosure prohibition exist. These exceptions include when any party to the message consents to disclosure, when disclosure is ordered by a court, or when the message appears to involve the commission of a crime (in which case disclosure is limited to the appropriate law enforcement officials).

A sysop does not violate the ECPA if the message is *accidentally* sent to the wrong person. (However, the sysop may be responsible for damages caused by negligence in operating the service.)

Law enforcement officials may access or disclose electronic communications only after receiving a court-ordered search warrant. Only certain officials may apply for this order, and a detailed procedure is set forth in the ECPA for granting the order (18 U.S.C. §§ 2516–2518). These provisions are relaxed for messages that have been stored in a system for over 180 days (18 U.S.C. § 2703).

Remember. Your e-mail message may be handled by several different online services during delivery. The sysop of each of these systems may view e-mail under the above exceptions to the ECPA. Additionally, the message may be intercepted if either the sender or recipient consents. So, even if you do not consent yourself, the person you sent the e-mail to may have consented to the disclosure of the message.

## CAN ONLINE SERVICES TRACK AND RECORD MY ACTIVITY?

In a word, yes. Many types of online activities do not involve sending e-mail messages between parties. Internet users may retrieve information or documents from sites on the World Wide Web (WWW), or from "gopher" or "ftp" sites. Or users may simply "browse" these services without any other interaction. Many users expect that such activities are anonymous. *They are not.* It is possible to record many online activities, including which newsgroups or files a subscriber has accessed and which Web sites a subscriber has visited. This information can be collected both by a subscriber's own service provider and by the sysops of remote sites which a subscriber visits.

Many kinds of Web-browsing software deposit on your hard drive information, called "cookies," about your visit to that site. When you return to that site, "cookies" will read your hard drive to find out if you've been there before. (See page 8 for more information about "cookies" filters.)

Records of subscriber "browsing patterns," also known as "transaction-generated information," are a potentially valuable source of revenue for online services. This information is useful to direct marketers as a basis for developing highly targeted lists of online users with similar likes and behaviors. It may also create the potential for "**junk e-mail**" and other marketing uses. Additionally, this information may be embarrassing for users who have accessed sensitive or controversial materials online.

The practice of collecting browsing patterns is increasing. Online users should be aware that this practice poses a significant threat to online privacy. It is a good idea to contact the service provider and ask whether this type of information is collected on the system. Additionally, online users should educate themselves about what information is transmitted to remote computers by the software that they use to browse remote sites. Most World Wide Web browsers invisibly provide Web site operators with information about a user's service provider, and with information about the location of other Web sites a user has visited. Some Web browsers are programmed to transmit a user's e-mail address to each Web site a user visits.

Users who access the Internet from work should know that employers are increasingly monitoring the Internet sites which an employee visits. Be sure to inquire about your employer's online privacy policy. If there is none, recommend that such a policy be developed.

In order for law enforcement officials to gain access to subscriber transactional records, they must obtain a court order demonstrating that the records are relevant to an ongoing criminal investigation (Communications Assistance for Law Enforcement Act, 18 U.S.C. § 2703(d)). This provision prevents "fishing expeditions" by government officials, hoping to find evidence of crimes by accident.

## CAN AN ONLINE SERVICE ACCESS INFORMATION STORED IN MY COMPUTER WITHOUT MY KNOWLEDGE?

Unfortunately, the answer to this question is yes. Many of the commercial online services will automatically download graphics and program upgrades to the user's home computer. News reports have documented the fact that certain online services have admitted to both accidental and intentional "prying" into the memory of home computers signing on to the service. In some cases, personal files have been copied and collected by the online services.

It is difficult to detect these types of intrusions. The online user should be aware of this potential privacy abuse, and investigate new services thoroughly before signing on. Always ask for the privacy policy of any online service you intend to use.

## WHAT CAN I DO TO PROTECT MY PRIVACY IN CYBERSPACE?

When you are sitting alone at your computer, "surfing" the Internet, sending electronic mail messages and participating in online forums, it's easy to be lulled into thinking that your activities are private. Be aware that at any step along the way, your online messages could be intercepted, and your activities monitored, in the vast untamed world of cyberspace.

1. Your account is only as secure as its **password**. Create passwords with nonsensical combinations of upper and lower case letters, numbers and symbols, for example tY8%uX. Change

your password frequently. Never write it down or give it to someone else. Don't let others watch you log in. Never leave your computer logged in unattended.

2. Contact the sysop of any online service you intend to use and ask for its **privacy policy**. Most of the commercial services have written privacy policies which are provided to new subscribers. Also, carefully read all messages which appear on initial login. Many sysops notify online users in login messages that e-mail is subject to inspection. Many services require new subscribers to allow e-mail to be monitored as part of the sign-up process. All sysops should have a well-defined, written policy concerning privacy. Those that do not should be avoided.

3. **Shop around.** Investigate new services before using them. A good way to do this is to post a question about a new service in a dependable forum or newsgroup. Bad reputations get around quickly in cyberspace, so if others have had negative experiences with a service, you should get the message.

4. Assume that your online communications are NOT **private** unless you use powerful encryption. Do not send sensitive personal information (phone number, password, address, credit card number, vacation dates) by chat lines, forum postings, e-mail or in your online biography.

5. Be cautious of "**start-up**" **software** that makes an initial connection to the service for you. Often these programs require you to provide credit card numbers, checking account numbers, Social Security numbers, or other personal information, and then upload this information automatically to the service. Also, these programs may be able to access records in your computer without your knowledge. Contact the service for alternative subscription methods.

6. Note that public postings made on the Internet are often **archived** and saved for posterity. For example, it is possible to search and discover the postings an individual has made to Usenet newsgroups. . . . This information can be used to create profiles of individuals for a variety of purposes, such as employment background checks and direct marketing.

7. Be aware that online activities leave **electronic footprints** for others to see, both at your own service provider and at any remote sites you visit. Your own service provider can determine what commands you have executed and track which sites you

visit. Web site operators can often track the activities you engage in on their site, particularly at sites which ask you to "register" or otherwise provide personal information. Some Web browsing software transmits less information to remote sites than other software. You can avoid leaving tracks when you send e-mail messages by using anonymous remailers. . . .

8. If your online service allows you to compile a list of **favorite newsgroups,** or lets you arrange newsgroups by priority, be aware that your sysop can monitor that list. Do not place controversial or sensitive newsgroups in this list if you want to avoid being connected to particular issues.

9. The "**delete**" **command** does not make your messages disappear. They can still be retrieved from back-up systems.

10. Be aware that others' **online identities** are not always what they seem. Many network users adopt one or more online disguises.

11. Your **online biography,** if you create one, may be searched system-wide or remotely "fingered" by anyone. If for any reason you need to safeguard your identity, don't create an online "bio." Ask the system operator of your service to remove you from its online directory.

12. If you publish information on a **personal Web page,** note that direct marketers and others may collect your address, phone number, and any other information that you provide.

13. Be aware of the possible **social dangers** of being online: harassment, stalking, being "flamed" (emotional verbal attacks), or "spamming" (being sent frequent unsolicited messages). Women can be particularly vulnerable if their e-mail addresses are recognizable as women's names. Consider using gender-neutral online IDs.

14. If your **children** are online users, teach them about appropriate online privacy behavior. Caution them against revealing information about themselves or your family. . . .

15. Take advantage of privacy protection tools. There are several technologies which help online users protect their privacy. Discussed here are **encryption, anonymous remailers and memory protection software.**

ENCRYPTION    Encryption is a method of scrambling an e-mail message or file so that it is gibberish to anyone who does not know how to unscramble it. The privacy advantage of encryption is that anything encrypted is virtually inaccessible to anyone other than the designated recipient. Thus, private information may be encrypted, and then transmitted, stored or distributed without fear that it will be scrutinized by outsiders.

An encrypted e-mail message cannot be read by the online service sysop, or anyone else who has obtained the message legally or illegally. Therefore, any message containing private or sensitive information should be encrypted prior to communicating it online. Various strong encryption programs, such as PGP (Pretty Good Privacy) are available online. . . .

Because encryption prevents unauthorized access, law enforcement agencies have expressed concerns over the use of this technology, and Congress has considered legislation to create a "back door" to allow law enforcement officials to decipher encrypted messages. Users should be aware that the legal status of this technology is still unsettled. Moreover, it is against the law to export encryption technology to other countries (International Traffic in Arms Regulations, 22 CFR § 120.1 et seq.). However, its use within the United States is not currently restricted.

ANONYMOUS REMAILERS   Because it is relatively easy to determine the name and e-mail address of anyone who posts messages or sends e-mail, the practice of using anonymous remailing programs has become more common. These programs receive e-mail, strip off all identifying information, then forward the mail to the appropriate address. There are several anonymous servers available on the Internet. . . .

MEMORY PROTECTION SOFTWARE   Software security programs are now available which help prevent unauthorized access to files on the home computer. For example, one program encrypts every directory with a different password so that to access any directory you must log in first. Then, if an online service provider tries to read any private files, it would be denied access. These programs may include an "audit trail" that records all activity on the computer's drives.

## GLOSSARY OF ONLINE TERMS

*BBS*—Stands for Bulletin Board System. A local computer that can be called directly with a modem. Usually they are privately operated, and offer various services depending on the owner and the users. Often a BBS is not connected to a network of other computers, but increasingly BBSs are offering Internet access.

*Commercial Online Service*—A service in which users pay a certain fee to dial into what is essentially a very large BBS. These services provide a wide range of conferences, forums, software files, news and information, as well as e-mail service. Examples include Prodigy, CompuServe, America Online, the Microsoft Network, and others. Many of these services offer at least limited access to the Internet.

*Cookies*—A feature of many Web browsers defined as client-side persistent information. Cookies allow Web sites to store information about your visit to that site on your hard drive. Then when you return, cookies will read your hard drive to find out if you have been there before.

*Cyberspace*—The "place" where online activities occur. Commentators have noted that many of the activities that take place online are analogous to activities that occur in physical space. These online activities are said to take place in cyberspace.

*FTP*—Stands for File Transfer Protocol. A system of file storage on the Internet that allows users to upload or download entire files.

*Gopher*—A software program that archives files of information and displays the files in an organized directory which may be accessed via the Internet. These archives are called "gopher sites." Named after the University of Minnesota mascot, the golden gophers, where the software was developed. Gopher sites are being replaced by Web sites (see below).

*Internet*—An immense global network of computers. The Internet is not owned by any one entity, but rather owners of individual computer systems agree to participate in it. Users with an account with one of these computers generally may connect with any other computer on the network.

*ISP*—Stands for Internet Service Provider. A service which provides subscribers with direct access to the Internet. Some of the larger ISPs include Netcom, Pipeline, and Panix. Many small, local ISPs exist.

*Modem*—Acronym for *modulator/demo*dulator. Equipment which converts the digital signals of your computer (the '1s' and '0s') into analog signals which can be transmitted over the telephone network, and vice-versa.

*Newsgroups*—Newsgroups are lists of messages from users grouped by specific topics. Usenet is a network of thousands of these electronic conferences which may be accessed on the Internet. Most commercial services and BBSs have similar public forums.

*Online*—Connected to a computer network.

*URL*—Stands for Universal Resource Locator. URLs are unique addresses assigned to every location on the Internet. URLs for Web pages begin with the letters "http."

*WWW*—Stands for World Wide Web. This powerful tool for accessing the Internet combines graphics, "point and click" navigation commands, and a method of linking many different sites to allow users to quickly and easily search for information on the Internet.

*Web page*—A location on the World Wide Web which can be visited by Internet users employing software called a *Web browser.* Every Web page is identified by a unique address, called a URL. Publishing information on a Web page is a relatively simple and low-cost process. A collection of related Web pages maintained on a single computer system, or sometimes just a single Web page, comprises a *Web site.*

## FOR MORE INFORMATION

Several **public interest groups** advocate on behalf of online users. They also have extensive information about privacy issues available via their online archives.

**Center for Democracy and Technology,** 1634 I St. N.W. #1100, Washington, DC 20006. Voice: 202-637-9800 Fax: 202-637-0968 E-mail: info@cdt.org. URL: http://www.cdt.org.

**Computer Professionals for Social Responsibility,** P.O. Box 717, Palo Alto, CA 94302. Voice: 415-322-3778 Fax: 415-322-4748 E-mail: cpsr@cpsr.org. URL: http://www.cpsr.org.

**Electronic Frontier Foundation,** 1550 Bryant Street #725, San Francisco, CA 94103. Voice: 415-436-9333 Fax: 415-436-9993 E-mail: eff@eff.org. URL: http://www.eff.org.

**Electronic Privacy Information Center,** 666 Pennsylvania Ave. S.E. #301, Washington, DC 20003. Voice: 202-544-9240 E-mail: info@epic.org. URL: http://www.epic.org.

**NetAction,** 601 Van Ness Ave. #631, San Francisco, CA 94102. Voice: 415-775-8674. E-mail: akrause@igc.org. URL: http://www.netaction.org.

Several **online newsletters** discuss cyberspace privacy issues:

*Computer Privacy Digest:* CPD can be read as a Usenet newsgroup, *comp.society.privacy.* Alternatively, to receive CPD via e-mail, send a request to the newsletter's moderator at: comp-privacy-request@uwm.edu

*Privacy Forum:* For subscription information, send an e-mail message consisting of the word "help" (without quotes) in the *body* of the message to: privacy-request@vortex.com

To see a **demonstration** of the kind of information that can be compiled about you when you surf the Web, visit the site of the Center for Democracy and Technology: http://www.cdt.org. This site also has information about "cookies." And it lists the privacy policies of the major online service providers: AOL, CompuServe, Msnet and Prodigy.

To learn more about **"cookies" blockers** and other types of online filters, visit these Web sites:

http://www.privnet.com

http://www.wizvax.net/kevinmca/

To learn more about **anonymous Web browsing,** visit the Web site http://www.anonymizer.com.

To see examples of powerful **search tools** available to find public postings made on the Internet, visit these Web sites:

*Alta Vista* at http://www.altavista.digital.com

*DejaNews* at http://www.dejanews.com

To learn more about the **encryption** program PGP, contact these online sources:

"Where to Get PGP," compiled by Michael Paul Johnson. ftp://ftp.csn.net/mpj/getpgp.asc

"PGP Frequently Asked Questions with Answers," compiled by Jeff Licquia, http://www.prairienet.org/~jalicqui/pgpfaq.txt

For information about **anonymous remailers**, the following online resource is helpful:

> "Anonymous Remailers FAQ," compiled by Andre Bacard, http://www.well.com/user/abacard/remail.html

If your **children are online users**, request the free brochure, "Child Safety on the Information Highway," from the National Center for Missing and Exploited Children. Voice: 800-843-5678. You may learn more about "parental control" software programs by visiting the following sites. These online filters both limit the types of sites children can visit and prohibit online users from disclosing certain information like name and address.

> Cyber Patrol: http://www.microsys.com
>
> Cyber Sitter: http://www.solidoak.com
>
> N2H2: http://www.n2h2.com
>
> Net Blocker: http://www.netblocker.com
>
> Net Nanny: http://www.netnanny.com/netnanny
>
> SurfWatch: http://www.surfwatch.com

The major **federal and state laws** affecting online privacy are:

> The federal Electronic Communication Privacy Act of 1986, 18 U.S.C. § 2511 et seq.
>
> California Penal Code § 631 et seq., regarding wiretapping and recording telephone messages (known as the Invasion of Privacy Act).

The resources of the **Privacy Rights Clearinghouse** are available online:

> Web site: http://privacyrights.org
>
> E-mail: prc@privacyrights.org

*   *   *

# 6

## Censors Take On the Net

Libraries are no strangers to censorship. Because they provide a wide range of intellectual materials to the general public, questions of appropriateness are part of the library stock in trade. Libraries are also well prepared to respond to attempts to limit access to materials based on content. The American Library Association began developing policy relating to the censorship of library materials as early as 1929 and has a well-crafted and detailed set of policies that cover both general issues and modern dilemmas. In 1996 the Office for Intellectual Freedom issued its latest interpretation of the Library Bill of Rights, *Access to Electronic Information, Services, and Networks*.

Many other institutions, including colleges and universities, seem less equipped to respond to new threats to intellectual freedom. As use of the Internet became widespread in higher education, concerns about its content arose. And a surprising number of institutions responded by censoring student and faculty access to selected online materials.

It seems that each new technology brings out new fears about the danger of speech. The Internet has caused us to relive some of the basic battles about free speech, much as television and radio did in their early days.

# The Great Porn Debate

Many people first became aware of the question of pornography on the Internet after the July 3, 1995, *Time* magazine cover story on "Cyberporn." The eye-catching cover showed the shocked face of a young boy, lit by the glow of a computer screen. The article gave astonishing figures regarding the percentage of graphical files on the Internet that contained hard-core pornography and revealed connections between the sleazier side of the pornography trade and online services.

Unfortunately, most readers never heard the other side of the story. Within days, members of the Internet community had done their own research. The study used as the basis of the *Time* magazine article was revealed to be greatly flawed, possibly to the point of fraudulence. The author of the study had leaked his figures to conservative legislators and religious groups at the same time that he denied the same information to noted legal experts and members of the press. The author of the *Time* article, Philip Elmer-DeWitt, lost his credibility with the online community, although he bravely defended himself in discussions that took place on the Internet.

Although *Time* reported briefly on the controversy that its article stirred up in the online community, most readers were left with a greatly exaggerated view of the nature of sexually explicit materials on the Internet. The story, without the disclaimer of the flawed study, was repeated in other media. Even worse, it became the basis for legislation that would impose government censorship on online communications far beyond that allowed for the same content in the print world. The damage had been done.

## *The Facts of Life*

Let's be clear about this: yes, there is sexual material on the Internet, in the form of both pictures and text. And it is true that some of that material would be considered pornographic by at least some members of our greater community. Ironically, much of the material, especially the displayable pictures, are scanned images from previously published materials—materials that are constitutionally protected in their paper form.

Both *Playboy* and *Penthouse* have Internet Web pages that include playmate-style pictures as well as the famed articles that everyone always claims is what he really buys the magazine for. Some other sex-oriented sites are decidedly amateur, created and maintained by individuals who are simply fans of the genre. The sites vary from those that are mainly suggestive in nature (Bianca's Smut Shack) with little actual display of nudity or sex, to others that do have sexually explicit photos of the type found in "adult" magazines. Sexually oriented sites are very popular and get some of the highest hit rates (that is, number of visitors) on the Internet.

Material that is more explicit than *Playboy* or Bianca sometimes has a warning screen about the content of the site. A few have an entry barrier consisting of a registration process (in which the user declares himself or herself to be over the age of eighteen). Others require a paid subscription using a credit card. It is important to remember that pornography is a business with a normal profit motive; few serious pornographers would give away their products for free over the Internet.

Does this mean that your library users won't find sexually explicit materials on the Internet? No, those who have the greatest interest in these materials will use their new-found search skills to find them. But it is important to understand that sexual content will not be forced upon innocent users of the Internet. Access to materials online is by a user-initiated search process. Unlike our broadcast media like television and radio, the user really does have some control over the content that appears on the screen.

There is also sexual material on the Internet that has nothing to do with pornography, yet which some patrons might find objectionable. The Internet includes discussion groups on sexuality and sexual orientation that may or may not discuss the actual sex act. It is also a primary information resource for all types of medical information and research, some of which touches on sexual issues. There are support groups for people with HIV as well as discussions of childbirth and menopause. Sex is a big topic, after all.

## Not Just Sex

And there is other material on the Internet that is not related to sex but that might be disturbing to some library users. White Power groups have sites on the Internet to give information about their beliefs, as do social, political, and religious groups of just about every stripe. At one point the Simon Wiesenthal Center called for the censoring of White Power sites, naming them hate groups. This led to an interesting discussion of censorship in a whole host of Internet forums as users struggled with the idea that the principle of free speech necessarily includes speech that you might find distasteful or even dangerous. As the discussions wound down, the voices calling for a ban on White Power sites were fewer and fewer, and most users had come to the conclusion that censorship was more dangerous than racist speech.

More than once bills have been introduced in Congress to ban bomb-making information from online systems. This same information is readily available in hard copy, some of it produced by the U.S. Department of Agriculture, and often available in libraries. The argument for censorship in one medium rather than another is often that online systems make the information more readily available, and to a larger audience. These people seem to think that information is all right as long as it is hard to find and therefore doesn't circulate widely. What they fail to recognize is that a well-crafted online system makes *all* information more readily available, including that which might lead people to find constructive, peaceful means to achieve their goals.

## The Communications Decency Act

In 1995, at the time of the *Time* "Cyberporn" article, only about 10 percent of the American public had access to the Internet. So naturally the article was quite convincing to those people who had no experience with online communications. Making use of this ignorance and fanning the fears that were fueled by the mental image of an uncivilized and debauched virtual world, some legislators, most notably Senator James Exon, drafted the Communications Decency Act (CDA).

The CDA was added to the huge telecommunications deregulation bill being worked on in both houses. In essence, it made it illegal to transmit obscene or indecent material to anyone under the age of eighteen. The bill immediately gained the support of organizations promoting a return to family values, and was vilified on the Internet itself.

In spite of numerous protests from members of the Internet public and the attempts by some legislators to amend the bill to be more in keeping with current laws relating to challenged materials (especially those of sexual nature), the CDA was included in the version of the Telecommunications Bill of 1996 signed by President Clinton on February 8, 1996.

That very same day a first lawsuit was filed by the ACLU and nineteen other organizations challenging the CDA on constitutional grounds and requesting the court to block implementation of the law until this issue had been decided. A longer lawsuit was filed on February 26 by the American Library Association and twenty other organizations representing libraries, publishers, educational organizations, and public interest groups.

While the ACLU lawsuit emphasized the purely legal aspects of the CDA in relation to the First Amendment, the ALA-led lawsuit addressed a different aspect of the battle for control of the online environment. This suit recognized that most legislators and members of the judicial system had little or no experience with this new medium. As a matter of fact, at the time the CDA was passed into law, only about 7 percent of our legislators, those same people who voted it into law, even had E-mail addresses, and many fewer had ever "surfed the net." Senator Exon had someone else find the examples of online pornography that he used in his defense of the CDA, and admitted that he himself had never actually been online. So the ALA lawsuit spent a number of pages educating the court in the nature of the Internet—how it is structured, how it is governed, and who uses it.

The ALA lawsuit spoke to some of the popular misconceptions about the Internet that many nonusers embraced. In particular, it explained that the attempt to treat the Internet like our broadcast media of television and radio was based on a misunderstanding of the technology. Online, users must actively seek out information, so nothing appears on their screen that they haven't requested. The Federal Communications Commission is given control of broadcast communications precisely because the audience is not able to control the incoming content.

The Internet is unlike broadcast media in many other ways. For example, the content of our mass media is controlled by a relatively small number of large companies. The Internet has millions of individuals, organizations, and companies providing a notably wide variety of content. There is no centralization of control. This means that information seekers have a vast universe that they can plug into, not just a few dozen channels. Without any monopoly on information, there is very little legitimate reason for regulation of the content.

But when it comes to passing laws to govern the Internet, there is another important issue that we have to keep in mind: about one-third of the computers connected to the Internet are not in the United States and are not under U.S. law. The Internet itself, in its technical design, is virtually ageographical—it really doesn't care where on the planet an Internet site is located. In this sense, cyberspace really is a different place from Earth. Each computer linked to the Internet has a location relative to the structure of networks and subnetworks on the Net. And that's the geography of cyberspace.

Many of those protesting the passing of the CDA, including the ALA, were concerned about the effect of the CDA on this nascent telecommunications technology. With only a small percentage of our population online it is much too early to be censoring this medium. Censorship, by its nature, will change even the technological direction that we take in the future, perhaps eliminating ideas and possibilities that could be greatly beneficial. If we start building in ways to hold back information from some of our users, we may have to overlook technologies that could improve our online communications but that don't conform to the more restrictive laws we have passed.

The ALA was particularly concerned with the immediate effect of the CDA on libraries in this country. It could mean that libraries would have to know the true ages of everyone who uses the Internet on the library's computer network. This is a burden that most libraries today could not shoulder. And the CDA would require libraries to treat online materials differently than printed materials, because the restrictions required by the CDA do not apply to books, magazines, or other analog information resources. This could restrict libraries in their choices of resources to acquire, perhaps forcing them to favor print materials and thus cutting them out of the upcoming communications revolution.

The education of the judges continued in the courtroom in the Philadelphia Federal District Court as witnesses showed the court how searching was done. In the end, the approach taken by the ALA-led coalition was key to obtaining a highly favorable judgment. The judges not only found the CDA to be unworkable and unconstitutional in the Internet environment, they included in their judgment much of the background information they felt that other courts would need to understand the case. At the time of this writing, the fate of the CDA has been passed to the Supreme Court, which will decide it in 1997.

Although the Communications Decency Act has been defeated in a Federal District court, other threats to online communication are arising at the state level. In 1995 alone, nine state bills were passed that place limitations on speech over online services, and many times that number were introduced in 1996. It may seem unlikely that the laws of an individual state could be used to hold the world of Internet users liable, but for those over whom these laws are enforced the result is as powerful as a Federal law or international treaty.

Some of the state laws may have been promoted by legislators with little detailed knowledge of online communication. At times these laws address criminal behavior online already covered by current law, as if the legislators did not understand that the Internet does not place its users above the law. This frenzy of legislation could leave us with a legacy of laws that do not conform to the reality of cyberspace—and that we may spend many years untangling at some future time.

## Filtering: a Better Solution

We still, however, have the problem of how to best assure that children are not presented with grossly inappropriate materials when they are online. Fortunately, the same technology that makes these inappropriate materials available can be used to allow individuals a choice in what they access over computer networks.

There are a number of programs that can run on a personal computer that will block access to networked materials based on certain criteria. Aimed mainly at parents for home use, programs like Net Nanny and CyberPatrol simply will not allow some material to show on the computer screen. Filtering software of this type allows home users to limit access to materials in a networked environment without putting constraints on others. This kind of solution adheres to the U.S. court's desire to use the "least restrictive means" to achieve the goal of protecting children from inappropriate material.

Not all filtering programs work in the same way. Some keep lists of undesirable Internet sites that will be blocked. These lists must be updated frequently, since new information is added to the Internet constantly and keeping up with it is a full-time job for a staff of employees. Because of this, these programs are usually sold as a service that includes a subscription to the updates. The disadvantage of these products is that you must accept the manufacturer's blocking list. An example of this is that one of the first programs on the market was blocking all Internet sites and discussion lists that had homosexuality as their topic. Many of these did not discuss the sex act itself but were support groups for persons trying to understand their own sexual nature. After users protested this blanket ban, a finer criterion was used for including these discussions, and many people were satisfied. However, there are parents who don't want their children to have access to any information about homosexuality, considering it against their moral beliefs. There will clearly not be a single list that satisfies all users.

Other filtering programs have selection criteria built into them that analyze each document retrieved over the Internet. These programs use lists of words as well as information about online sites to make their selection on an ad hoc basis. Though this means that they can filter new sites that haven't yet been reviewed by the software producer, they can be quite imprecise because computers aren't at all good at understanding the context of human discussion. So at one point the White House online site was banned by a program because it discovered pictures on one page that had the names *couples* and *children.* This apparently was a red flag indicating possible child pornography. And there was the famous case of America Online's banning of the word *breast,* which then made it impossible for the breast cancer survivor's discussion group to function, and even caused some consternation in the culinary forums where breast of chicken is not an uncommon phrase.

There are also some hidden dangers in using a filtering program. Most of the manufacturers of commercial filtering programs do not reveal the list of sites that they block, considering that something of a trade secret. This means that parents are not really in control of what their children view online, the software manufacturer is. Since "appropriate" is a very value-laden concept, it could be hard to predict what actually gets filtered when you purchase a product. Users of Cybersitter, for example, reported that they were surprised to learn that they were unable to access the site of the National Organization for Women, even though it seemed not to contain any sexually explicit material. Many filtering services include nonsexual topics such as drugs, firearms, and violence. Depending on the service, parents can choose which topics are included in the filtering, but do not have a choice as to how the topic itself is defined by the software.

All of these solutions have the disadvantage that you are limited by the selection criteria of just a few services. To remedy this, the standards body of the Internet has approved the Platform for Internet Content Selection or PICS. PICS is a proposed software device that would allow any group to develop its own rating scheme for online resources. This means that you could make use of the rating scheme of your church, the PTA, or any other group with which you find you share a basic set of values relating to the information that you want members of your family to be exposed to. There could be as many filtering schemes as there are points of view in this country, at least in theory.

In practice, the PICS standard has not yet been implemented, though some software providers are working to incorporate it into their Internet browsers. The job of rating materials on the Internet is a large one, and it may be a while before organizations are able to develop their methodology for making their selections.

Filtering isn't just for families with children. It could be used in any situation where there is a reason to restrict Internet access to a limited set of resources. Employers are interested in making use of filtering to keep employees "on the job." They want to limit access to recreational sites, such as the sites that give up-to-date sports information and that are among the heaviest accessed sites on the Internet. Teachers could conceivably create filters that keep students' access related to their course materials, at least during class time.

## Using Filters in Libraries

Futurists talk about a time when each of us will have *bots*— intelligent programs that know us and understand our information needs. We will no longer spend our time surfing the Net because our bots will do it for us. Until that time (if it should ever come), we need a way, or many ways actually, to match up information seekers and information in the digital world. Filtering the incoming content isn't just an act of censorship—it can also be part of providing each user with the right materials. After all, we have children's books and adult books and the main reason for this isn't to keep children away from sexual materials. It's to give our younger readers books that they can understand and enjoy.

The filters that exist today are far, far from the vision of intelligent bots. And they aren't even as effective as the existence of the children's reading room. There is currently no way to individualize online resources for our patrons. Installing filters on library computers means limiting the access of all patrons to those materials deemed suitable for some patrons. The portion of the Internet that will be accessible will only be appropriate for a limited segment of the library's population. This definitely violates the library's philosophy of the intellectual autonomy of patrons, and puts the library in the untenable position of deciding what is right for everybody. A library with multiple online stations may be able to designate some for children and others for adults, only installing filtering software on the children's computer. Of course, childhood is not a single moment, and it may be difficult to satisfy the information needs of teenagers while providing a safe online environment for the youngest Net surfers.

If a library does decide to install one of the online filters, it will not have solved the problem of presenting inappropriate materials to its patrons. No one set of criteria will satisfy all patrons. Some parents will be concerned if their children are able to access any information about sex; others may be strongly opposed to their child reading about evolution. Already on the Internet some people have called for the elimination of sites advocating White Power, labeling this as hate speech. If these sites aren't blocked by the filtering program, the library may come under fire.

There is a danger that the use of filters will give libraries and their patrons a false sense of security. In fact, no filtering software is perfect and it shouldn't be trusted to be so. Parents who have been assured that their child will not be exposed to certain materials at the library will be doubly upset when this turns out to be untrue.

It would be foolish to assume that these filtering programs only block the inappropriate materials. In fact they can and do sometimes also block appropriate and useful information. And as we know from our library experience, it's very hard to know what you miss when information isn't retrieved. An example of this is with the Usenet discussion groups, of which there are well over ten thousand on the Internet, covering every possible topic of interest. The discussions in these groups are generally not under anyone's control, so they can cover a wide ground. Each group will probably have some instances of profanity or sexual reference, while the remainder of their content could be highly valuable discussions of science, politics, or the arts. Groups that deal predominantly with sexual themes are usually on the banned list, though only some percentage of the messages may actually contain offensive content. When the list of groups that falls under the hierarchy "alt.sex" is banned, it also eliminates "alt.sex.not," which is the discussion group for those who favor celibacy.

The use of filtering software in libraries, given the current state of that technology, would have a high probability of preventing library users from taking full advantage of the Internet. Considering the individuality of our information needs, these programs may be suitable in a home situation but may not further the mission of the library.

# Libraries As Leaders
# in the Censorship Debate

Because of our history as defenders of free speech, libraries have the potential to become true leaders in the debate over online censorship. Already the American Library Association has proven itself to be a major force through its work on the anti-CDA lawsuit. Libraries are working with a new generation of allies such as the Electronic Frontier Foundation and the Center for Democracy and Technology to fight against threats to free speech in cyberspace.

The lawsuit that ALA took to the Philadelphia court against the Communications Decency Act was a prime example of modern librarianship, and it proved that there is nothing more powerful than our libraries' role in educating the public and our officials in the value of free speech, both online and off.

**IN THEIR OWN WORDS**

**Frequently Asked Questions (FAQ) about the 1995 Communications Decency Act**
Voters Telecommunications Watch, August 26, 1995

> The Communications Decency Act itself was only a few lines of legal text in the midst of the more than two hundred pages of the Telecommunications Act. Those few lines, however, had far-reaching implications. This FAQ, written at the time by a strongly anti-CDA organization, attempts to explain some of the reasons for opposition to the Act.

**Internet Parental Control Frequently Asked Questions (FAQ)**
Voters Telecommunications Watch, 1995
http://www.vtw.org/pubs/ipcfaq

> This digital pamphlet turns the discussion of Internet content from one of censorship to one of individual choice. Though by now out of date in its details, it provides a useful categorization of the types of content control that are available.

**Access to Electronic Information, Services, and Networks: An Interpretation of the Library Bill of Rights**
American Library Association, 1996
gopher://ala1.ala.org:70/00/alagophx/
alagophxfreedom/electacc.fin

> An affirmation of the Right to Read extended to the digital environment. This document is essential policy for any library providing public Internet access.

### Further Reading

*Access to Electronic Information, Services, and Networks: An Interpretation of the Library Bill of Rights—Questions and Answers.* American Library Association, Draft 1.1. gopher://ala1.ala.org:70/00/alagophx/ alagophxfreedom/electacc.q%26a

> Based on the Interpretation, this series of questions and answers helps put the Library Bill of Rights policy on access to electronic

information in the context of actual questions one might be asked in a library setting. This should be essential reading for any member of library staff who has contact with the public.

American Library Association et al. ALA *Plaintiffs' Memorandum of Law in Support of Their Motion for a Preliminary Injunction*, March 1, 1996. http://www.cdt.org/ciec/injunction_brief.html

> This document explains in clear and plain English what the Internet is, and what is unique about it as a communications and information system. It then explains why it is that censorship of this medium is not only undesirable, it probably is not feasible. I like to think that this explanation was what won the case in the Philadelphia Federal court.

Hoffman, Donna L., and Thomas P. Novak. *The Cyberporn Debate.* http://www2000.ogsm.vanderbilt.edu/cyberporn.debate.cgi

> Hoffman and Novak chronicle the investigation into the career of Marty Rimm, the Carnegie-Mellon graduate student whose report on pornography on the Internet served as background material for the *Time* magazine cover story on July 3, 1995. Rimm comes across as no more than a shyster, and revised figures give a more balanced picture of sexually explicit materials on the Internet.

National Law Center for Children and Families. *Brief Filed by the National Law Center for Children and Families [et al.] in Support of Janet Reno, Attorney General, and the U.S. Department of Justice,* Philadelphia, 1996. http://www.cdt.org/ciec/NLC_brief.html

> If you followed some of the discussion of the CDA case on the Internet, you know that the case for the government (that is, pro-CDA) came off very badly, with some of the witnesses clearly not expert in Internet use or content. But some of the argument in support of the CDA was well thought out and clearly expressed, as you can see in this brief from the National Law Center for Children and Families.

## Internet Resources

American Civil Liberties Union. http://www.aclu.org

> The ACLU site is the best for keeping up with a variety of current court cases relating to censorship of online speech, especially those happening at a state level or below.

Larry Magid's Kids Page. http://www.larrysworld.com/kids.html

> Larry Magid writes for a number of computer-oriented publications and can always be counted on to take on the difficult social and political issues that others might shun. He authored the pamphlet "Child Safety on the Information Highway," which is distributed by the National Center for Missing and Abandoned Children. He was one of the first to defend both free speech and the concerns of parents.

Citizen's Internet Empowerment Coalition. http://www.cdt.org/ciec

> The CIEC formed in response to the passage of the Communications Decency Act and served as a focus for Internet opposition to the legislation. Its Web site carries a full history of the CDA and the battle to prevent it from becoming law.

---

# FREQUENTLY ASKED QUESTIONS (FAQ) ABOUT THE 1995 COMMUNICATIONS DECENCY ACT

## Voters Telecommunications Watch

### INTRODUCTION

The following FAQ contains everything you need to know to argue about the Communications Decency Act. The subtleties are easily lost on most people who think they know these issues, so please take the time to digest this information. Next time you get a call from a reporter, or are asked to do a radio show, keep a copy of this handy.

Changes/additions/corrections should be sent to vtw@vtw.org.

### BRIEF ANALYSIS

The Communications Decency Act (CDA) is a poorly thought-out piece of legislation intended to restrict the access of minors to indecent and obscene material on the Internet.

It fails to meet those goals. It would, however, succeed in chilling free speech such that public discussions would be diluted to the level

---

of that which is acceptable to children. Furthermore its whole approach is to treat computer communications as a broadcast medium, which fails to take into account the unique possibilities for parental control and "self-filtering" that are available to us in this medium.

Please watch these newsgroups and subscribe to vtw-announce @vtw.org if you want to stay abreast of these issues.

## DEFINITIONS

It's important when arguing that you're familiar with the terminology. This isn't an all-inclusive discussion of these issues; please refer to the relevant caselaw for more information.

OBSCENITY    Obscene material was determined as not deserving of Constitutional protection in *Miller v. California* (1973). In that decision, the Supreme Court provided a three-part test for determining if material was obscene.

1. Would the average person, applying contemporary standards of the state or local community find that the work, taken as a whole, appeals to the prurient interest?

2. Does the work depict or describe in a patently offensive way sexual conduct specifically defined by the applicable state law?

3. Does the work lack serious literary, artistic, political, or scientific value?

If a work satisfies all three of these tests, then a court may determine it to be obscene. Notice that the three-part test above does not specify which media the work might be viewed, created, transmitted or stored in. This means that every time a new technology that allows expression is invented, the laws governing obscenity are automatically in force for it.

INDECENCY    Indecent material is sexually-explicit material which may be offensive to some or may be considered by some to be inappropriate for children, but which is protected by the First Amendment. In *Sable Communications v. FCC,* the Court found that any regulation of indecent material must use the "least intrusive means" for accomplishing the government's goal of protecting children. The Court has stated that restrictions on indecency cannot have the effect that they "reduce the adult population to only what is fit for children."

Given the existence of software and hardware that enable parents to block children's access to indecent material the regulation here does not constitute the "least restrictive means" requirement set out by the Supreme Court.

What are some examples of "indecent" content? The most famous example probably is the George Carlin comedy monologue that was the basis of the Supreme Court case *FCC v. Pacifica Foundation* (1978). In that monologue, Carlin discusses the "Seven Dirty Words" (i.e., certain profane language) that cannot be uttered in broadcast media. Other examples of "indecency" could include passages from John Updike or Erica Jong novels, certain rock lyrics, and Dr. Ruth Westheimer's sexual-advice column. Under the CDA, it would be criminal to "knowingly" publish such material on the Internet unless children were affirmatively denied access to it. It's as if the manager of a Barnes & Noble bookstore could be sent to jail simply because children were able to wander the store's aisles and search for the racy passages in a Judith Krantz or Harold Robbins novel.

LEWD/FILTHY/LASCIVIOUS EXPRESSION OR SPEECH    These are all also Constitutionally-protected expression, although there currently exists no legal definition for what constitutes this type of speech.

PORNOGRAPHY    Unless this is deemed as "obscene," this is Constitutionally protected as well.

## MYTHS SURROUNDING THE (CDA) COMMUNICATIONS DECENCY ACT

**M** = Myth        **R** = Reality

**CDA** = the Communications Decency Act, aka the Exon bill, the Exon/Gorton bill, the Exon/Coats bill S 314, the Internet Censorship bill

### *Myths about Expression and Online Systems (Such as the Internet)*

**M:** Obscene material is currently legal in electronic form. The CDA is needed to bring electronic networks in line with telephone and broadcast media.

**R:** Distribution of obscene material is already illegal in any medium, existing or in the future. No new legislation is needed.

**M:** There's lot of "dirty stuff" on the Internet that's protected because current law doesn't work there. The CDA would fix that.

**R:** Obscene material is already illegal on the Net (or anywhere else). There's nothing for the CDA to fix.

**M:** The government has the right to control all speech in any electronic media through the FCC (Federal Communications Commission). They have previously done the very same thing for television and radio. This is just an extension to a new medium.

**R:** This is indeed a new medium. It is not a broadcast medium and should not be treated like the broadcast mediums the FCC currently is allowed to regulate. The government (and in particular the FCC) has only had content control over two specific types of media: (1) broadcasting media like TV and radio (and broadcasting-related technologies, such as cable TV), and (2) the narrow class of telephone-based commercial services that requires the assistance and support of government-regulated common carriers. (e.g., 900 chat lines).

In all other communications media, the government has no constitutional authority to impose broad regulation of indecent content.

**M:** The CDA is just an extension of the already Constitutional "Dial-A-Porn" statutes into this new medium.

**R:** The Dial-A-Porn statutes were specifically written for telephone communications. They deal in a communications medium that is specifically point-to-point. Online communication on the other hand is many-to-many and cannot fit the same model. In particular, the Dial-A-Porn statutes do not criminalize speech between two adults in a non-commercial conversation, whereas the CDA does.

**M:** The only effect the CDA will have is to stop obscene material on the net.

**R:** Since the CDA would be a US law, and networks do not acknowledge geographical borders, it is unlikely that the CDA will stop anyone outside the US from sending lewd, lascivious, filthy, obscene, or indecent information into networks that traverse the United States.

More importantly, the effect of the CDA will be to impose a chilling effect on speech on the Net, where only that which is appropriate for children is acceptable in public. Any discussion of

Shakespeare or safe sex would not be allowable except in private areas, where someone can be paid for the task of rigidly screening participants.

M: There's no way to control what my child can see, and I cannot be bothered (nor am I capable) of monitoring them while they're using the computer. This is the only way.

R: Several large service providers (such as America Online, Prodigy, and CompuServe) have special areas specifically for kids on their systems. In addition there are a growing number of products for restricting access to the Internet. Software that filters all forms of Internet content including World Wide Web, Gopher, News, and Email is already available for some platforms.

M: The government is the best person to tell me what my child can see.

R: Parents are the best people to evaluate what they want their children to see, whereas government censors are probably the least appropriate. In *Wisconsin v. Yoder* (1972), the Supreme Court acknowledged that the right of parents to determine what is appropriate for their children is Constitutionally protected.

M: This will encourage other countries to extradite their citizenry back to the US, if the citizen violates this law.

R: Non-US citizens will be theoretically liable if they commit any element of the crime in the United States (e.g., if the indecent content reaches a minor in the United States). Normally, this theoretical liability won't translate into an actual attempt at prosecution unless the defendant has a high Noriega Quotient. (There has to be strong political pressure backing the prosecution.)

## Myths about Harassment

M: The CDA simply makes it illegal to harass another person electronically ("knowingly makes transmissions that are indecent or obscene with the intent to threaten or harass another person").

R: Obscene or harassing speech which "threatens," is not Constitutionally protected. However, the CDA goes farther than that, prohibiting lewd, lascivious, filthy, obscene, or indecent speech even when it is intended to be "annoying" which is a Constitutionally-protected form of speech.

For example, if you wrote a letter to your Senator about his or her poor vote on the Exon bill, you might intend to annoy him.

### Myths about Liability of Service or Content Providers

**M:** The CDA makes each individual sysop responsible for the content they carry and provide to their users. This is not unreasonable, as you should be responsible for the material you store on your disks.

**R:** Even if a service provider took their entire staff and devoted them to reading all the email, news forums, and chat forums, that provider still could never be expected to keep up with the huge volume of information that travels the Internet every day. It is unreasonable to expect a service provider to be responsible for each piece of content that travels through or onto its systems.

**M:** The CDA says you're liable only if you "knowingly transmit or make available" this information to a minor. If you ask everyone on your system their age, won't this keep you from being liable?

**R:** No, it is a reasonable assumption that someone might not be telling you the truth. Simply asking age would not be strict enough measures.

**M:** I can claim I don't know the content of the stuff on the Net, because I can't possibly be required to read it all. Won't that protect me from "knowingly" transmitting it to a minor?

**R:** No, Senator Exon said he's found lewd, lascivious, filthy, indecent, and obscene material on the Internet during his investigation for the bill. If a Senator has noticed this, then you, an Internet Service Provider, should have too.

**M:** I don't actively send any data out, I simply leave it on a Web page for people to pick up. Therefore neither I nor my service provider are liable if a minor gets access to my web page and decides it is lewd, lascivious, filthy, indecent, and obscene.

**R:** The statute clearly states that you are responsible if you "make available" such information. You don't even have to be aware it is being downloaded to be liable.

**M:** If I'm providing a Fidonet or netnews relay for someone else, and I don't examine all the content, will I still be liable if someone downstream from me provides indecent content (that I carried for a time, however brief) to a minor?

**R:** Probably yes, though the statute leaves some room for interpretation.

### Typical Questions Asked by Reporters

This section is currently being completed. Please be patient.

## Bill Chronology

No more actions have been scheduled as of June 27, 1995.

Jun 21, '95 Several prominent House members publicly announce their opposition to the CDA, including Rep. Newt Gingrich (R-GA), Rep. Chris Cox (R-CA), and Rep. Ron Wyden (D-OR).

Jun 14, '95 The Senate passes the CDA as attached to the Telecomm reform bill (S 652) by a vote of 84–16. The Leahy bill (S 714) is not passed.

May 24, '95 The House Telecomm Reform bill (HR 1555) leaves committee in the House with the Leahy alternative attached to it, thanks to Rep. Ron Klink of (D-PA). The Communications Decency Act is not attached to it.

Apr 7, '95 Sen. Leahy (D-VT) introduces S 714, an alternative to the Exon/Gorton bill, which commissions the Dept. of Justice to study the problem to see if additional legislation (such as the CDA) is necessary.

Mar 23, '95 S 314 amended and attached to the telecommunications reform bill by Sen. Gorton (R-WA). Language provides some provider protection, but continues to infringe upon email privacy and free speech.

Feb 21, '95 HR 1004 referred to the House Commerce and Judiciary committees.

Feb 21, '95 HR 1004 introduced by Rep. Johnson (D-SD).

Feb 1, '95 S 314 referred to the Senate Commerce committee.

Feb 1, '95 S 314 introduced by Sen. Exon (D-NE) and Gorton (R-WA).

## ORGANIZATIONS OPPOSING THE CDA

In order to use the net more effectively, several organizations have joined forces on a single Congressional net campaign to stop the Communications Decency Act. The following list of groups are coordinating to stop the Communications Decency Act.

American Civil Liberties Union • American Communication Association • American Council for the Arts • Arts & Technology Society • Association of Alternative Newsweeklies • BiancaTroll productions • Californians Against Censorship Together • Center for Democracy and Technology • Centre for Democratic Communications • Center for Public Representation • Citizen's Voice—New Zealand • Computer Communicators Association • Computer Professionals for Social Responsibility • Cross Connection • Cyber-Rights Campaign • CyberQueer Lounge • Dutch Digital Citizens' Movement • Electronic Frontier Canada • Electronic Frontier Foundation • Electronic Frontier Foundation—Austin • Electronic Frontiers Australia • Electronic Frontiers Houston • Electronic Frontiers New Hampshire • Electronic Privacy Information Center • Feminists for Free Expression • First Amendment Teach-In • Florida Coalition Against Censorship • Friendly Anti-Censorship Taskforce for Students • Hands Off! The Net • Human Rights Watch • Inland Book Company • Inner Circle Technologies, Inc. • Inst. for Global Communications • Internet On-Ramp, Inc. • Joint Artists' and Music Promotions Political Action Committee • The Libertarian Party • Marijuana Policy Project • Metropolitan Data Networks Ltd. • MindVox • National Bicycle Greenway • National Campaign for Freedom of Expression • National Coalition Against Censorship • National Gay and Lesbian Task Force • National Public Telecomputing Network • National Writers Union • Oregon Coast RISC • Panix Public Access Internet • People for the American Way • Rock Out Censorship • Society for Electronic Access • The Thing International BBS Network • The WELL • Voters Telecommunications Watch

## WHERE YOU CAN GO FOR MORE INFORMATION

### Web Sites

URL: http://www.vtw.org/

URL: http://epic.org/

URL: http://www.eff.org/pub/Alerts/

URL: http://www.cdt.org/cda.html

### FTP Archives

URL: ftp://ftp.cdt.org/pub/cdt/policy/freespeech/00-INDEX .FREESPEECH

URL: ftp://ftp.eff.org/pub/Alerts/

### Gopher Archives

URL: gopher://gopher.panix.com/11/vtw/exon

URL: gopher://gopher.eff.org/11/Alerts

## E-mail

vtw@vtw.org (put "send help" in the subject line)

cda-info@cdt.org (General CDA information)

cda-stat@cdt.org (Current status of the CDA)

## Credits

Significant legal input came from Mike Godwin (mnemonic@eff.org) and Shari Steele (ssteele@eff.org) of the Electronic Frontier Foundation and Jonah Seiger (jseiger@cdt.org) and Danny Weitzner (djw@cdt.org) from the Center for Democracy and Technology.

Several coalition members contributed large amounts of text and suggestions to the document, including Andy Oram (CPSR Cyber Rights campaign), Bob Bickford (Libertarian Party), Anne Beeson (ACLU), Steven Cherry (Voters Telecommunications Watch) and Stanton McCandlish (EFF).

\*   \*   \*

# INTERNET PARENTAL CONTROL FREQUENTLY ASKED QUESTIONS (FAQ)

## Voters Telecommunications Watch (VTW)

## INTRODUCTION

Within the last few years the Internet has gained in popularity. With that growth came a whole host of mainstream issues, such as the growing presence of children and minors on the Internet. In order to assist parents, legislators, educators, and the public in learning what is available to you "today" we have put together this document.

In the solutions mentioned below, it is important to note not just what is desirable to parents, but to free speech advocates as well. A

---

solution agreeable to both parties will successfully flourish, while a solution highly unpopular with one or the other will never catch fire in the industry due to legal challenges or customer unhappiness.

The solutions below have been judged purely on their workability. Changes/additions/corrections should be sent to vtw@vtw.org.

## CURRENT METHODS

### Parental Guidance

As will always be true, the most effective method of getting comfortable with your child's Internet access is to guide them as a parent. No other human being except you knows best what is and isn't appropriate for them. By learning to use the Internet with your child (either one of you can teach the other) you can instill in them the values that you want them to use when selecting material in the Internet, or on television, radio, or in print media. The respect built between you and your child will function when no one is around, and will survive software upgrades, eternally-changing international law, and other unpredictable events.

This solution is supported as the best one by most reasonable parents and free speech advocates.

### Governmental Restrictions

Some members of Congress have introduced legislation to criminalize certain types of speech throughout the medium in order to shield minors from objectionable material. Although this plays well at the polls, it is not effective at addressing the issue of children's access to such material. As long as the Internet continues to be a global network, there will always be some one or more countries in which one can provide material that is out of the reach of US law and flies afoul of US expression standards.

In addition it is very difficult to write constitutional restrictions on speech, as we have learned from almost ten years of court testing of the Dial-A-Porn statutes. Governmental restrictions are not the answer to those serious about addressing the issue.

### Author Ratings Systems

On the technical side, several people have proposed "tagging" all items on the Internet with a rating similar to the American motion picture ratings. This scheme is also not a workable one, since even well-intentioned content authors will have difficulty rating their material in a manner that agrees with your values as a parent. In addition, malicious authors are under no pressure to rate their content correctly if at all. Although the next logical step would seem to be to make rating of content a statutory requirement, this quickly enmeshes one in all the problems described above in "Governmental Restrictions."

### Proof of Age/Shielding Systems

Recently there has been a growth in the number of systems that require proof of age before providing access to their content. This system still requires a judgement call on the part of those providing the content. This judgement call is by someone who has probably nothing in common with your ideals as a parent.

In addition, because they are a content provider they have a "disincentive" to make that judgement call impartially, since every user that cannot see their content reduces their audience (and potential revenues) by one person.

Similarly, many have suggested "encrypting" all traffic that might be objectionable to minors. Ignoring the lack of ubiquity and general exportability of encryption, this begs the question. Who decides what should be encrypted? If they assume everything, you still need to decide who is allowed to receive the keys to decrypt the traffic.

### Proprietary Environments

Several online systems have proprietary environments where content is screened as being available for the lowest common denominator of children. You, the parent, request that your child's account be placed into this environment. Because you the parent are paying the service provider for the child's account, they have an incentive to do it correctly as opposed to the ratings systems previously presented.

The major systems are treating this option as a customer-driven feature, fueled by requests from paying parent customers. It is a growing market and not likely to fade in the near future.

### Phrase Detection Systems

String detection systems are a method for setting up, ahead of time, trigger phrases and words. When these phrases or words are detected in the data stream (whether they're in a Web page, a file being ftp'd, or even in a chat session) the software can take an action to counter it.

It could shut down the computer, choose not to show it, hang up the modem, or many other things configurable by the parent.

### Third Party Ratings Systems

This is an extremely popular method of controlling children's access to content that has both the support of the market and free speech advocates. In all the previous ratings systems (the proprietary system notwithstanding) you have only two parties, the content producer (i.e., author of a Web page or a Usenet posting) and the content consumer (the child). In the third party ratings system the third party is an entity trusted by the parent of the consumer (the child) who goes out on the Internet and rates pages.

The parent has specially tinkered versions of Internet access software that understands and enforces the ratings system. Raters could be either the authors of the software themselves, or yet different third parties that are chosen by the parent. Indeed, the third party ratings system possesses the unique quality of allowing you to choose a ratings body that is closely principled with what you believe as a parent.

For example, the Metropolitan Community Church might wish to shield young people from any images of sexual images involving food, but explicitly allow pages about gay and lesbian teenage support groups. The Christian Coalition, on the other hand, may wish to place both types of information on their "not for children" list.

A crucial element to this is how you as a parent would want the software configured. Would you rather have every part of the Internet be unavailable unless deemed "appropriate for children" by your ratings groups? Or would you rather have every part of the Internet deemed "appropriate for children" unless a ratings body (that you trust to consistently net-surf) deems it "inappropriate for children"?

Most software packages allow you to do both. And that's the best part: unlike other communications technologies, consumer demand has driven entrepreneurs to produce third party ratings products far ahead of government calls for regulation, attempting to head off the problem before Congress feels the need to legislate a solution. You can obtain these products now, and in some cases, your child's school can obtain them free of charge.

## APPENDICES

## WHAT IS AVAILABLE RIGHT NOW

### *Parental Control*

Parental control (i.e., you giving your child guidance on what is appropriate) has been available for hundreds of years and continues to be the best approach to the issue of monitoring your child's use of the Internet.

### *Governmental Restrictions on Content*

*Federal level*

> June, '95: The Senate has passed the Communications Decency Act which addresses the issue from a governmental restriction approach. It does not avoid any of the pitfalls described in the above section.

> July, '95: The House has passed the Internet Freedom and Family Empowerment Act (420–4) which encourages industry solutions and third party solutions over censorship. Both bills (and other Title 18 amendments snuck in at the last minute) will have to be worked out in conference.

*State level*

> The following states have passed laws restricting content online: Connecticut (6/95), Georgia (3/95), Maryland (4/95), Montana (3/95), Oklahoma (4/95), Virginia (5/95).

### *Author Ratings Systems*

Several proposals for author self-rating of content on the Internet have been floated. Here is the list of proposals we are aware of:

> RSAC (Recreational Software Advisory Council on the Internet): this is a system whereby a webmaster can rate his or her pages by filling out a questionnaire at http://www.rsac.org/ which then returns sets of HTML tags. Authors can add these tags into their documents which can then be read by compatible browsers.

RSAC is compatible with PICS (see below). See the RSAC WWW site for more information.

"Voluntary Internet Self Rating" by Alex Stewart
(riche@crl.com) http://www.crl.com/~riche/IVSR/proposal.html

## Proof of Age/Shielding Systems

Many content providers are now requiring you to have a registration on file that proves you are over 18 before accessing their content. Some are using a credit card or an Internet FirstVirtual account number as proof of age. However, the same original problem applies: what incentive does the content provider have to keep objectionable material out of the hands of minors? (None; more restrictions diminish their advertising audience.)

## Proprietary Environments

**America Online** (AOL) offers parental blocking that allows the parent to limit a child's distinct screen-name to either a "Kids Only" area (recommended for children under twelve) or to just disallow Chat Rooms and Internet Newsgroups (for pre-teens and teens). "Kids Only" is a collection of educational resources and entertainment areas specifically designed for kids—it includes a range of AOL content areas as well as a pre-selected collection of child-oriented Internet sites. Message boards and chat rooms in Kids Only are monitored by AOL staff, who are recognizable by the prefix "KO" in their screen-names. A Teens-Only area is in development as well as tools that will allow the parent to select appropriate Internet sites at their discretion. AOL provides telephone help, detailed instructions and advice for parents who are the only ones who can change the control settings. In addition, parents can contact AOL to set billing limits on accounts. There is no additional cost for the service.

**Bess** (a.k.a. Bess.Net) is an Internet service provider designed specifically for kids, families, and schools. Bess provides access to most popular Internet services, including World Wide Web, FTP, Gopher, and e-mail. Bess blocks access to areas of the net that are inappropriate for children. Bess monitors new sites and adds them to the list of blocked sites on a daily basis; no maintenance is required on the part of the subscriber. Bess costs about $35/month for 30 hours of online time. Bess can be reached at:

Phone: 206-971-1400
E-mail: bess@bess.net
WWW: http://demo.bess.net/about_bess/the_service.html

**Netcom,** not a proprietary system, provides SurfWatch built-in to the NETCOMplete product. See the SurfWatch entry below for more info.

**Prodigy** subscribers are restricted from posting messages either in public forums or in chat rooms that are deemed inappropriate for children. This includes George Carlin's famous "Seven Dirty Words." Internet access from Prodigy is not allowed except with authorization from the parent account holder (using a credit card). In addition, Prodigy keeps a log of which sites the child has visited for parental review. Prodigy's parental control service is free.

**CompuServe** does not yet have parental control features available, but has announced two projects called KidNet and Internet In A Box For Kids. KidNet is planned to be a "child-safe" online service that will contain closely monitored interactive games, shopping, messaging, and chatting areas. Internet In A Box For Kids will contain a program called Crossing Guard, which will allow parents to control their children's access by blocking access to sites that may contain inappropriate materials. Crossing Guard will also allow parents to monitor their children's online activities and set timers to control when and how long their children can surf the net. Both products will not be available until Fall of 1995. The cost is not yet known.

## Phrase Detection Systems

**Net Nanny** is a parental control tool that allows screening of World Wide Web sites, newsgroups, and text messages. It is specifically parent configurable and screens material not only coming from the Internet but information your child sends back out to the Internet as well. It can also be configured to block access to files on the PC's hard drive, floppy drive and CD-ROM, to prevent a child from accessing and altering the parent's financial records, work related files, and programs and files intended only for adults. Net Nanny contains a log of all the child's activities for later parental review. You can contact the makers of Net Nanny at:

Trove Investment Corporation
Main Floor, 525 Seymour Street

Vancouver, BC, Canada V6B 3H7
E-mail: netnanny@netnanny.com
URL: http://www.netnanny.com/netnanny/

Net Nanny is generally available for less than $50.

## Third Party Ratings Systems

**Cyber Patrol** allows parents to restrict access to certain times of day, limit the total time spent on-line per day and per week, block access to specific Internet resources and sites by content (using Cyber Patrol's objectionable sites list), block or allow specific Internet resources and sites according to your own preferences, and control access to major on-line services and other local applications such as games and personal financial managers. You can contact the makers of Cyber Patrol at:

Microsystems Software, Inc.
600 Worcester Rd.
Framingham, MA 01701
Phone: 800-489-2001 or 508-879-9000
Fax: 508-626-8515
E-mail: info@microsys.com
URL: http://www.microsystems.com/

Cyber Patrol is generally available for $49.95 which includes a 6-month subscription to their blocked site list. Subsequent 6-month subscriptions are $19.95; 12-months, $29.95.

**CYBERsitter** filters pre-defined offensive Internet sites (WWW, Newsgroups, Chat Lines, FTP, etc.) that are maintained in a filter file that is updated regularly (almost daily) and available for all users to automatically upload as often as they like, for free. It also uses smart phrase technology to anticipate offensive sites as well as to block offensive words and language in incoming and outgoing e-mail. CYBERsitter also monitors and maintains an alert file of any offense that occurs and optionally can track every Internet site visited for the parent to review. You can contact the makers of CYBERsitter at:

Solid Oak Software, Inc.
Post Office Box 6826
Santa Barbara, CA 93160

Sales: 800-388-2761; Fax: 805-967-1614
E-mail: info@solidoak.com
URL: http://www.rain.org/~solidoak/

CYBERsitter is generally available for $29.95.

**INTERNET FILTER** is a parental control tool for Windows and Windows 95 that can be configured to block or log all data transfers including World Wide Web pages, newsgroups, types of messages within any newsgroup, Internet hosts known to have material objectionable to children, and Internet Relay Chat (IRC) sessions. You can contact the makers of INTERNET FILTER at:

Turner Investigations, Research and Communication
Box 151, 3456 Dunbar St.
Vancouver, BC, Canada V6S 2C2
Phone/Fax: 604-733-5095
Internet: bturner@direct.ca
URL: http://www.xmission.com/~seer/jdksoftware/

INTERNET FILTER 1.0 is generally available and costs $49.95 (Canadian funds). INTERNET FILTER Version 0 blocks everything but E-mail and can be obtained free of charge. To obtain Version 0 go to:

http://www.xmission.com/~seer/Turner/netfilt1.exe

**SurfWatch** is a parental control tool that blocks access to Web, gopher, and ftp sites that SurfWatch's team of net-surfers have deemed objectionable. SurfWatch's list of "not-for-children" sites is a subscription service updated through their site on the Internet. Updates are done automatically; frequency of updates is configurable by the parent. SurfWatch has announced a partnership with AOL and will be incorporated into AOL's proprietary interface. You can contact the makers of SurfWatch at:

SurfWatch Software
105 Fremont Avenue, Suite F
Los Altos, CA 94022
Phone: 415-948-9500; Fax: 415-948-9577
E-mail: press@surfwatch.com *or* info@surfwatch.com
URL: http://www.surfwatch.com

SurfWatch is generally available for less than $50 with updates available for $5.95. Netcom's NETCOMplete subscribers receive the initial software free of charge when they sign up for either a six or twelve month subscription to SurfWatch site updates. The NETCOMplete price for a six month subscription to the Surf-Watch site updates is $19.95 or twelve months for $29.95.

**ISCREEN** from NewView Communications is a third party ratings system that is coming up to speed. Although their WWW site has a lot of information, it still does not seem to answer the burning questions: is there a product, how much does it cost, and where can I download it? Nevertheless, the product, which employs a client/server approach, looks exciting. NewView can be contacted at:

NewView Communications
558 Brewster Ave.
Redwood City, CA 94063
Phone: 415-299-9157; Fax: 415-299-0522
E-mail: cji@newview.com *or* als@newview.com
URL: http://www.newview.com/demo/

**Netscape Communications** sells a proxy server which can be configured to restrict access to the gopher, the World Wide Web, ftp, and telnet on the Internet. Users are prevented from accessing sites which have been explicitly disallowed. No pre-screened list of sites is provided with the product, as the product is aimed at institutions. You can contact the makers of the Netscape proxy server at:

Netscape Communications
Phone: 415-528-2555
E-mail: info@netscape.com
URL: http://www.netscape.com/

The cost of the Netscape proxy server is unknown.

**WEBTRACK** is designed to allow institutions to provide their employees with restricted Internet access. Sites on the Internet are classified into 15 categories of World Wide Web, Gopher, and ftp sites (including sexually explicit material, games, gambling. job search information, drugs, online merchandising, sports, humor, and others). Institutional administrators then choose which categories they wish to restrict (if any). Logs of Internet access are also kept for later review. You can contact the makers of WEBTRACK at:

Webster Networks Strategies
1100 5th Avenue South, Suite 308
Naples, FL 33940
Phone: 800-WNS-0066 *or* 813-261-5503

Fax: 813-261-6549
E-mail: info@webster.com
URL: http://www.webster.com/

WEBTRACK is generally available for about $7,500. Updates of the site list are available on a subscription basis for $1,500 per year. WEBTRACK is free to all K-12 schools (kindergarten through 12th grade).

**Automated Collaborative Filtering** (ACF) is a proposal for linking up different users with common tastes (and distastes) and helping them share their collective Web page ratings. The proposal is extremely interesting to fans of filtering technology, but offers no immediate assistance to parents wishing to control their children's access to the net. The proposal can be found at URL: http://wex.www.media.mit.edu/people/wex/rate-proposal.html

The **Home & School Internet Foundation** is being created under a charter that would include both third-party ratings and an Internet author ratings system. They can be contacted at:

David Porte, Sr. Managing Partner
Astrolabe Group, Inc.
Phone: 206-814-9441 *or* 800-910-0227
Fax: 206-814-9442
E-mail: astrolabe@astrolabe.com
URL: http://www.astrolabe.com/home_and_school

**NoCeM** (pronounced "No See 'Em") is a system whereby a person can post metadata to Usenet about other people's postings. Given the amount of spamming that's been happening lately, NoCeM is certainly an exciting possibility for controlling not only that, but all forms of content without actually impacting the poster of such information. Don't take our word for it though, learn about NoCeM at URL: http://www.cm.org/faq.html

**Platform for Internet Content Selection** (PICS) is an industry-endorsed proposal from the World Wide Web Consortium for author and third-party ratings done in a standard format. The press releases can be found at URL: http://www.w3.org/pub/WWW/PICS/

An **IETF Working Group** has been formed to address the possibility of advancing an Internet Draft for providing ratings of Internet resources. The working group mailing list moderator can be contacted at owner-vac-wg@naic.nasa.gov.

**Safesurf** is a proposed rating system and software development effort. The software is not available yet, but you can self-rate your pages through their WWW site. You can learn more about it at URL: http://www.safesurf.com/wave/

## CREDITS

Almost all of the original product research for parental control tools was done by the Center for Democracy and Technology (info@cdt.org). Carl Kadie (kadie@eff.org), Jonah Seiger of CDT (jseiger@cdt.org), Anne Beeson of the American Civil Liberties Union (beeson@aclu.org) and Steven Cherry of the Voters Telecommunications Watch did heavy editing and proofing. Contributions were made by many people, including Alan Wexelblat <wex@media.mit.edu> and Andy Oram (andyo@ora.com).

Feedback and questions about reuse of this FAQ should be sent to the authors at: <vtw@vtw.org>

\* \* \*

# ACCESS TO ELECTRONIC INFORMATION, SERVICES, AND NETWORKS: AN INTERPRETATION OF THE LIBRARY BILL OF RIGHTS

## American Library Association

## INTRODUCTION

The world is in the midst of an electronic communications revolution. Based on its constitutional, ethical, and historical heritage, American librarianship is uniquely positioned to address the broad range of information issues being raised in this revolution. In particular, librarians address intellectual freedom from a strong ethical base and an abiding commitment to the preservation of the individual's rights.

Freedom of expression is an inalienable human right and the foundation for self-government. Freedom of expression encompasses the freedom of speech and the corollary right to receive information. These rights extend to minors as well as adults. Libraries and librarians exist to facilitate the exercise of these rights by selecting, producing, providing access to, identifying, retrieving, organizing, providing instruction in the use of, and preserving recorded expression regardless of the format or technology.

The American Library Association expresses these basic principles of librarianship in its *Code of Ethics* and in the *Library Bill of Rights* and its Interpretations. These serve to guide librarians and library governing bodies in addressing issues of intellectual freedom that arise when the library provides access to electronic information, services, and networks.

Issues arising from the still-developing technology of computer-mediated information generation, distribution, and retrieval need to be approached and regularly reviewed from a context of constitutional principles and ALA policies so that fundamental and traditional tenets of librarianship are not swept away.

Electronic information flows across boundaries and barriers despite attempts by individuals, governments, and private entities to channel or control it. Even so, many people, for reasons of technology, infrastructure, or socio-economic status do not have access to electronic information.

In making decisions about how to offer access to electronic information, each library should consider its mission, goals, objectives, cooperative agreements, and the needs of the entire community it serves.

## THE RIGHTS OF USERS

All library system and network policies, procedures, or regulations relating to electronic resources and services should be scrutinized for potential violation of user rights.

User policies should be developed according to the policies and guidelines established by the American Library Association, including *Guidelines for the Development and Implementation of Policies, Regulations and Procedures Affecting Access to Library Materials, Services, and Facilities.*

Users should not be restricted or denied access for expressing or receiving constitutionally protected speech. Users' access should not be changed without due process, including, but not limited to, formal notice and a means of appeal.

Although electronic systems may include distinct property rights and security concerns, such elements may not be employed as a subterfuge to deny users access to information. Users have the right to be free of unreasonable limitations or conditions set by libraries, librarians, system administrators, vendors, network service providers, or others. Contracts, agreements, and licenses entered into by libraries on behalf of their users should not violate this right. Users also have a right to information, training, and assistance necessary to operate the hardware and software provided by the library.

Users have both the right of confidentiality and the right of privacy. The library should uphold these rights by policy, procedure, and practice. Users should be advised, however, that because security is technically difficult to achieve, electronic transactions and files could become public.

The rights of users who are minors shall in no way be abridged. (See: *Free Access to Libraries for Minors: An Interpretation of the Library Bill of Rights; Access to Resources and Services in the School Library Media Program;* and *Access for Children and Young People to Videotapes and Other Nonprint Formats.*)

## EQUITY OF ACCESS

Electronic information, services, and networks provided directly or indirectly by the library should be equally, readily, and equitably accessible to all library users. American Library Association policies oppose the charging of user fees for the provision of information services by all libraries and information services that receive their major support from public funds (50.3; 53.1.14; 60.1; 61.1). It should be the goal of all libraries to develop policies concerning access to electronic resources in light of *Economic Barriers to Information Access: An Interpretation of the Library Bill of Rights* and *Guidelines for the Development and Implementation of Policies, Regulations, and Procedures Affecting Access to Library Materials, Services, and Facilities.*

## INFORMATION RESOURCES AND ACCESS

Providing connections to global information, services, and networks is not the same as selecting and purchasing material for a library collection. Determining the accuracy or authenticity of electronic information may present special problems. Some information accessed electronically may not meet a library's selection or collection development policy. It is, therefore, left to each user to determine what is appropriate. Parents and legal guardians who are concerned about their children's use of electronic resources should provide guidance to their own children.

Libraries and librarians should not deny or limit access to information available via electronic resources because of its allegedly controversial content or because of the librarian's personal beliefs or fear of confrontation. Information retrieved or utilized electronically should be considered constitutionally protected unless determined otherwise by a court with appropriate jurisdiction.

Libraries, acting within their mission and objectives, must support access to information on all subjects that serve the needs or interests of each user, regardless of the user's age or the content of the material. Libraries have an obligation to provide access to government information available in electronic format. Libraries and librarians should not deny access to information solely on the grounds that it is perceived to lack value.

In order to prevent the loss of information, and to preserve the cultural record, libraries may need to expand their selection or collection development policies to ensure preservation, in appropriate formats, of information obtained electronically.

Electronic resources provide unprecedented opportunities to expand the scope of information available to users. Libraries and librarians should provide access to information presenting all points of view. The provision of access does not imply sponsorship or endorsement. These principles pertain to electronic resources no less than they do to the more traditional sources of information in libraries. (See: *Diversity in Collection Development: An Interpretation of the Library Bill of Rights*)

\* \* \*

# 7

# Accessing the
# Digital Universe

Everyone is for universal access. The telephone companies, the cable companies, the entertainment megacompanies, the libraries, and the public interest groups all have stated their desire for universal access. When you see so much agreement among a range of institutions, you wonder if they are all talking about the same thing.

Some of the confusion in discussions about the Information Highway is that the parties aren't always referring to the same technology. People involved in the telephone system are usually thinking primarily of point-to-point communications, like the telephone; those in the broadcast industries naturally emphasize the functions that bring audiovideo entertainment to the public; and we in the library and education fields see mainly the information delivery aspects. The fact is that in the future all of these functions may be rolled into a single digital service, and may not even be seen by users as separate.

The principle of universal access that appears in *The National Information Infrastructure: Agenda for Action* (see In Their Own Words, Chapter 2) recognizes that it is access to the content that is important:

> Extend the "universal service" concept to ensure that information resources are available to all at affordable prices. Because information means empowerment, the government has a duty to ensure that all Americans have access to the resources of the Information Age.

Note that the document says information resources are to be available, not just the highway itself. While we cannot know how conscious this was on the part of the authors of that document, it is a common assumption that the future of communications is a mixture of transport and content. The telecommunications companies today have expressed a strong interest in being content providers, not just message transport systems. So the universal access of the future will not be the same as the telephone's universal service, which consists solely of the wiring that messages will travel across. What it will look like, however, is yet to be determined.

## Universal Access/Universal Service

In 1934 Congress passed telecommunications legislation that mandated equal access to telephone service for all U.S. residents. The concept of universal service in the telephone market had as much to do with the natural monopoly of the telephone system as it did with the belief that everyone in the country "deserved" phone service. The telephone today is more than a luxury, and universal service is now seen as being a reflection of the importance of the telephone in our society. We know that having a telephone at home makes a difference in terms of economic opportunities (for example, it is very hard to apply for employment if you can't receive phone calls from your prospective employer). And the telephone is everyone's primary access to emergency services.

Universal telephone service does not guarantee that every home will have a working phone. As a matter of fact, only 93 percent of U.S. households do have a telephone. Instead, universal service regulates the cost of service so that prices are equally applied to customers, regardless of the cost of providing service to any one area or individual. This means that rural customers pay the same as urban ones even though the actual cost to the telephone companies is greater for providing access to their rural customers. The more expensive rural service is subsidized by an overcharge on other services, such as business services or long-distance rates.

### Universal Access and the Information Highway

The Information Highway was not always seen as a candidate for universal access. Not so long ago, computers and computer networks were only used by a small portion of our population. As a matter of fact, when Senator Albert Gore first used the term Information Highway, he was not referring to a popular technology. He used the phrase to describe an elite telecommunications system that would serve the nation's supercomputer centers and the sciences that employ them. It was 1988, and he was introducing the High Performance Computing Act that would create a high-speed connection between U.S. supercomputer centers. The bill was amended to include the higher education community and from then on referred to as the National Research and Education Network, or NREN.

Before the NREN bill reached a vote, Congressman Frederick C. Boucher (D-Va.) introduced amendments that would extend the benefits of the NREN to the remaining educational levels. He argued that in this modern world it is not sufficient to limit access to computer networking to universities—all of our students need to learn how to use this technology and can benefit from the resources it makes available. Senator Boucher's bill also included access for medical services and for libraries.

Though Boucher's amendments were not included in the version of the NREN bill that passed in late 1991, he had planted the idea that the Information Highway has a public role to fulfill. Over the next few years, with the rapid growth of the Internet, his vision of a broader role for computer networks in our society became a commonly held assumption.

## Defining the Information Highway

Not unlike the early days of the telephone, we don't yet know how computer technologies will develop as they are used. Alexander Graham Bell originally expected the telephone to be a broadcast medium, and he demonstrated it in halls and parlors as a way for people to listen to music being played in another part of town. When it became clear that the telephone was more suited to one-to-one communication, it was marketed to businesses and professionals as a business tool. The first users were doctors and shops, and later upper-middle-class housewives were encouraged to use the phone to conduct their household duties more efficiently.

In the early part of this century, telephone companies were horrified to learn that the phones installed in private residences were being used as frequently for social purposes as for practical activities. Campaigns were waged to discourage this "frivolous" use of the valuable telephone resource. But it wasn't long before the phone companies realized that their market was driven by the human need to keep in touch with others and that catering to this need gave them the widest possible market for their product.

Telecommunications technology in the computer age may undergo a similar transformation. While online systems advertise their large libraries of files and informational databases, time and again users have shown that communications functions like real-time chat, discussion groups, and electronic mail are the ones with the greatest appeal. One commercial database system, Prodigy, was nearly driven out of business because it misjudged the services that users would prefer and assumed that online shopping revenues would pay for free electronic mail services. Instead, users sent hundreds of thousands of E-mail messages each month, and Prodigy had to start charging for E-mail use just to stay alive.

Though there is much that we can learn from the history of the telephone, computer communications technologies undoubtedly still hold their own surprises for us. These new digital technologies differ from the telephone in that they offer a much wider range of services and functions. While nearly all telephone communication is one-to-one, with one person at each end of the line, computer communication is frequently one-to-many, as when a user posts a discussion list that is read by anywhere from a handful of others to thousands. The telephone is designed only for conversation, and for that to take place both participants in the conversation must be connected at the same time. Computer communications are primarily "asynchronous," that is, the sender and the recipient perform their roles at different times. Electronic mail is an example of asynchronous communication—the recipient does not need to be logged on at the time that the mail is sent. Instead, the mail waits in the receiver's mailbox until it is retrieved at her convenience. Although electronic mail may take the form of a conversation, it is different from the conversation that takes place when two people can speak at the same time.

The information retrieval function of computer systems is also much more sophisticated than any analogous function over the telephone. Using the telephone, the IRS voicemail system allows you to key in a number and hear a prerecorded report on a particular tax question, but the total number of questions that can be answered in this way is actually quite small. Computer systems can provide access to highly complex databases, to pictures and diagrams, and to documents that would be much too lengthy to be presented orally.

## POTS on the Information Highway

Many discourses on access to the Information Highway emphasize wiring our cities for data communications and getting computer equipment into every home. But it would be a mistake to define access in terms of hardware—a definition of this type becomes out of date in a matter of a few years, if not months. At best we can describe access in terms of services or functions.

Universal service and universal access may not be the same thing, though the expressions are often used interchangeably. The Clinton administration's document *Agenda for Action* calls for universal access to the information infrastructure but doesn't define what either *universal* or *access* mean in this context. In the language of telephone service, universal service means equal access to plain old telephone service or POTS. The telephone company is not obligated to provide all services to all customers beyond the basic POTS.

We don't know what POTS will be on the Information Highway, but it will have to be more than just the plain voice communication that the telephone provides today. And although we talk about the *Information* Highway, the future technology will most certainly provide for information services, broadcast media, and a variety of communication capabilities using text, voice, and pictures. This complicates the assessment of universal access because there will probably be many levels of service, some of which will be used for entertainment as well as information and communication services. Defining basic service requirements is going to be very difficult.

# The Functions of Universal Access

### Personal Communications

Personal communications on today's Internet are conducted in writing though electronic mail. But already there are the beginnings of voice and video communication technologies that will allow us to use the Internet much as we use the telephone and video conferencing.

A RAND report (see In Their Own Words in this chapter) suggests that at the very least we need the capability of universal E-mail. Electronic mail is generally considered to be the most basic function for participation in online services. It can be done with the least expensive of today's computer equipment, even equipment that is out of date for other activities like accessing the World Wide Web. Many

Internet functions that were not originally usable through an E-mail interface have been modified so that E-mail users can take advantage of them. For example, systems offering documents for downloading over the Internet can make these available through E-mail by accepting a request and returning the document to the E-mail account of the requester.

### Group Communications

It is also through the E-mail function that online users participate in discussion groups of various types. Each person in the group can write an E-mail message that can be read by anyone else participating in the discussion. Others can then reply to that message, and reply to the replies ad infinitum. Discussions take place on a wide variety of topics, and there are tens of thousands of such groups on the Internet today.

This communication is known as many-to-many, as opposed to the one-to-one of the telephone or even of private electronic mail. Discussions range from the academic to the practical; from the professional to the personal. There are support groups for people suffering from illness, groups that serve as alert services on current events, and groups for a wide variety of pastimes and hobbies. It is through this many-to-many interaction that online communities are formed. These communities transcend the normal boundaries of geography and are also known for allowing persons of different ages and backgrounds to find a common ground.

### Information Retrieval

There are two basic requirements for information retrieval services to be successful: first, the information you need has to be available through the service; and second, you have to be able to find that information.

New users of the Internet often come to it expecting that it contains all information in the known universe. They are disappointed to find that isn't so. As an information system, the Internet is still somewhat idiosyncratic since nearly all content is provided by the users themselves. There is no global plan that guides the content of the Internet, and no such policy is planned for the Information Highway. Yet so much depends on the quality of our future information services that leaving it up to chance does not seem wise. Great numbers of documents are insufficient if they don't provide the quality and variety of information that is needed by the users.

It doesn't matter if the information you need does exist if you can't find it. We hear the expression *information overload* in reference to the huge amount of material on the Internet, but what overloads us is that we cannot retrieve relevant information resources from the many thousands of nonrelevant or less relevant ones. Well-crafted information retrieval is an essential component of the Information Highway, but it is one we have yet to achieve. Because creating such systems is likely to be expensive, we could find ourselves in a situation where the information retrieval function is beyond the reach of some people unless it is included in a universal access package.

### Information Providing

Many users are able to make their information accessible to the entire Internet community with a minimum of expense or technical effort. An example of this is the personal Web page. A personal Web page can carry any content that the user chooses to make available, and can point to other pages on other computers that the person wishes to highlight. In the academic community researchers use this capability to advertise their current research to others in their field. Other Internet users develop Web pages that relate to their hobbies or personal interests.

It is this ability for users to place their own content on the Internet that sets this era of communications technology apart from that which has gone before. Until now we have had personal communication media—where we communicate privately by mail or over the telephone often to only one other person—and we have had the broadcast media, which are one-to-many communications with a limited number of channels dominated by very large, corporate content providers. Traditional publishing allows more individuals to make their ideas public, but the number of us who can participate is still very small.

With computer networks there is no limitation on how many people can be information providers. Unlike television or radio, there can be as many channels as there are users on the system. With this technology we can hear the voices of many members of our society who have not been represented by mass media. For this reason, today's definition of universal access must include the ability to be a provider of information as well as a consumer. The Internet model, where everyone has the capability to provide information at a reasonable cost, assures the wide range of information needed in a diverse society. If the technology and the costs do not inhibit the provision of information, even the smallest communities of interest will be able to respond to their own information needs. Our success at achieving universal access could be measured by the extent to which the information needs of all of our communities are met: rural and urban; ethnic and linguistic groups; and communities of interest.

### Civic Participation

Many people tout the Information Highway as having the potential to open a new era of democracy. As our country has grown, it has become increasingly difficult for individuals to have a voice in the running of the nation, and we have even lost some of our mechanisms for participation in our own communities. We know that there are many fewer community newspapers today than there were fifty years ago. This means that community information is less readily available since it is unlikely to be covered by the large metropolitan daily papers that most of us read. Radio and television stations have also undergone a consolidation, and each covers a wide geographic and social area. Community networks can re-create the traditional town meeting by providing a forum for open discussion of local issues.

The Internet has shown that online networking can be used for political organizing on a national scale. Most of the campaigns waged there so far have been ones of specific interest to the Internet community, such as the protests against the adoption of the Clipper Chip encryption standard in 1995, and the battle against the Communications Decency Act. The kind of rapid communication that networking allows has proven to be a powerful tool through which notices of votes in legislatures have the potential of reaching many thousands of interested people in a matter of seconds.

The more that we use electronic communications for this kind of political activity, of course, the more vital it is that it be accessible to everyone. Otherwise those people who are not online will find themselves outside the political debate that is a fundamental characteristic of our particular form of democracy.

# Paying for Universal Access

## Funding Models

Universal service, in the telephone world, is funded through an elaborate system of robbing Peter to pay Paul. Services beyond the plain old telephone service are surcharged to keep the rates of the basic service artificially low. Many people object to these subsidies because they are not made explicit, and most telephone users are unaware that their long-distance charges might be lower if universal service were not required by Federal regulation.

This model of subsidized funding does not work outside the monopoly of the telephone system. The problem is that when different companies compete in the wide variety of services that we envision for the Information Highway, Peter and Paul will most likely be competitors who have no interest in funding each other's basic rates. Definitions of universal service and how that will be funded are being discussed at a national level. The decision will be finalized through a series of Federal Communications Commission rulings that have resulted from the passage of the Telecommunications Act of 1996. These rulings are significant because they will affect the development and affordability of the Information Highway.

None of these rulings tell us how we will finance the content of the Information Highway. While entertainment content will undoubtedly thrive through consumer payments and advertising, we have no plan to help us deliver the many kinds of critical information that won't be of interest to the commercial information vendors. This includes public health information, the full range of community social services, and information of interest only to small communities. It will be of no use to build the highway if we can't afford to run our content on it.

## Funding Public Access in Libraries

I would like to have a dollar for each time a public official has declared that libraries will be the online access for our country's have-nots. I'm sure I could fund a few library connections with the money I would gather in that way. It's obviously unreasonable to expect libraries to make networked resources available without additional funding. And if the libraries aren't connected, they can't provide universal access.

Funding for libraries will necessarily come from a number of different sources. At this writing at least a dozen states have programs that will grow to provide online service to schools, libraries, health care institutions, and local government. Agencies at the county level are forming cooperative partnerships with local businesses to bring technology into their area with an eye to improving their economic standing. The Federal government authorized $136.4 million in funding for the Library Services and Technology Act (LSTA) in October 1996. LSTA funds will be delivered to states which will allocate the funds to these and other projects.

Another Federal funding project, the Telecommunications and Information Infrastructure Assistance Program (TIIAP), administered by the National Telecommunications and Information Administration, provides funding for projects that involve public/private partnerships. TIIAP funds demonstration projects that are intended to stimulate other partnerships between nonprofit organizations and the private sector. And the American Library Association has formed its own public/private partnerships with Microsoft and MCI to fund technology projects in libraries.

A project called NetDay was first implemented in California in March of 1996. NetDay brought together volunteers to wire the state's classrooms for computer networks. High technology businesses in the state contributed the necessary materials and encouraged their skilled employees to join with parents, teachers, and local citizens for a single afternoon that would make a vast difference to thousands of students. Since then, NetDay activities have taken place in more than forty states, and others are planned for the future. While NetDay wiring only takes care of one piece of the overall technology need, it is an example of how community action can be part of steps we must take toward universal access.

The Telecommunications Act of 1996 directed the Federal Communications Commission to determine what telecommunications services should be provided at a discount to schools and libraries. To counter the idea that some version of plain old service is sufficient for libraries, ALA argued that the role of libraries as the primary providers for some segment of our population means that they must be able to carry the full range of telecommunications and online services that other members of our society are enjoying. After all, we don't stock libraries with only the least expensive of printed materials, we use them to give equal access to the full range of our published cultural heritage.

In addition, ALA called for further discounting for those libraries in rural or high cost areas so that they would be able to have affordable connections to the Information Highway. These libraries are often in communities that are themselves economically challenged and therefore they will not be able to take advantage of the kind of local support that other libraries may have.

The November 1996 FCC ruling on universal access gave libraries discounts ranging from 20 to 90 percent with deeper discounts for libraries and schools in rural high-cost and low-income communities. These discounts are capped at $2.25 billion annually. And the ruling would allow schools and libraries to choose the services they deem most appropriate to their individual needs, ranging from the most basic to the most advanced technology services commercially available.

While these funding sources are a good step ahead toward getting libraries and schools connected to the Information Highway, libraries will need ongoing funding in order to take advantage of the discounts on telecommunications. They will need computers, internal wiring, and staff who have been trained to incorporate the new technologies into the basic functions of their institutions. Some of this funding can come through sources like LSTA, but some must by necessity come from the immediate community.

## Universal Access and Libraries

There should be no question about the willingness and ability of libraries to provide full public access to the information resources of the Information Highway. In this sense, the Information Highway is no different from any other source of information in our environment. Libraries have not been limited to print-on-paper resources for a number of decades—they have embraced video and CD-ROM, have provided access to online databases, and many are already using the Internet to answer questions at the reference desk.

At the same time we need to make it clear that the library should not be used to excuse telecommunications companies from fulfilling their universal access obligations. Many of the services that will be included in the new telecommunications offerings will require private accounts. Electronic mail, as an example, can theoretically be retrieved from any networked computer, but each individual must have a personal account, as advocated in the RAND study. These accounts must be administered by the telecommunications agencies before the library's computer can serve as an access point for the individual to retrieve her or his mail. And just as the corner pay phone is no real substitute for home telephone service, the library's public Internet access will not provide the convenience and privacy that one has with home access.

The best service that libraries can provide today is to allow a greater portion of our public to have hands-on experience with computer communications. In our role of facilitating the ongoing education of the American people, we can be assured that an informed public will make better decisions about the future of telecommunications than one that has not had the opportunity to personally experience this new technology.

## IN THEIR OWN WORDS

**Libraries As Vehicles of Universal Service: Discounted Telecommunications Rates for Libraries**
American Library Association Washington Office, 1996

> This article is a chronicle of the American Library Association's involvement in the development of the universal service requirements that were included in the Telecommunications Act of 1996. It can be read as a case study in the use of legislative action to achieve public goals.

**Universal Service and the Information Superhighway**
Benton Foundation
http://www.benton.org/cgi-bin/lite/Catalog/Brief1/brief1.html

> The document from the Benton Foundation, listed on its Web pages on universal access as "Policy Briefing No. 1," begins by asking many of the more difficult questions on equity of access, such as what universal should really mean, and how can we pay for it? There are no easy answers, but this report does an excellent job of presenting the scope of the problem from a public policy perspective.

**Equity on the Information Superhighway: Problems and Possibilities**
American Library Association, 1996
http://www.ala.org/alanow/equitybrochure.html

> "Before there was talk of an information superhighway, there were libraries." And now that there is talk of the Information Highway, the role of libraries in connecting people to information resources is as vital as ever. This document, issued as a Library Advocacy Now brochure, gives advocates plenty of good arguments on the importance of libraries in the digital age.

**People with Disabilities and the NII: Breaking Down Barriers, Building Choice** *(Part I)*
U.S. Department of Commerce, September 1994
http://nii.nist.gov/pubs/sp868/disabled.html

> In its broadest sense, disability really means a degree of differentness, and as Deborah Kaplan of the World Institute on Disability points out when she speaks, most of us will experience

that differentness at some point in our lifetimes, whether it be the temporary disability of a sprained ankle or the gradual changes of old age. How well we accommodate differences in ability is key to making the Information Highway truly universal.

**Universal Access to E-mail: Feasibility and Societal Implications**
Center for Information Revolution Analyses-RAND, 1995. 267 pp. MR-650
http://www.rand.org/publications/MR/MR650

While the universal service activities of telecommunications companies and the FCC focus on technical infrastructure and wiring, this RAND report proposes that electronic mail is a basic function that needs to be accessible to all, and that this can be achieved with a wide variety of low-cost technologies.

## *Further Reading*

*Latinos and the Information Highway.* The Tomas Rivera Center. Telecommunications Project. N.d. http://www.cgs.edu/inst/trc_super1.html

Each community will have its own needs and its own problems to solve in getting on the Information Highway. The Tomas Rivera Center at the Claremont Graduate School in Claremont, California, has identified key issues for the Latino community.

*Estimated Cost Profiles for Connecting Schools and Libraries to Advanced Networks.* Washington, D.C.: U.S. Department of Commerce, 1996.

This is an NTIA response to the FCC request for comments on Universal Service following the passage of the Telecommunications Act of 1996. Rather technical in nature, it brings together a handful of studies and a variety of possible scenarios. Estimates for connecting our public libraries are about $1.6 billion, with ongoing costs of $1.3 billion per year.

## *Internet Resources*

The Federal Communications Commission. http://www.fcc.gov

Many of the changes to our national communications and broadcast systems still must be regulated by the Federal Communications Commission. This site announces upcoming decisions and requests for comment and chronicles changes that may be highly significant for our information future. Much of it is written in a rather thick Federalese, unfortunately, but there is no better source than this.

Computer Professionals for Social Responsibility. http://www.cpsr.org/home.html

Of all of the public interest groups working in the area of the Information Highway, CPSR has the greatest interest in community activities. Its pages on community networking are a good starting point for learning about this important grassroots movement.

---

# LIBRARIES AS VEHICLES OF UNIVERSAL SERVICE: DISCOUNTED TELECOMMUNICATIONS RATES FOR LIBRARIES

## American Library Association Washington Office

## LIBRARIES AND UNIVERSAL SERVICE

A precedent-setting recognition of the role of libraries in a democratic society was achieved in the Telecommunications Act of 1996 due to major work by the ALA Washington Office and the help of legislative and grass roots champions. This act, the first ever signed into law in the magnificent nineteenth-century Library of Congress Jefferson Building amid twenty-first-century digital library technology, mandates for the first time that our nation's universal service policies for telecommunications incorporate libraries and schools.

While this historic act, the first comprehensive rewrite of the Communications Act of 1934, is aimed at deregulation and at spurring competition within and among industries in the provision of

---

This article was written by the following members of the ALA Washington Office staff: Carol C. Henderson, Executive Director; Lynne E. Bradley, Deputy Executive Director; J. Andrew Magpantay, Director, ALA Office for Information Technology; Fred W. Weingarten, Senior Policy Fellow.

telephone and advanced telecommunications services, it also includes a major revision of universal service policy. First, the definition of what universal service includes (previously just POTS—"plain old telephone service") is to evolve over time as technology evolves. Second, institutions—schools and libraries—are now seen as vehicles of universal service. Libraries and schools will receive discounted rates, and the availability to them of advanced telecommunications services will be enhanced.

How did this happen? ALA made preferential rates for libraries a specific legislative priority; then, once telecommunications reform became a serious priority for Congress, ALA's Washington Office swung into action. Getting and keeping libraries in the legislation was not an easy matter. First came years of persistent educational effort with key congressional committee staff, contacts by home district library advocates with key legislators, and congressional visits in Washington by knowledgeable librarians already using new technologies to benefit the public. The first requests to testify were turned down. We filed testimony for the record more than once. ALA issued "Principles for the NII" and passed resolutions. We kept at it and ALA was finally able to testify in person at Senate hearings in 1994.

Supportive senators developed the Snowe-Rockefeller-Kerrey-Exon amendment to provide for discounted telecommunications rates for schools and libraries. The amendment had an up-and-down history as industry opposition or questions by legislators led to its inclusion, exclusion, and revision over time. However, it was included in the Senate-passed bill in 1995. ALA worked hard to secure passage, and even harder to retain this provision in the final version of the bill. House opposition was stronger; interest in helping schools did not extend as solidly to libraries, and the library inclusion was often in danger. No similar provision was included in the House-passed bill.

By this time, ALA had a much-expanded Washington presence in place as a result of ALA Goal 2000, including an Office for Information Technology Policy and senior policy expertise. The ALA Washington Office also mounted for the first time, with the help of ALA's media consultant, a media campaign targeted to a specific legislative goal: keeping discounted rates for libraries in the final House-Senate compromise bill. Working with library advocates in the districts of key House conferees on the bill, ALA sought editorials supportive of discounted rates for libraries in local newspapers. A dozen key newspapers did express published support, and in the end, House conferees agreed to the Snowe-Rockefeller-Kerrey-Exon provision.

As a result of all this involvement, ALA was looked to as the major voice for the next stage, currently under way. A major legislative victory has now become a major regulatory project for ALA in Washington. Congress left most of the details to federal and state regulators of telecommunications, including what services to discount, and how much of a discount to provide to libraries and schools. The Federal Communications Commission (FCC), with the help of a Federal-State Joint Board, is to determine answers to these questions for interstate telecommunications, while the appropriate regulatory commission in each state will answer these questions for intrastate telecommunications.

## PROPOSED RULEMAKING

The FCC issued what's known as an NPRM, or a Notice of Proposed Rulemaking, on March 8 and set a due date of April 12, 1996 for questions and proposals. ALA filed (1) a set of joint comments with several K–12 education organizations, such as the National School Boards Association, the National Education Association, the Council of Chief State School Officers, and other groups; and (2) separate comments that elaborated on recommendations for libraries.

Preparation of ALA's comments, totaling 93 pages, required the combined resources of the Washington Office, the Office for Information Technology Policy, and a vast network of advocacy and legislative contacts who provided valuable data, input, and comment from the field. ALA members were able to provide information about what libraries are doing on the Information Superhighway, the need for high-speed connections in libraries, telecommunications costs, the problems faced by libraries in rural areas, the kinds of cooperative networks in which libraries participate, and even innovative stories of wireless applications for bookmobiles.

ALA also sought assistance from experts in telecommunications, economics, and law. ALA was orchestrating in this regulatory proceeding an effort to achieve meaningful discounts that would maximize the benefit to schools and libraries; efficiency in administration of the discounts; and a mechanism that would evolve as technology evolves and would hold up over time.

## ALA'S RECOMMENDATIONS

ALA recommended that any telecommunications service offered by a carrier commercially under tariff or through contract in a region should be made available to libraries and schools at a discount. The rationale for this expansive definition is that since libraries must be able to provide to their users the full range of electronic information resources available either commercially or in the public domain, they need high-level telecommunications to fulfill their missions. This mission flows naturally from the traditional role of libraries to provide information, regardless of the format. Libraries serve this mission in the digital age by providing access to global electronic resources such as the Internet's World Wide Web (WWW), by creating and offering their own public information services, and by developing community information infrastructures.

ALA said that libraries must be viewed, not as recipients of universal service benefits, but as institutional providers of public access and, hence, as instruments of universal policy. The global information infrastructure has several characteristics that make traditional universal service concepts ineffective or insufficient. It offers a vast array of services and a wide selection of connectivity options, some of which are relatively expensive under any system of pricing. Technology is changing rapidly, and many of the most interesting and useful information services are at the leading edge. As a result, the concept of the residence as the sole focus of universal service is much too limited. It is not just a matter of cost, but also of sharing scarce resources within communities.

If the policy goal is to see that everyone has full, equitable, and affordable access to the rich resources of the infrastructure, then public institutions such as libraries, schools, health care institutions, and community networks will play a vital role in providing effective access. Access is not all that libraries provide. Libraries bring organization and structure to the morass of information resources now available electronically. They train users to navigate the networks on their own, expanding libraries' age-old responsibilities in improving literacy by teaching electronic information skills needed in the modern world.

Providing discounted access for libraries will also generate tangible and significant economic benefits to the telecommunications providers and to the broader information industry in the forms both of avoided costs and increased demand. Benefits to the industry include:

1. increasing market demand for specialized information services
2. providing public exposure for new services

3. providing user test-beds for new services
4. improving user literacy
5. saving providers at least some advertising and related expenses
6. providing these benefits in a competitively neutral manner

## HOW MUCH OF A DISCOUNT?

ALA recommended discounts for libraries and/or schools at the lower of the lowest price offered to any customer, or a rate called the Total Service Long Run Incremental Cost (TSLRIC). The TSLRIC rate has similarities to wholesale rates and covers a carrier's cost plus a return on investment. Because it covers a carrier's cost, it should not require reimbursement from the universal service fund nor offsets to a carrier's contribution to universal service obligations except for libraries in rural, insular, and high-cost areas.

Libraries in high-cost areas should, ALA said, receive further discounts on telecommunications services through whatever mechanism is established to average the rates in these areas through the universal service fund. Libraries in rural, insular, and high-cost areas have encountered many special barriers to affordable connections due to the same characteristics of these areas that require special attention for residential consumers. For these libraries, telecommunications costs are a much higher percentage of overall library budgets, and wholesale rates may not be low enough to be affordable. These circumstances justify a below-cost deeper discount for libraries and schools in these areas.

ALA developed its discount methodology proposal based on several factors. The methodology maximizes the benefits to libraries and schools; minimizes the impact on the universal service fund; evolves as technology evolves; is competitively and technologically neutral; and is equitable, efficient, and flexible to administer across the nation and among demographic groups.

## BETTY TUROCK TESTIFIES

The Federal-State Joint Board held a hearing on April 22, 1996 on universal service issues, chaired by FCC Chairman Reed Hunt. Secretary of Education Richard Riley testified on the importance of the new information technologies to school children and library users. A panel of education and library witnesses included then ALA President

Betty Turock, who testified on how discounted telecommunications rates for libraries and schools should be implemented. "Libraries need more than a telephone and modem," she said. "They need discounted access to the full range of telecommunications services."

Turock's testimony noted that the potential and real benefit of recognizing libraries as instruments of universal service is evidenced by the penetration of library services throughout the nation and by public access to electronic information through our nation's libraries. Her presidential theme, Equity on the Information Superhighway, decided two years earlier, was on target for this period of telecommunications development.

## PUBLIC LIBRARIES

There are 15,946 public library facilities and 97,976 libraries in public and private schools. A 1990 survey conducted by Louis Harris and sponsored by Equifax, Inc., found that six out of ten Americans interviewed—representing 66 percent or 122 million people—used public library services.

According to research led by Dr. Charles R. McClure for The National Commission on Libraries and Information Science (NCLIS), considering all sizes of public libraries, only 20.9 percent had some Internet access as of 1994. This falls to approximately 13 percent for rural libraries. In this same study, the cost of connection remains the dominant factor affecting library involvement with the Internet. This is especially so in the Midwest and West. A Public Library Association/ PLDS 1995 Survey showed that in libraries serving communities of 100 thousand or more, 68.3 percent have some type of Internet access, but only 23.3 percent provide public access terminals.

## SCHOOL LIBRARIES

The opportunities and the challenges for telecommunications applications in school library media centers (LMCs) is demonstrated in the research conducted by the U.S. National Commission on Libraries and Information Science and ALA in a twelve-state survey. The study determined that only one state, Massachusetts, reported more than half of its elementary school LMCs have computers with modems. Seven of the twelve states reported that more than half of their secondary school LMCs have computers with modems. Only one state, again Massachusetts, reported that more than half of its elementary school LMCs had Internet connections; the rest of the states fell below

15 percent for elementary schools with Internet capability. Three states reported that only a quarter of secondary school LMCs had Internet connections.

Another survey by the Illinois State Board of Education, Center for Learning Technologies, found that, while the average number of computers per school for student instruction was 46, the average number of modems attached to computers was only 1.6. That means only about 3 percent of school/LMC computers had modem capability. Even where a school or LMC had dial-in access to outside computer resources, it was used for learning, on average, only 4.3 hours per week. "Furthermore, while the Internet and Illinet On-line were available in about one-third of the schools, these information resources were available to only 16 percent of their students. . . . Only one-third of the schools had access to regional library system databases, Illinet On-line, library catalogs of other libraries in the area, and the Internet."

Mere access to a simple modem and computer is not effective public access to the Information Superhighway. Libraries must respond to the need for high bandwidth, greater speed capabilities, and so forth. Consider how few public libraries are currently able to mount web sites. The St. Joseph County Public Library in Indiana has been collecting information since November 12, 1994, on public library World Wide Web sites. They list nearly two hundred public libraries that maintain WWW sites in the United States. But this represents only 2.25 percent of the 8,929 public library systems.

Some of the two hundred libraries offering web sites include the Alachua County Library District in Gainesville, Florida <http://www.acld.lib.fl.us/>; the St. Charles City–County Library District in St. Peters, Missouri <http://www.win.org/library/scccld.htm>; and the Seattle Public Library in Seattle, Washington <http://www.spl.lib.wa.us/>. Like their counterparts, they maintain WWW sites and make full use of this medium's graphical capabilities to provide information about the libraries' materials, to act as hosts to community information, and to provide neighborhood gateways to national and international resources such as:

- the Gettysburg Address (Library of Congress)
- an early draft of the Declaration of Independence (Library of Congress)
- clips of the 1996 U.S. Presidential candidates (CNN AllPolitics Web page)
- the Dead Sea Scrolls (University of North Carolina)

- a movie showing the sun's corona (University of Amsterdam, Netherlands)
- a history of traditional Japanese pottery (NJK Company, Japan)
- The Heart: A Virtual Exploration (a Web page put up by the Franklin Institute Science Museum in Philadelphia)
- StockMaster (graphs of stock market activity including the S&P 500 and NASDAQ Composite indexes along with data on 452 individual companies hosted at the Massachusetts Institute of Technology Artificial Intelligence Laboratory)

These sites and applications are just a few of the thousands of sites that make use of multimedia formats to provide access to information. Libraries, both as access points and hosts to this type of information, require high-speed telecommunications services. It is clear that text-based access to the Internet is not effective public access. Broadband connections are required to provide timely and reasonable public access for all library users and for libraries to develop and mount unique sources of electronic information. According to *The Wall Street Journal* (Dec. 26, 1995, B1), it takes approximately 2.3 minutes to download a simple 2 megabyte (Mb) image over a 14.4 kilobytes per second (Kbps) line. A more complex image of 16 Mb would take 18.5 minutes over that same line, while a short animation or video clip could take 1.4 hours. Over a 56 Kbps ISDN line, a simple image takes 35.7 seconds, a complex image 4.8 minutes, and a short video clip approximately 21.5 minutes to download. Even a 30-second clip of one of the U.S. presidential candidates takes approximately 4 minutes to download over 10 Mb ethernet LAN, with a 56 Kbps connection. A State of the Union address would take considerably longer.

The ALA Office for Information Technology Policy will provide information about good state models, data, and help to librarians and library advocates in the states as state public utility commissions embark on similar proceedings for setting discounted rates within each state. To review work done to date, see the universal service web pages on ALA's Web site at <http://www.ala.org/oitp/univserv.html>.

## WHAT'S NEXT?

The response of Joint Board members and of FCC staff to ALA's recommendations has been very positive. ALA's comments have been publicly praised by the FCC chair and others as positive, thoughtful and helpful. On November 7, 1996 the Federal-State Joint Board made final recommendations to the full FCC regarding universal service, recommending that discounts for libraries and schools extend to all telecommunications services, as well as to internal connections and Internet access. The Joint Board recommended discounts ranging from 20 to 90 percent off the prices charged comparable to nonresidential customers, with total support capped at $2.25 billion annually. Bigger discounts would go to rural, insular, high cost, and low income libraries and schools. Under the Joint Board's recommendations, libraries and schools could self-certify that they have a technology plan in place. The FCC is mandated by law to issue final rules on implementation by May 8, 1997 so that discounts may be implemented in time for the beginning of the 1997–98 school year.

Without technologically sophisticated libraries in every community, the evolving infrastructure will only widen the gulf between the information rich and the information poor. Establishing effective universal service policies is absolutely necessary to prevent an uneven playing field. Libraries contribute to economic vitality and increased productivity; they expand literacy; they broaden the horizons and opportunities for people of all ages and backgrounds—youth, scholars, emerging minorities, new immigrants, and our growing number of older Americans. ALA has made significant advances in representing and securing the public interest in the developing information infrastructure; but we must and will continue to intensify our efforts to reach our goal of complete Equity on the Information Superhighway.

\* \* \*

## UNIVERSAL SERVICE AND THE INFORMATION SUPERHIGHWAY

### Benton Foundation

For years, universal telephone service has meant providing person-to-person voice communications to all Americans—at prices made affordable through a system of subsidies. Today, converging commu-

Reprinted from Benton Foundation, *Communications Policy Project Briefing 1*, "Universal Service and the Information Superhighway," Washington, DC, 1994.

nications technologies are expanding the concept of universal service beyond "plain old telephone service"—to extend the benefits of new communications capabilities to most Americans. But growing competition in the telecommunications business is making it increasingly difficult to preserve universal service by undermining the traditional funding mechanisms. So, just when the concept of universal service is expanding, the funding mechanisms to support it are crumbling.

## KEY POLICY QUESTIONS

- What telecommunications services should be universal in the "information age"?
- What criteria should govern that choice?
- What funding mechanisms should be put in place to make service universally available and affordable?
- Who should answer the first three questions?

## WHY GETTING THE ANSWERS RIGHT IS IMPORTANT

The rhetoric of the National Information Infrastructure promises improved health care, broader opportunities for enriched education and lifelong learning, and an informed populace active in its own governance. It also promises an internationally competitive economy supporting new jobs with good pay. But without a program to make sure this advanced infrastructure serves everybody, these promises will not be realized. Instead, the new technologies will widen the gap between those who enjoy access to information and communications services and those left behind.

## WHAT'S GOING ON

- The Administration proposes to preserve the goal of universal service while allowing it to evolve with technology, so that all Americans are guaranteed access to essential information and communications services.
- Congressman Ed Markey, Chairman of the House Subcommittee on Telecommunications and Finance, recently introduced a bill to develop a plan to define universal service and create the funding mechanisms necessary to support it.

- The Commerce Department's National Telecommunications and Information Administration is holding hearings around the country to elicit concerns and proposals from interested groups for defining and supporting universal service.
- The National Association of Regulatory Utility Commissioners has put together a working group on universal service.
- New providers of local telephone service, such as MFS Communications and Teleport, have developed proposals for universal service that they are promoting with state and federal policymakers.

## WHAT PUBLIC INTEREST GROUPS CAN DO

Public interest groups should join the debate to set high expectations for access to the new technologies, to stake out noncommercial public space in this new communications environment, and to make sure that the new information superhighway serves everyone with more than movies, games, and home shopping.

To start learning about the issues, read the Administration's The National Information Infrastructure: Agenda for Action and the Benton Foundation's Communications Policy Briefings and Working Papers. To stay informed, get on the Benton Foundation's mailing list and join news groups on the Internet where these issues are discussed. To influence the debate, take part in hearings and other public meetings and talk to state and federal policymakers.

## THE SUPERHIGHWAY'S PROMISE

Once, telephones stayed in one place, TV had three channels, and no computer was personal. Today, the convergence of telephone, television, and computer technologies is changing how we learn, stay healthy, shop, amuse ourselves, and work.

The promise of the information superhighway—the National Information Infrastructure—is vast. In education, it could extend the reach of students to resources far outside the classroom and school library. It could connect parents to teachers and decisionmakers in schools. And it could complement education in the home. All these are important in a country where half the population is functionally illiterate and in a global economy that demands higher and higher skills.

In health, the information superhighway could connect patients to care-givers. But it could also make the delivery of health care more cost-effective. It could expand the scope of preventive health. It could smooth the processes for billing and for managing personal health records. All these are perhaps essential if universal health care is to become a reality.

In the workplace, the superhighway could connect job-seekers to training and jobs, and workers to their colleagues. It could also reduce the need for commuting—and the emissions from cars. And it could help revive communities, connect constituents with public servants, and bring people together in deciding what's important to them.

According to Nolan Bowie, Professor of Communications at Temple University, "we are creating the nation's nervous system. But we need to promote an educated, enlightened, and literate society. Treating information as a commodity could give access only to those who can afford it."

## WHAT SHOULD UNIVERSAL SERVICE BE

All agree on the desirability of universal service, which today means making "plain old telephone service" available to all Americans. But there is much debate about what universal service should be in the future. With today's new communications technologies, many people are setting their sights on a higher standard of service.

Heather Hudson, Director of the Telecommunications Management and Policy Program at the McLaren School of Business at the University of San Francisco, says that if the standard is to be raised, a new and improved basic package for universal service should include:

> *Single-Party Touch Tone*—Single-party service should be universally available not just for voice communications but also for facsimile and data communications. All switching should be digital, so that everybody has the option of touch-tone phones to gain access to information services.
>
> *Line and Service Quality*—Line quality should be adequate for voice, fax, and data transmission. Maintaining service quality will require new approaches that accommodate today's many providers.
>
> *Enhanced 911*—All subscribers should have enhanced emergency service access, in which telephone numbers are linked to a data base, so that operators can see the caller's address on the screen.

Lisa Rosenblum, Commissioner for New York State's Public Service Commission, asks whether all consumers should have affordable access to technologies that permit caller ID, call blocking, video services, high-speed digital transmissions, and so on. With access dependent on computers, modems, and televisions, should that equipment be included in any basic service package? If not, will universal service continue to divide society into the information-rich and information-poor?

Susan Hadden of the LBJ School of Public Affairs takes a different stance: "The universal service debate must be framed not in terms of technologies such as telephone and cable TV, but in terms of services or features of the network that should be available in the public interest."

She notes two opposing views on the future of universal service. "We could be limited to responding to messages designed by others. Or everyone could be a provider as well as a recipient of information." Hadden feels that the ability to originate information is central to the future of universal service.

Steven Wildman, Associate Professor of Communication Studies at Northwestern University, suggests that "we need to think about the nature of the public services that will emerge as the universal service frontier opens up. We need to come to some agreement on what information services must be universally available." Because public health and education services are less profitable businesses than, say, entertainment, they are likely to be provided only with government intervention. Rosenblum adds, "demand should show us what is required through subscription levels, and we should look at what consumers want as part of basic service."

If universal service soon means much more than access for all to a telephone, this will add greatly to the demands on the National Information Infrastructure. According to Hudson, the following criteria should govern its construction:

Equitable—Nobody should be penalized because of where they live.

Compatible—Americans should be able to communicate with each other and with major sources of information, regardless of who provides the services or what technology links them to networks.

Secure—With the proliferation of new technologies and decentralized access to limitless information sources, safeguarding privacy should be at the top of everybody's list.

*Flexible*—Changing technologies and the introduction of new services require flexibility in setting universal service targets and adjusting to change.

## TELEPHONE SERVICE STILL FAR FROM UNIVERSAL

Even with plain old telephone service, achieving universal service is a problem. Research by Jorge Schement at Rutgers' Department of Communications shows that about six million U.S. homes do not have direct access to a telephone. Who lacks direct access?

- 50 percent of households headed by single women with small children at or below the poverty line.
- 16 percent to 18 percent of Black and Hispanic households.
- 10 percent of renters.
- 40 percent of Americans living in boarding houses or hotels.
- 21 percent of Americans living in public housing.

These are precisely the homes that have the most to gain from universal service, especially if it is redefined to include health, education, and government benefit programs. Ironically, for these groups, television and radio use is higher than that of telephones because televisions and radios are one-time purchases. The telephone has a charge that must be paid—and reconsidered—each month.

## PAYING FOR UNIVERSAL SERVICE

Providing universal service has involved a web of subsidies. Commercial users subsidize residential users. Urban users in lower delivery cost areas subsidize rural users in high delivery cost areas. Those able to pay subsidize those unable to pay.

Federal and local policies have long helped fund universal service through pooling arrangements and cost allocations. Today, however, having many providers rather than a single provider means that paying for the full cost of universal service is going to be difficult and complicated.

"If you eliminate the support level for subsidies," Rosenblum says, "rates would rise, and that would undercut the states' universal service objectives." Even so, there are pressures on all state commissions to reduce these subsidies as competitive providers enter the market.

The New York State Public Service Commission and New York Telephone are meeting the pressure to cut subsidies by doing two things. First, they are adopting a more targeted approach. Subsidies are provided only to those who are income-eligible. New York Telephone has started an automatic verification program to test eligibility. Second, the Public Service Commission has also initiated policies to preserve reasonable financial support to the universal service program in the new multiprovider environment. Any provider of competitive telephone services using local networks will be assessed a charge that will support universal service programs.

But one of the largest competitive access providers, MFS Communications of Omaha, is applying pressure to change the current system of funding. It has proposed to the FCC that thousands of existing pooling arrangements be scrapped and replaced by a single national pool.

## THE FUNDING CRUNCH

The public policy question is how to preserve universal service when growing competition threatens its funding. Eli Noam of the Columbia Institute for Tele-Information identifies three reasons for the funding crunch.

First, monopolies formerly bore the cost of internal cross-subsidies and invested to establish a critical mass of capital equipment and technology. Now, other service providers can tap into that critical mass at little cost to themselves, making it more difficult to maintain the system of internal cross-subsidies and to encourage those new providers to make long-term investments in the customers' interest. Solutions include higher interconnection charges and government subsidies.

Second, competition reduces the likelihood of some customers subsidizing others because subsidy-paying customers who pay above-cost rates to cover the subsidies are easy targets for competitive service providers that charge lower rates.

Third, if there is competition among carriers, the common carrier is vulnerable to the private carrier, who can reject or accept customers and use discriminatory pricing to underprice the common carrier.

Beyond such problems, some see great possibilities. According to Gail Garfield Schwartz of the Teleport Communications Group, competition is the key to sustaining universal service. "All competitive access providers must be willing to bear the burden of universal service, which would encourage lower costs for consumers."

Schwartz outlined some other requirements for a universal service plan. All carriers should have access to the subsidies. And to be sure that all subsidies are visible and accountable, there should be a universal service pool that all carriers contribute to, perhaps administered by a bank. As Hudson says, "Most end-users do not know how the lifeline or the rural or residential subsidies work—or even that they are paying for them."

So, what are the choices? Will competition make things more efficient? Will having more choices keep the costs down? Only to a point, for the issue is not merely one of the efficiency of production—it is also one of the allocation and distribution of services. Noam says, "because the price tag for universal service will never be zero, either politically or socially, new ways of funding need to be found."

## ENSURING NEUTRAL TREATMENT

In deciding on the instruments for funding universal service, policy-makers must ensure neutral treatment of all carriers in the telecommunications business. All should have equal financial rights and obligations. Noam outlined seven neutralities for all carriers in the telecommunications business:

1. Competitive neutrality: support payments do not skew the relative market strength of any carrier.
2. Structural neutrality: neither integrated nor unbundled services are favored.
3. Technological neutrality: no type of transmission technology is favored.
4. Applications and content neutrality: even-handed treatment for all uses of telecommunications.
5. Geographical neutrality: no discrimination by region.
6. Transitional neutrality: no shocks or windfalls to any participant from transition to a new system.
7. Jurisdictional neutrality: successful integration of the new system into the federal and state regulatory systems.

## PROPOSALS FOR FUNDING

The notion of imposing some form of "tax" to sustain universal service is generally accepted—if the burdens are seen as fair and if the revenues are plowed back into the telecommunications system. Some of the models being proposed today include taxes on a network's equipment, taxes on all retail sales of equipment and services, taxes on revenues from value-added services, and a mix of debits for services and credits for universal service contributions.

NETWORK TAXES    Taxes could be assessed on property and equipment owned by network competitors. The equipment tax could cover items on customer premises that originate or process voice or video signals (wireless and wireline handsets, fax machines, personal computers, modems, televisions, ATM machines, "inside wire" that connects phones to the network, and so on). "With a network tax," says Michael Einhorn of the Department of Justice's Antitrust Division, "there would be no distortion of the designs that network competitors choose."

The prospective base of network components that could be symmetrically taxed also includes calling and access revenues from local companies, interexchange carriers, competitive data networks, cellular carriers, cable companies, satellite operators, and competitive access providers.

TELECOMMUNICATIONS SALES TAXES    Sales taxes could be assessed on all carrier use and access revenues. Imposing sales taxes on the services of every carrier would avoid creating incentives to switch carriers.

Because a sales tax on purchases of carrier equipment cannot realistically be assessed on network equipment already in place, a tax on carrier equipment might disadvantage new entrants and aggressive incumbents, which tend to install disproportionately more new equipment than their rivals. An alternative sales tax strategy that does not disadvantage these parties could be assessed on sales of carrier services and customer equipment used to interconnect with the network.

Schwartz argues against the use of sales taxes for three reasons. First, further taxes on telecommunications would disadvantage the industry in global competition. Second, putting the taxes in place would be politically difficult. And third, once introduced, they are impossible to scrap. She prefers a voluntary contribution to a universal service pool.

VALUE-ADDED SERVICE SURCHARGES    Proposed by Bruce Egan of the Columbia Institute for Tele-Information and Steve Wildman of

Northwestern University, these surcharges could be a fixed percentage of the gross revenues of all providers of value-added services. These are the services of all service providers interconnecting with the public switched network (except local loop services provided to residences by state-certified common carriers with provider-of-last-resort obligations). The size of the fixed charge would be adjusted annually to reflect expected needs for the coming year and projected revenues for the contributing services.

For the equivalent tax revenues, the surcharges offer a greater consumer surplus than levies calculated per unit, such as the minute-of-use switching charges by local exchange companies. Such surcharges are efficient because they are proportional to revenue, and they reduce the possibility of users bypassing a service whose higher price includes the universal service contribution. The surcharges should also be more politically sustainable because big users can't avoid them. The disadvantages, according to Egan and Wildman, are that they are imposed from the top down and are not flexible enough to allow local variation.

NET TRANSMISSION ACCOUNTS   Dubbed NetTrans Accounts by Eli Noam, this telecommunications-specific instrument draws on value-added-tax principles. In an independently administered universal service account, each carrier would be debited a flat percentage of its transmission path revenues and credited for its universal service contributions for subsidized users choosing its service. This credit mechanism is important because it means that the existing mechanism does not have to be scrapped immediately but can be phased out.

As Noam describes it at its most basic, a system of NetTrans Accounts is not primarily a new form of transferring money. It is a way of keeping score, so that all carriers pay a proportionately similar share to maintain the type of universal service that the political process decides on. Only if some carriers contribute less than others would the NetTrans accounting result in transfers to and from the accounts. This system also removes the need to eliminate or change existing contribution programs (though it could). Those programs are simply taken into account and credited in the process.

The system would be initiated when local competition is fully permitted, with full interconnection rights. It would also be tied to the cost-reduction from competition, so that inefficient carriers could not shift their costs to more efficient ones.

Implementing a NetTrans Account system requires opening the market to full competition and making the system politically accountable. All players would be part of the system: local exchange companies, the Bell operating companies, competitive access providers, interexchange carriers, AT&T and other common carriers, wireless and independent cellular carriers, trunk-line providers, international record carriers owning their own facilities, carriers operating their own facilities, cable television operators offering two-way telecommunications services, private radio service operators offering two-way services to other parties, and satellite carriers serving nonbroadcast users.

Any new plan to reform funding for universal service is "unlikely to find approval if it means major disruptions, price changes, or shifts of financial burden among companies, customer classes, industry segments, and regions of the country," says Noam. It must be acceptable to state and local governments, such as public utility commissions and local regulators.

## A BIG ROLE FOR PUBLIC INTEREST GROUPS

Interesting arguments, but how do we get them before policymakers? By getting more people into the debate, something public interest organizations have typically done on behalf of their constituencies. Nonprofits play a big role in health, education, and civic participation. And they have a long-standing commitment to social values that runs deeper than the fiscal bottom line—such values as equity, diversity, opportunity, and participation.

"We need to develop recommendations useful to policymakers and give options to people working in public advocacy, and we need to do this fast. These issues have emerged at center stage and many of these policies may be set in the next year or two," says Andrew Blau, Coordinator for the Benton and MacArthur Foundations' Communications Policy Project.

"We need to get the message out to public interest groups that universal telecommunications service is in their strategic interest and that they should jump into the debate over what it is and who is going to pay for it. Why? Because this is not just an issue for the telephone industry. It's an issue for social policy."

Susan Hadden has suggestions for what public interest groups might do to further their aims. They should demand specific physical features of the National Information Infrastructure. They should define policy in terms of features, not technologies. And in worrying about costs, which will fall as demand increases, they should ensure the development of public service applications that are not as profitable as movies, games, and home shopping—applications in health, education, and public participation in national, state, and local decisionmaking.

\*   \*   \*

# EQUITY ON THE INFORMATION SUPERHIGHWAY: PROBLEMS AND POSSIBILITIES

## American Library Association

### AN IMPORTANT MESSAGE

As we approach the 21st century, a momentous telecommunications revolution is taking place.

Electronic technology can help you find a job in another state or read the Congressional Record online. It can connect a student to the local library—or the Library of Congress.

But what if that child's parents or school can't afford a computer? What if you don't have one in your home—or don't know how to use one? The information superhighway promises vast riches of information, but it also threatens to widen the gulf between the "information rich" and "information poor."

Our forefathers and mothers knew it made good sense to invest in libraries as a shared community resource for books. It makes even more sense to support libraries in acquiring the powerful and expensive technology needed to obtain electronic information.

Nothing is more important to the future of our democracy than ensuring public access to information. That is why we need our nation's public, school, college and university libraries online.

The technological revolution is happening **now**. And now is the time to support your library and all libraries in their efforts to ensure equity on the information superhighway.

Betty J. Turock, President, 1995–96
American Library Association

## RIDING THE INFORMATION SUPERHIGHWAY

Before there was talk of an information superhighway, there were libraries.

In fact, you might say librarians paved the way for the information superhighway. Many children and adults have their first hands-on encounter with a computer at their school or public libraries. College and university libraries, in particular, have been leaders in making their collections available online not just to their students but to researchers around the globe.

Today, an increasing number of public and school libraries offer access by computers to their own collections and to worldwide databases. And librarians are experts at helping others navigate the myriad of electronic networks known as the information superhighway.

Some examples:

In Seattle, a mother researched her daughter's chronic ear condition online at the library before deciding whether to proceed with surgery.

In Clinton, Iowa, library users can view more than 1,500 job listings throughout the state via an electronic bulletin board, then print out the listings that interest them.

In Macedon (N.Y.), third-graders joined explorer Will Steger on a walk to the North Pole via online connections at their school library media center.

In Maryland, residents obtain online stock market reports, travel advisories and job listings at their homes, schools and businesses via the federally-funded Sailor project, which provides free statewide access to the Internet via libraries.

In New York, a physician saved an infant's life using techniques for treating a rare form of meningitis that he found online in a medical journal published in India.

In Rock Island, Ill., students at Augustana College can call up an original Civil War diary thanks to federal funds which enabled the library to make its collection of photographs and other rare, historical documents available online to students and researchers worldwide.

In Columbia, Mo., residents send e-mail and participate in listservs and "chat" lines via the Columbia Online Information Network (COIN) at the Daniel Boone Regional Library.

## NEEDED: EQUAL ACCESS

New technology threatens to widen the gap between the "information rich" and "information poor" even as it promises to revolutionize how we live, learn, work and govern. Statistics such as these underscore the need for policies to ensure equal access to electronic information:

About one in three U.S. households owns a computer. Those living in rural areas and central cities are least likely to be connected.

Families with incomes over $50,000 are five times more likely to have access to computers and ten times more likely to have access to online services than other families.

African-American and Latino school children are less likely to have access to computers, both at home and at school, than other children.

## SOLUTION: LIBRARIES

Libraries have always connected people of all ages and backgrounds with the resources they need for their education and enjoyment. This role is more critical than ever in the new era of electronic information.

At a time when only one of three American households owns a computer, our nation's public, school, college and university libraries are uniquely positioned to serve as the public's on-ramp to the information superhighway—a place where all people can tap into new technology with the expert assistance of a librarian.

Libraries that are online support equal access in many ways. These include:

- providing free public access to vital information resources
- teaching people of all ages to use new technology
- serving as a hub for their community's electronic information

- making collections accessible online in their communities and around the world
- staying abreast of new technology
- advocating free and open access to electronic information.

Unfortunately, the high cost of technology makes it difficult for some libraries to keep pace.

The number of libraries connected to the information superhighway is growing rapidly thanks to the leadership of librarians and support from savvy communities. But there is still a long way to go before equity is achieved. A new infusion of support from both public and private sources is needed if Americans are to enjoy the same access to information in the next century as they do today.

The most recent statistics show that:

- only 11 percent of public elementary school libraries and 21 percent of high school libraries are connected to the information superhighway
- about 2 in 5 public libraries are connected
- 78 percent of academic libraries are connected to the information superhighway with the number ranging from 93 percent for Doctorate granting institutions to 76 percent of Baccalaureate colleges to 61 percent of Associate of Arts colleges.

## RULES OF THE ROAD

The new era of electronic information raises many issues of special concern to the nation's libraries and librarians. The American Library Association believes that development of the information superhighway should be guided by the following principles:

1. *Equity* must be ensured via libraries to make information available, accessible and affordable to all Americans.
2. *Open access* to information must be assured in the electronic environment. A balance must be struck between financial return to copyright owners and the rights of library users to reproduce copyrighted materials.
3. *Affordable* telecommunication rates must be provided for libraries, similar to existing postal rates. These rates must be predictable and stable.

4. *Privacy* must be protected. Individuals should have the right to inspect and correct data files about themselves. Library records must remain confidential.

5. *First Amendment* rights guaranteed by the U.S. Constitution must be protected. Individuals must have the right to choose the information they wish to receive.

6. *Easy access* must be encouraged through uniform standards of operation by government, telephone companies, computer manufacturers and other providers. Electronic information must be organized to maximize accessibility.

## WHAT YOU CAN DO

Become a member of the Library Advocacy Now! Network.

Attend or organize a Library Advocacy Now! training session.

Let your librarian and library board know you want your library online and offer your support.

Join the Friends of the Library. Almost every library has a support group of concerned citizens.

Attend local government meetings to urge city and county legislators to invest in libraries as public on-ramps to the information superhighway.

Urge school boards and college administrators to make information technology a priority for their libraries.

Stay informed about the latest developments in information technology and their impact on libraries and public access to information.

Share your concern with friends, family, neighbors and co-workers. Many people are not yet aware of the importance of ensuring public access to the information superhighway.

Speak up at campus or community groups you belong to—the PTA, Chamber of Commerce, League of Women Voters, faculty groups. Invite your librarian to speak.

Write a letter to the editor or call in to a radio talk show to express your concern.

Write or visit your local officials, state legislators and Congressional representatives to demand that they support libraries in providing public access to the information superhighway.

Plan to attend Library Legislative Day in Washington, D.C., or your state capital. Ask your librarian for information.

## SIGN ME UP

The Library Advocacy Now! Network consists of library supporters nationwide who are willing to speak out about urgent issues facing our nation. Members receive action alerts and other materials to support them in advocating for the public interest in library and information issues.

☐ I wish to be a member of the Library Advocacy Now! Network.

☐ Please send information about Library Advocacy Now! training.

*Please print*

Name _____

Position _____

Mailing address (street, city, zip) _____

_____

Telephone _____ Fax _____

E-mail address _____

Your signature _____ Date _____

*Send this form to:*   Library Advocacy Now!
American Library Association
50 East Huron Street
Chicago, IL 60611
Telephone: 312-944-6780, ext. 5044/5041
Fax: 312-944-8520
E-mail: aladnow@ala.org

The American Library Association (ALA), with 57,000 members, is the oldest and largest library association in the world. Its members include school, public, college, university and special librarians, trustees, Friends, publishers and other library staff and supporters. ALA's mission is to protect and promote the public's participation in a free and open information society and to advocate the highest quality library and information services.

\*   \*   \*

## PEOPLE WITH DISABILITIES AND NII: BREAKING DOWN BARRIERS, BUILDING CHOICE

### U.S. Department of Commerce

DRAFT FOR PUBLIC COMMENT

> In a competitive global economy, our country does not have a single person to waste. Opportunity must be open to everyone. . . . I believe our entire nation will share in the economic and social benefits that will result from full participation of Americans with disabilities in our society.
>
> —President Clinton, 12/1/92

*PART I*

*What Is the Application Arena?*

On September 15, 1993, the Administration issued "The National Information Infrastructure (NII): Agenda for Action," which formalized several federal NII policy development mechanisms and enumerated the guiding principles and goals for future policy development. A portion of the vision is as follows:

> A major objective in developing the NII will be to extend the Universal Service concept to the information needs of funda-

mental fairness; this nation cannot accept a division of our people among telecommunications or information "haves" and "have-nots." The Administration is committed to developing a broad, modern concept of Universal Service, one that would emphasize giving all Americans who desire it easy, affordable access to advanced communications and information services, regardless of income, disability, or location.

*The National Information Infrastructure: Agenda for Action* addresses responsiveness to the usage requirements of people with disabilities as a founding principle. Providing choices in the modes of information representation and manipulation will break down existing barriers and accelerate progress toward the full participation of people with disabilities in society as envisioned by the Americans with Disabilities Act (ADA). The technologies that deliver for the NII will be the technologies that LEAD the way in Liberating Expressiveness, Amplifying Dignity for all Americans.

### LEAD by Design: Breaking Down Barriers, Building Choice

Ensuring that the NII accommodates the rights of the 49 million Americans with disabilities to equitable communication and information access amplifies innovations and economic returns from national investment in the NII. Existing Federal, State, and local investment activities underway are demonstrating that accommodating people with disabilities is finally gaining recognition as a driving force for advances in human and organizational performance. As this investment strategy gains momentum, information technology developers are weighing in on the broad-based, competitive advantages of this universal design approach, that readily accommodates individual needs associated not only with disability, but also worker re-training, aging, illiteracy, and high performance, critical mission information environments. Adoption of universal design will stimulate the deployment of applications that all consumers will value for convenience, customer choice, and equal opportunity.

Americans with disabilities represent a large customer base already discussing with industry and government how they envision the information infrastructure will work for them. Most important is customer choice. Until now, choice of the mode or form in which information is presented or communications conducted has not been available. Due to this inflexibility, many people with limitations of hearing, vision, or information processing have been inconvenienced by, or excluded from using these single modality services. Newspapers and documents available in a visual mode only excluded or inconvenienced customers who were blind until the choices of auditory or Braille modes became available. Auditory-mode-only telephones excluded deaf individuals until multi-modality telephone services were developed that today incorporate hearing relay operators who convert communications between users of auditory-only devices and visual-only devices.

If future telephones or information appliances accommodated the choice of either visual mode (typing) or auditory mode (speaking), direct communications could be achieved and communicating parties would no longer be handicapped by single-modality services that are not compatible. Greatly anticipated as well are visual communications appliances that accommodate a range of needs from sign language transmission to handwritten note-sharing as an alternative to auditory mode only for conversations.

As the NII takes shape, being in the minority in terms of information mode requirements, due to a disability, need not be a significant handicapping condition, if a useful alternative mode is available. People who flexibly accommodate to either auditory or visual modes of information transmission, frequently fail to realize how single-modality services hamper and inconvenience access by people who are unable, due to a sensory mode limitation, to also alternate between both modes.

Many people who can accommodate either visually presented information or auditorially presented information, but not both, due to hearing or vision loss, are now high demand users of on-line services that readily accommodate their choice of mode(s) and media, including visual display (standard or magnified), Braille display, or machine-generated speech. This pattern of early and sustained demand by people with disabilities can enhance the evolution of NII services. It will ensure that the full range of information mode choices unavailable in the past, can now be provided to enhance learning and communications by individuals and organizations.

### Historical and Current Evidence of the Benefits

Two of the world's most valuable information technologies, the typewriter and the telephone, emerged from early efforts to accommodate greater choice in information mode by people whose disabilities made them less adaptable to mode differences. The typewriter was invented as a private writing device for a blind member of a royal family. Other developers of early typewriters also designed for blind people. Modality choice of writing device was critical to these early users. Realization of commercial advantages and transfer of this technology to business came much later.

When Alexander Graham Bell invented the telephone, he was attempting to convert speech to a visual representation in order to accommodate a greater choice of information modalities for his wife who had a hearing loss. Unfortunately Bell's invention failed to accommodate conversion of information from auditory to visual mode as intended. Instead the telephone extended the range of the auditory mode and broke down distance as a barrier to spoken communication. The originally intended benefits to deaf people have been late and inadequate. Only in the last 30 years has a usable choice for telephone access by deaf people become available. At that time, deaf people began purchasing and adapting old Western Union teletypewriters (TTYs) that only enabled communications with other TTY users. Communications between TTY users and standard telephone users has only become widely available in the last 2 years due to the establishment of ADA mandated state relay services.

Like the typewriter, transfer and extension of text messaging took a long time and could have taken even longer. One of the lead engineers of the original Advanced Research Projects Agency Network (ARPANET), the predecessor of Internet, was very accustomed to modality choice because he used a text messaging device (TTY) when communicating with his wife by telephone due to her hearing loss. This exposure positively influenced the inclusion of text messaging as an ARPANET application even though it was not part of the original planning. Today the value of this electronic text messaging or e-mail capability to people around the world is beyond estimation and choice of information mode is becoming an inherent feature in well-designed information applications.

Another contemporary ARPANET example of choice driving innovation is infrared-based eye-tracking. This technology has been matured and commercialized by a small business, that targeted individuals with severe disabilities as the first customers of this hands-independent and body-movement-independent intelligent interface device. Today, this eye-tracking product is being sold around the world to a small, but growing number of people with extensive mobility limitations for whom keyboard use is not an option.

This product, after being commercialized and matured by users who demanded high performance and reliability, is now being purchased by federal and private sector laboratories. Oak Ridge Laboratories is exploring its use to control tele-robotic vehicles in hazardous environments. A number of usability laboratories world-wide have purchased a related product that enables user performance measures to drive advanced designs of visual interfaces. A head-mounted display incorporating eye-tracking is next; it will accommodate not only people with disabilities but anyone in high demand, high performance environments, including national security.

Speech recognition, a technology increasing in power and potential, also originated through ARPANET resources. Quadriplegic individuals have become recognized by the speech recognition industry for the significant contributions they've made to maturing a technology that is likely to revolutionize human-computer interactions in the near future. These pioneer users, without functional use of a keyboard, were driven not by device novelty, but by true performance demands and the need for choice of information input mode that accommodated effective interactions with a computer. Other user groups who have begun to derive significant benefits from speech recognition are people with learning disabilities and people whose repetitive strain injuries preclude continued use of a keyboard.

Another powerful telecommunications advance was spearheaded recently by a person with a profound hearing loss who worked with an engineer to overcome her dependence on text telecommunications. She wanted another choice. The resultant product is elegant in its simplicity and cost effectiveness. With this product, she is able to use both standard and cellular phones directly. All amplification is provided by her existing hearing aid. While the cost-per-unit is approximately $80, there are immense long-term benefits and value of this technology to a segment of the hearing impaired population around the world.

### Federal Evidence of Benefits

THE GENERAL SERVICES ADMINISTRATION   Clearinghouse on Computer Accommodation (COCA), has been tracking these little-known innovation synergies for a number of years. Through the Congressionally chartered Federal Laboratory Consortium for Technology Transfer, COCA has recently begun serious discussion with the Army Research Laboratory and other labs that exhibit strong interest in user interfaces that accommodate choice.

COCA became aware of this innovation dimension during the past decade while assisting federal agencies in identifying and shaping their investments in technology to fully accommodate people with disabilities. Public Law 102–569, Section 508 (1992 Amendments to the Rehabilitation Act of 1973), is the source of this federal policy.

As implementation of federal accessibility statutes proceeds, federal agencies are discovering that purchasing information systems that accommodate a wide range of user interface requirements promotes productivity and ensures access to work-related and public information by people with disabilities. Organizations are benefiting from the ability to recruit and retain quality employees and the ability to effectively interact with all clients, including those with disabilities.

Agency experiences with user interface options that incorporate maturing technologies such as speech synthesis, speech recognition, or infra-red technologies also provide an effective means for evaluating near-term applications with potential benefit to all users. Many employees in "hands-busy," "eyes-busy," or noisy environments can benefit today from flexible interface alternatives that have already been adopted by people with disabilities.

Applications with user interfaces that accommodate choice of alternative displays and keyboards are also being employed to minimize or prevent the visual fatigue and repetitive strain injuries associated with keyboard-intensive environments. As the work-force ages, accessible information services must support the requirements of people who develop age-related limitations of vision, hearing, or mobility. As planning by the Federal Government increasingly addresses a comprehensive information infrastructure, planning for choice represents a solid foundation to maximize the value of information applications and acceptance by users.

### *LEAD by Design As an NII Innovation Driver*

As awareness of disability-driven innovations becomes recognized, and societal dependence on technology for community participation and economic growth continues, breaking down barriers and building choices will become recognized as an innovation driver globally. E. H. Sibley summarizes this strategic opportunity:

> In reflecting on the problems of the multiple language and character sets faced by the world, it appears that a large portion of the potential computer user population is at a disadvantage. They must use difficult interfaces or learn another language. When we add up the cost of not having good input/output

devices for the many people who can compute but find it cumbersome, we can conclude that the cost of efficient new devices would pay for themselves many times over. Particularly at a time when the world's political barriers are being removed, perhaps our new opportunity frontier should be to remove the barriers to computing for all humanity, be they different in language, representation, or device needs [endnote 1].

The recent report on High Performance Computing and Communications: Toward a National Information Infrastructure by the Office of Science and Technology Policy also acknowledges this opportunity. Addressing intelligent user interfaces, the report states, "A large collection of advanced human/machine interfaces must be developed in order to satisfy the vast range of preferences, abilities, and disabilities that affect how users interact with the NII."

The NII affords a unique opportunity in the design of human interface technologies to formalize collaborations among early demand user groups with a wide range of preferences, abilities and disabilities in order to reduce the lag time between technology transfer and user acceptance.

The Electronic Industries Foundation has reported that "manufacturers who have found ways to simplify the user interface have seen positive consumer response in terms of increased sales and decreased product returns. . . . A growing body of research suggests that there are ways to design products that can accommodate functional limitations, and actually enhance their ease of use for everyone" [endnote 2].

The use of generic performance benchmarks such as those developed by Pirkl and Babic (1988) would stimulate the design needed to ensure customer choice. The benchmarks include:

- cross-sensory redundant cuing, feedback, and modes of operation that support choice
- reduced complexity of operations
- adjustable product/user interfaces designed for a variety of populations and accommodation levels
- designing beyond basic needs in a manner that enhances user's independence, self-respect, and quality of life

These findings are congruent with the growing recognition that technological advance only provides a competitive advantage for a short time; superior design and manufacturing—doing it right for the customer and quickly the first time—ensures true economic advantage in a customer driven, global economy.

## What Is the Public Interest in Investing in NII and People with Disabilities?

This section outlines how significant benefits are anticipated in at least five areas. The public will be particularly interested in how building choice in NII:

- removes communications and information access barriers that restrict business and social interactions between people with and without disabilities
- removes age-related barriers to participation in society
- reduces language and literacy-related barriers to society
- reduces risk of information worker injuries and
- enhances global commerce opportunities

## Removes Communications and Information Access Barriers That Restrict Interactions between People with and without Disabilities

An individual with limited mobility may not have easy access to public libraries, places of employment or business, or retail outlets. Although these facilities may be "accessible" for the wheelchair user, getting to and from such locations often poses a serious challenge. Loss of hearing or sight are obvious barriers to information access.

The capacity to communicate with, and collect information from almost any point on the globe from one's home has already expanded the ability of persons with disabilities to participate in an information oriented society more effectively than ever before.

Federal policy promoting the coordination of an NII holds great promise of protecting the gains already made in information access by persons with disabilities. However, if the design and development of the NII does not accommodate the technical requirements for choice needed to provide universal access, then information utilization by persons with a variety of disabilities will be set back to the days before the development of computers.

At present, even without the development of a coordinated infrastructure, people with disabilities are carrying out electronic banking, shopping on-line, telecommuting, providing information services to others, all from their homes. In the office setting via electronic document processing, visually impaired and blind employees have access to vital information equal in some cases to their sighted colleagues. The economic impact of developing an information system that fails to accommodate the choice of modes of operation including access devices that convert electronic information into a form that can be used by a person with a disability (i.e., Braille displays, speech synthesizers, or voice input processors) will be far greater than the cost of ensuring this universal access in the infrastructure from its inception.

### Removes Age-Related Barriers to Participation in Society

According to the U.S. Bureau of the Census, by the year 2000, the U.S. population of those over 65 years will be greater than 34 million, this figure world wide will be over 419 million. The Bureau projects that in the next 50 years, the U.S. population will increase overall by 19.8 percent; however, the population of those 65 years or older will increase by 117 percent, more than doubling from 31.6 million to 68.5 million. By designing the NII to meet the needs of people with disabilities, the NII will also have the flexibility and competitive advantage of accommodating the freedom of choice and independence desired by this unprecedented number of older people. A well-designed NII that accommodates a wider range of vision, hearing, and mobility differences will normalize and not stigmatize our aging society. Personal and economic loss associated with past age-discriminatory designs can be minimized.

The NII will increasingly be a key factor in the independence, productivity, commerce, and community participation of a significant percentage of older people in our society. User acceptance will be accelerated by designs that make the NII easier and simpler to use. Those over the age of 50 control over 50 percent of America's discretionary spending funds (Ostroff 1989), and those over 65 control 77 percent of all assets (Pirkl and Babic 1988).

### Reduces Language and Literacy Related Barriers to Society

Full implementation of the Television Decoder Circuitry Act of 1990 will ensure not only full access to broadcasting by deaf Americans, but will also provide the choice of text captioning that may serve as a powerful application to reduce illiteracy in this country. According to the most comprehensive literacy study ever done by the U.S. government, the literacy levels of 90 million people in the United States are deficient [endnote 3]. This situation represents a direct threat to the U.S. economy. Another significant benefit of television with text captioning will be its usefulness as an effective learning technique for people who are learning English as a second language.

### Reduces Risk of Information Worker Injuries

With 70 million personal computers in use, strain injuries have skyrocketed. The U.S. Department of Labor figures show repetitive stress injuries represent 60 percent of all job-related illnesses. Estimates of the annual cost to business are $20 billion [endnote 4]. Pilot demonstrations of speech recognition for all workers are underway in several large companies as a strategy to increase productivity and decrease keystrokes. Again, pioneer users of this technology have been people with disabilities who needed a choice other than a standard keyboard. NII applications must interoperate with intelligent user interfaces accommodating a wide range of user needs and preferences such as speech interfaces.

### Enhances Global Commerce Opportunities

There are approximately 750 million people with disabilities in the world. Meeting the needs of people with disabilities in the NII will provide U.S. companies an early competitive advantage in the global marketplace.

The global advantages of the increasing U.S. market responsiveness to people with disabilities was noted in the 1993 report of the Commission of the European Communities. The report, European Technology Initiative for Disabled and Elderly People—Call for Proposals, states as follows:

> Technology transfer from the major European Information Technology industry to the Small and Medium-sized Enterprises, with the knowledge of the customer, will be critical to the competitiveness of the European Information Technology industry. This technology transfer opens new markets for European technology. It also helps counter the threat posed to European industry by US legislation in favor of people with disabilities which is both forcing the Information Technology industry to take their needs into

account and stimulating a strong rehabilitation technology industry in the US.

Deploying technologies such as real-time captioning, originally developed to accommodate deaf individuals, could also enhance international commerce activities. For example, U.S. economists working on General Agreement on Tariffs and Trade (GATT) spent many hours transcribing and comparing notes from working sessions before strategizing on next steps. Delegates with limited English proficiency may experience even greater difficulties processing meeting content when it is only presented in spoken English. This situation may tend to increase misunderstanding and decrease trust, resulting in costly negotiation delays. Deploying real-time captioning would provide all delegates with a written English transcript of the proceedings at the end of the meeting. The captioning equipment would also provide to the entire group a real-time text display of the speaker's words that would serve to enhance language comprehension by delegates with limited English proficiency.

The technical solutions employed today to magnify text displays for low vision users are identical to solutions being evaluated in Saudi Arabia to make English software applications readily translatable to Arabic. This approach can be applied to any foreign language and may reduce barriers to market entry for U.S. software developers.

## CONCLUSION

Full participation by citizens with disabilities in the design, pilot demonstrations, and implementation of NII applications is a national priority. Collaborative support mechanisms within the Federal and State Governments and private sector need to be strengthened to serve as communication conduits between citizens and NII developers. NII investments need to include performance benchmarks to ensure that applications can be fully utilized by people with disabilities.

The NII must accommodate choice in order to deliver on its promise of universal access. The unprecedented convergence of information technologies only amplifies the possibilities—accommodating choice provides a focal point for early and far reaching benefits.

### Endnotes

[1]  E. H. Sibley, Communication of the ACM, May 1990

[2]  EIA Seal of Accessibility Development Plan Version 1.0 09/17/93

[3] U.S. Department of Education, National Center for Education Statistics, National Adult Literacy Survey, funded by Federal and State Governments

[4] Smithsonian, June 1994

\*    \*    \*

# UNIVERSAL ACCESS TO E-MAIL: FEASIBILITY AND SOCIETAL IMPLICATIONS

## Center for Information Revolution Analyses-RAND

*Summary*

One of the most intriguing inventions that visitors see at Monticello—Thomas Jefferson's magnificent home outside Charlottesville, Virginia—is a contraption that allowed him to write on many sheets of paper simultaneously. The device holds several pens in place attached by a series of hinged levers to a central pen. As Jefferson wrote with that main pen, the others moved in unison, providing him several copies of the same correspondence with only a single effort.

Jefferson's writing device was an 18th century high-tech wonder. It freed him from the drudgery of copying. It allowed him to concentrate on composition rather than on production. And it permitted him to mail multiple copies of letters in his own hand as soon as he finished writing.

Jefferson's device never caught on with the public at-large, in part because it could be used by only a small information elite of literate letter writers. Today's technological equivalent, electronic mail—commonly referred to as e-mail—holds that same promise, but it also runs the same risk of catering to a small elite. This time, however, the risks hold far broader implications than in Jefferson's day.

E-mail has swept the communications and information world during the past decade, providing instantaneous global information and data exchange. People who send e-mail via the Internet—the amorphous network that links computers worldwide via telephone lines—can correspond with individuals 10,000 miles away as easily, quickly,

Robert H. Anderson et al., *Universal Access to E-mail: Feasibility and Societal Implications*, MR-650-MF. Santa Monica, CA: RAND, 1995. Used by permission.

and inexpensively as they can with neighbors next door. They can communicate with one or many people at the same time. And they can distribute information to any other user as soon as they create it.

However, even though this revolution has broadened and changed the ranks of people with access to information, it has not altered one fundamental feature: An information elite still exists, made up of those with access to and knowledge about computers and e-mail. And as e-mail becomes more pervasive, as more commercial and government transactions in the United States take place on-line, those information haves may leave the have-nots further behind, unless we make concerted efforts today to provide all citizens with access to the technology.

The topic of universal access to electronic mail has demographic, technical, economic, social, and international perspectives. Our study has touched on all of these to various degrees, resulting in many observations and conclusions. We highlight those we believe to be most important below, followed by a set of research topics whose study could provide additional data about and answers to the questions addressed in this report.

## POLICY CONCLUSIONS AND RECOMMENDATIONS

We find that use of electronic mail is valuable for individuals, for communities, for the practice and spread of democracy, and for the general development of a viable National Information Infrastructure (NII). Consequently, the nation should support universal access to e-mail through appropriate public and private policies.

The goal of achieving universal access has two main subgoals: (1) achieving interconnectivity among separate e-mail systems, and (2) widespread accessibility of individuals to some e-mail system.

Universal connectivity among systems appears to be occurring through market forces, although the portability of e-mail addresses and current regulations that distort the prices among potentially competitive communication offerings are likely to remain issues.

Individuals' accessibility to e-mail is hampered by increasing income, education, and racial gaps in the availability of computers and access to network services. Some policy remedies appear to be required. These include creative ways to make terminals cheaper; to have them recycled; to provide access in libraries, community centers, and other public venues; and to provide e-mail "vouchers" or support other forms of cross-subsidies.

The literature reviewed plus information gathered and analyzed in Chapters Two and Five make clear the central role of e-mail in the use of electronic networks; the role of these networks as a social technology is salient. Interpersonal communication, bulletin boards, conferences, and "chat rooms," of course, also provide information and help individuals find or filter information from other sources.

Much study and discussion, both within our government and elsewhere, focus on the content, design, and policies related to an NII. If this report demonstrates anything, it is the importance of person-to-person, and many-to-many communication within such an infrastructure. Therefore,

> It is critical that electronic mail be a basic service in a National Information Infrastructure.

To the extent that public policy guides the evolution of the U.S. NII, it should consider universal access to e-mail as a cornerstone of that policy. Specifically, one-way information-providing technologies—whether broadcasting systems or technologies that provide only search and retrieval—are inadequate. Two-way technologies supporting interactive use and dissemination by all users are key. And everyone should be able to participate:

> It is important to reduce the increasing gaps in access to basic electronic information system services, specifically, access to electronic mail services.

Implementation of such policies should begin as soon as possible, since it will undoubtedly take as much as a decade before full implementation is accomplished, no matter what strategy is envisioned. We recommend that the gaps that are greatest now and that are still widening be addressed first. Specifically, these are deficits in access to computers and electronic networks found in the low-income and low-education segments of the population.

Directory services and addressing mechanisms must be considered core components. Additionally, any obstacles to full connectivity and interoperability must be minimized.

Virtually every study of electronic mail establishes that immediate convenient access is the single most powerful predictor of use. To the extent that national or other policies attempt to redress imbalances caused by the market for electronic access, we conclude that

> Policy interventions should give priority to widespread home access.

[*Author's Note:* References to Chapters Two and Five (and others cited later) have to do with parts of the report not included here in this Summary.]

In addition, and not as a substitute, multiple options for network access located in convenient places (including, for instance, libraries, schools, public buildings, hotel lobbies, business centers, and the like) are important auxiliary access sites. Such common facilities could be considered good locations for help or training centers as well.

Prior studies as well as information presented in Chapters Two and Five show little reason to be concerned that citizens will abandon the needs of their local (physical) communities in favor of virtual communities in cyberspace. Rather, communications are typically addressed to a community of concerned individuals, and either for reasons of subject matter or prior acquaintance, these concerns are often (although not necessarily) geographically bounded. Thus, network access can be expected to enhance rather than detract from community involvement.

> Provision of community services and activities on-line should be actively supported.

Local nonprofit providers experience many of the same resource constraints—costs, technical expertise, and so on—that households and individuals face. Engaging people in participatory democracy is not just a problem of giving citizens access but also a problem of enabling the service and information providers. Specific policies might be designed to facilitate and support the development of on-line civic activities offered by government agencies and nonprofit organizations.

Our study of the technical considerations in providing universal access to e-mail concluded that

> There are no fundamental technical barriers to providing universal access to electronic mail services.

We concluded that current and evolving Internet standards for e-mail (SMTP and MIME, in particular), although perhaps not the definitive standards for electronic mail, provide a good basis for further evolution of a universal system. To the extent possible, gateways among dissimilar e-mail systems should be avoided, or be regarded as only temporary measures, because information is lost at least one way, and possibly both ways, in such transactions. Therefore, migration of Internet standards down into organization-level systems appears preferable.

We find that access to and the location of physical devices for e-mail use significantly impede universal access. With only about half of U.S. households containing personal computers by the year 2000, a robust set of alternative devices and locations is needed, including keyboard attachments to TV set-top boxes and video game machines, and extended telephones providing e-mail (and likely integrated voice mail) access. Public access is vital, with libraries, post offices, kiosks, and government buildings each playing a role. There might well be a market for "pay" terminals analogous to the ubiquitous pay telephones.

The state of software for "user agents," "knowbots," and similar filtering programs appears capable of handling, sorting, prioritizing, and presenting the large volumes of e-mail that may result from universal access. Similar technologies can give the user sufficient control over content (at least initially using the address or site that is the physical source of the material as an indicator of content; later "filters" may use other cues), so that avoiding objectionable materials should pose no greater problem than it does in other aspects of contemporary life.

We have concluded that e-mail white pages or yellow pages directories will be developed by market forces and therefore conclude that

> There appears to be no need for governmental or regulatory involvement in the development, or centralization, of directories for universal e-mail addresses (both white and yellow pages).

In considering the architecture of a universal e-mail system, we were strongly influenced by the recommendations developed by the Computer Science and Telecommunications Board (1994):

> The design of a universal e-mail system should follow "open data network" guidelines, with a small number of transport services and representation standards (e.g., for fax, video, audio, text).

Upon this base, a larger but still quite bounded set of "middleware" services such as file systems, security and privacy services, and name servers may be built. An evolving, growing set of applications can then thrive without requiring redesign of the underlying "bearer" and "transport" portions of the network. This model closely resembles that developed over the last several decades within the Internet development community.

Until more is known about appropriate user-computer interfaces for all segments of our society (see our "Recommendations for Further Research," below), we believe that—to the extent inexpensive computing devices can support it—the "Web browsing" model for user interactions, including access to e-mail services, is an important, highly usable, interface model. Within the foreseeable future, it is an important means of access to a burgeoning amount of on-line information and services. Because the cost of computing power continues to drop, we cautiously recommend

> The "Web browser" model of user-computer interaction should at least be considered a candidate for the minimum level of user interface for e-mail access as well as other hypertext-style access to information.

This report has considered the need for a simple e-mail address system that gives every U.S. resident a "default" e-mail address by which they can be reached. Such a development would "jump start" a universal access system, because governmental and other organizations could then assume that "everyone" was reachable by this means and design procedures and systems accordingly. The advantages of this approach lead to our recommendation:

> A simple e-mail address provision scheme should be developed giving every U.S. resident an e-mail address, perhaps based on a person's physical address or telephone number.

If such a universal addressing scheme were developed, services would then be needed, at least in transition, to "migrate" electronic materials received into paper form for persons not capable of, or not desiring to, access them electronically. Such services could be provided by third-party entrepreneurs or established agencies and companies such as the U.S. Postal Service or one's local telephone service provider.

The economic analysis presented in Chapter Four suggests that economies of scope and scale on the supply side, together with the easy substitutability among messaging and communications services on the demand side, may result in both vertical and horizontal integration—and the formation of strategic alliances—of suppliers in related markets. The growing use of bundled offerings and term and volume discount pricing are consistent with that analysis. The convergence of previously distinct messaging and communications services and the emergence of a unified communications/messaging environment raise a number of significant public policy issues. The following are two major areas in which policy may need to be reformed.

## Uniform Regulatory Treatment

It is virtually impossible to distinguish among video, voice, and data services in a modern digital environment. As the discussion of MIME in Chapter Three makes clear, an e-mail message may contain audio and video clips, and might substitute for video-on-demand offered by a cable television provider. However, video services can support data communication. Real-time interactive voice conversations can be carried by the Internet using a variety of commercially available software products, and many consumers access the Internet using modems and ordinary telephone lines.

Nevertheless, given their very different histories, voice, data, and video communications services have been treated very differently by regulators. With the convergence of the communications/messaging market, regulatory distinctions are creating artificial distortions in the marketplace and may be creating incentives for customers to use economically inefficient messaging options. The discussion in Chapter Four about access charges and the enhanced service provider exemption provides one example of artificial cost differences that arise from regulations designed for one application (standard telephony) that must now compete with other applications. We conclude that

> Policies developed separately for telephony, computer communications, broadcasting, and publishing that create artificial distinctions in the emerging information infrastructure should be reviewed, and a consistent framework should be developed that spans all the industries in the unified communications/messaging industry.

Address portability provides an example of the need for a consistent regulatory framework. Portability reduces the switching costs of consumers and increases market competitiveness. Chapter Four shows that with the use of bundling, the portability of telephone numbers could be negated through the use of nonportable e-mail addresses.

> Policymakers should develop a comprehensive approach to address, number, and name portability.

Efforts at implementing the above recommendation should be compatible with and cognizant of our earlier recommendation that "default" electronic addresses be provided for all U.S. residents. Although there may be some important tradeoffs between address portability and simplicity of routing, policymakers should attempt to make this tradeoff consistently across all competitors.

## Open Network Architectures

As technologies converge, each business and residence will have the choice of several access technologies and providers who will offer circuit- and packet-based services. In addition, multiple long-distance and international service providers will offer a comparable range of services.

Given the large sunk costs and the nominal marginal usage costs of facilities-based providers, competition in raw transport is likely to be unstable. Providers are likely to integrate vertically or form alliances that allow them to differentiate their products. Regulations requiring the nondiscriminatory sale of unbundled transport may not be consistent with emerging vertical relationships and competition.

In the near term, regulation should adopt a light-handed approach that specifies minimum capabilities that can be transferred across networks to allow providers sufficient flexibility to develop enhanced features that differentiate their products. In the longer term, when technologies have more fully converged, subscription to multiple networks by each customer may be inexpensive and widespread, and regulations governing interconnections may not be necessary. Providers may then be free to differentiate their offerings based on market demand.

Our study of the economics of e-mail provision concluded that subsidization for current household access could require approximately $1 billion per year, but we have mentioned (in Chapter Four) interesting commercial experiments providing "free" e-mail to those willing to accept advertising; similarly, "near-free" computers might be provided to those willing to subject themselves to additional advertising (e.g., on a built-in "screensaver" display). So the $1 billion amount may possibly be a mid-level estimate, not a minimum required.

Although e-mail penetration is expanding rapidly, some program of economic assistance to marginal consumers may be necessary to achieve universal levels of services. Obligating service providers to offer subscriptions to large classes of customers at low rates that are financed by contributions from other services is unlikely to succeed in the competitive messaging industry. Instead,

> Any e-mail assistance will require public funding from an industry-wide tax or from general revenues. Subsidies will need to be narrowly targeted to reach consumers who would not otherwise subscribe.

There are international dimensions to "universal" e-mail within the United States. Policies to influence the development of a national e-mail system should recognize the borderless nature of this technology. Perhaps more than other national systems, an e-mail system will affect and be affected by worldwide standards, policies, and events.

The analysis in Chapter Six leads to the conclusion that democracy in the nations of the world is positively correlated with interconnectivity. For nations emerging into democracy, or attempting to, connectivity is likely to have a positive influence on democratization. We conclude that

> The United States should support increased interconnectivity abroad, since this may aid the spread of democracy.

The results of this study support the conclusion that important results and benefits accrue to those becoming internetted, and that the problem to be addressed is the growing disparity among some society segments in access to that internetting. Universal access to electronic mail within the United States is an important solution strategy; achieving universal access will require dedication, focus, and cooperation by individual citizens, commercial companies, nongovernmental organizations, and government at all levels.

## RECOMMENDATIONS FOR FURTHER RESEARCH

Our research has uncovered inadequacies in the statistical data describing the phenomena we studied. We encountered other shortfalls in the existing literature or in current field experiments. We therefore recommend that the following research initiatives be undertaken to permit a better understanding of problems and issues related to universal access to e-mail and related interactive information systems.

> Cost-benefit analysis should be initiated to answer the question: What mass of the U.S. population, if it were network-accessible, is necessary to support electronic delivery of major government services (e.g., filing Medicare claims or income tax forms, delivering at least some of the postal mail, or distributing Social Security benefits or disability benefits) in a cost-effective manner? It is possible that the benefits to many government agencies and other organizations could outweigh costs of subsidization, so that a straightforward business case could be made for universal access.

A sizable and diverse number of grass-roots civic networks (i.e., those not designed, like HomeNet, and supported as field research) should be selected and followed from conception through efforts to raise start-up funding, and so on until they have been operating for some years. Getting comparable information across such activities about what works and what does not through early to later stages in the introduction of these networks (including what proportion of them do not make it), plus the kinds of civic, social, and economic roles they play, would vastly enhance what we have been able to learn from cross-sectional studies and site visits at a single point in time.

Current Population Survey (CPS) data should be collected on a panel basis to monitor access to and uses and effects of computer networks. In particular, the success of policies and markets to close the identified gaps should be tracked and social benefits assessed. This may require revision or extension of CPS questions and administration schedules.

Most e-mail systems have been designed for use in academic or business settings. Better understanding of the capabilities and limitations of current user-computer interfaces is needed, especially those related to electronic-mail handling. Existing interfaces rely on metaphors and analogies common to current users: multilevel "filing cabinets," commands to be issued, "Rolodex"-type address files, and forms to be filled out. How should these interfaces (including perhaps modest extensions of Web point-and-click browsers) evolve so that they can serve the entire range of users, including those in bottom-quartile income and education households? Field experiments concentrating on interface design for these prospective user groups are needed.

\*   \*   \*

# Organizations and Their Addresses

**American Library Association**

50 E. Huron
Chicago, IL 60611
Phone: 800-545-2433
TDD: 312-944-7298
Fax: 312-440-9374
URL: http://www.ala.org

*Washington Office*

1301 Pennsylvania Avenue N.W.,
    Suite 403
Washington, DC 20004
Phone: 202-628-8410
Fax: 202-628-8419
URL: http://www.ala.org/washoff

*Office for Information
    Technology Policy*

1301 Pennsylvania Avenue N.W.,
    Suite 403
Washington, DC 20004
Phone: 202-628-8421
Fax: 202-628-8424
URL: http://www.ala.org/oitp

**Benton Foundation**

1634 Eye Street N.W., 12th Floor
Washington, DC 20006
Phone: 202-638-5770
Fax: 202-638-5771
E-mail: benton@benton.org
URL: http://www.benton.org

**The Center for Democracy
    and Technology**

1634 Eye Street N.W., Suite 1100
Washington, DC 20006
Phone: 202-637-9800
Fax: 202-637-0968
E-mail: info@cdt.org
URL: http://www.cdt.org

**Center for Media Education**

1511 K Street N.W., Suite 518
Washington, DC 20005
Phone: 202-628-2620
Fax: 202-628-2554
E-mail: cme@cme.org
URL: http://www.cme.org/cme

**CommerceNet**

*East Coast Office*

3209-A Corporate Court
Ellicott City, MD 21042
Phone: 410-203-2707
Fax: 410-203-2709

*West Coast Office*

4005 Miranda Avenue, Suite 175
Palo Alto, CA 94304
Phone: 415-858-1930
Fax: 415-858-1936
URL: http://www.commerce.net

**Computer Professionals for
Social Responsibility**

P.O. Box 717
Palo Alto, CA 94302
Phone: 415-322-3778
Fax: 415-322-4748
E-mail: cpsr@cpsr.org
URL:
    http://www.cpsr.org/home.html

**Digital Future Coalition**

P.O. Box 7679
Washington, DC 20004-7679
Phone: 202-628-6048
Fax: 202-628-8419
E-mail: dfc@alawash.org
URL: http://www.dfc.org/dfc

**Electronic Privacy
Information Center**

666 Pennsylvania Avenue S.E.,
    Suite 301
Washington, DC 20003
Phone: 202-544-9240
Fax: 202-547-5482
E-mail: info@epic.org
URL: http://www.epic.org

**Federal Communications
Commission**

1919 M Street N.W.
Washington, DC 20554
Phone: 202-418-0200
E-mail: fccinfo@fcc.gov
URL: http://www.fcc.gov

**International Federation of
Library Associations and
Institutions (IFLA)**

P.O.B. 95312
2509 CH The Hague,
The Hague, Netherlands
Phone: 31-70-314-0884
Fax: 31-70-383-4827
E-mail: ifla.hq@ifla.nl
URL: http://www.nlc-bnc.ca/ifla/

**National Center for Missing
& Exploited Children**

2101 Wilson Boulevard, Suite 550
Arlington, VA 22201-3052
Phone: 703-235-3900
Fax: 703-235-4067
E-mail:
    74431.177@compuserve.com
URL: http://www.missingkids.org

## National Telecommunications and Information Administration

Office of Telecommunications
and Information Applications
(OTIA)
U.S. Department of Commerce,
Room 4096
14th and Constitution Avenue,
N.W.
Washington, DC 20230
Phone: 202-482-5802
Fax: 202-501-8009
URL: http://www.ntia.doc.gov

## National Writers Union

*National Office East*

113 University Place, 6th Fl.
New York, NY 10003
Phone: 212-254-0279
Fax: 212-254-0673
E-mail: nwu@nwu.org

*National Office West*

337 17th Street, Suite 101
Oakland, CA 94612
Phone: 510-839-0110
Fax: 510-839-6097
E-mail: nwu@nwu.org
URL: http://www.nwu.org/nwu

## Privacy Rights Clearinghouse

5384 Linda Vista Road,
Suite 306
San Diego, CA 92110
Phone: 619-298-3396
Fax: 619-298-5681
E-mail: prc@privacyrights.org
URL:
http://www.privacyrights.org

## Progress and Freedom Foundation

1301 K Street N.W.,
Suite 650 West
Washington, DC 20005
Phone: 202-289-8928
Fax: 202-289-6079
E-mail: mail@pff.org
URL: http://www.pff.org

## RAND

1700 Main Street
P.O. Box 2138
Santa Monica, CA 90407-2138
Phone: 310-451-7002
Fax: 310-451-6915
E-mail:
correspondence@rand.org
URL: http://www.rand.org

## Tomas Rivera Center

241 E. Eleventh Street
Steele Hall, Third Floor
Scripps College
Claremont, CA 91711-6194
Phone: 909-621-8897
Fax: 909-621-8898
E-mail: trc@cgs.edu
URL:
http://www.cgs.edu/inst/trc.html

## Voters Telecommunications Watch

233 Court Street,
Suite 2
Brooklyn, NY 11201
E-mail: vtw@vtw.org
URL: http://www.vtw.org

# Index

Photo credit: Mary Engle

**Karen Coyle** is a librarian with nearly twenty years' experience developing computer systems for libraries. She currently works at the University of California in the Library Automation Unit where she designs databases for the MELVYL® system. She is also active in Computer Professionals for Social Responsibility, a public interest group concerned with the impact of computers on society. She lectures and writes on a number of topics that relate both to libraries and computers, including privacy, intellectual property, information literacy, and gender issues. Other essays can be found on her Web page at http://www.dla.ucop.edu/-kec.